George W. Cable:
the Northampton Years

Yours truly
G. W. Cable

George W. Cable: the Northampton Years

by PHILIP BUTCHER

1959 NEW YORK

COLUMBIA UNIVERSITY PRESS

FIRST PUBLISHED IN BOOK FORM 1959
PUBLISHED IN GREAT BRITAIN, CANADA, INDIA, AND PAKISTAN
BY THE OXFORD UNIVERSITY PRESS
LONDON, TORONTO, BOMBAY, AND KARACHI
LIBRARY OF CONGRESS CATALOG CARD NUMBER: 59-6213
MANUFACTURED IN THE UNITED STATES OF AMERICA

For Ruth, Wendy, and
Laurel

PREFACE: "Regret Me When I Die!"

In 1866, when he was twenty-one years old, George Washington Cable was an intense young man, thoughtful about postwar problems in turbulent New Orleans, industrious in his efforts to support his mother and sisters, ambitious for security and an honorable profession. He was as egocentric as other youngsters, and despite his seriousness and his religious upbringing his was not an ascetic spirit, but he had a sense of dedication and he aspired to something more than material success. His compulsion to achieve some worthy accomplishment, to win a notable reputation, he expressed when he wrote to his mother in January of that year, "May the world regret me when I die!" [1] I believe Cable rarely lost sight of this goal during the years that followed. As his circumstances and environment altered, there were changes in his convictions, in his standards, even in his character, and there was a natural waning of his idealism. But when he died at eighty he had realized his principal ambition, for his fiction about ante bellum Louisiana had been accepted as an important contribution to American literature and his labors for civic betterment had made him an acknowledged public benefactor.

This book is particularly concerned with Cable's role as a

[1] Biklé, *George W. Cable: His Life and Letters,* p. 31.

social critic, his advocacy of civil rights for the Negro, and his sponsorship of the Open Letter Club and the Home Culture Clubs. These are matters which have not been exhaustively treated elsewhere, and I am interested in them largely because I believe a knowledge of them can contribute to an understanding of Cable as an author and as a man. This is not a biography, or a history of a social service agency, or a critical appraisal of Cable's literary work, or an analysis of his social and political philosophy, although all of these are involved in my approach. The core of the study is the twenty-year association of Cable and Adelene Moffat, who gave important assistance to his Open Letter Club and Home Culture Clubs.

The responsibility for this book, of course, is my own; whatever credit it may deserve must be widely distributed. I can acknowledge here only my major obligations. I began research on Cable at Howard University at the instigation of Professor Sterling A. Brown, the poet, scholar, teacher, and friend whose inspiration and instruction provided the original motivation for my choice of American literature as a field of graduate study. At Columbia University, I came under the stimulating influence of Professors Dorothy Brewster, Ralph L. Rusk, and Lionel Trilling, to each of whom I am indebted for many personal kindnesses. The late Professor Paul Spencer Wood, who conducted my doctoral seminar, focused my attention on Cable as a social critic, and it was he and Professor Marjorie Nicolson who led me to the discovery of much of the new material on which this study is based. At their suggestion, I wrote to various people in Northampton, Massachusetts, who might have known Cable personally. Some of the replies were helpful, and finally a letter from Miss Anna Gertrude Brewster informed me that Adelene Moffat was alive and enclosed her New York address. My request for an interview was granted, and my wife and I visited her on April 12, 1949.

Adelene Moffat was then eighty-six years old. Her eyes were weak and her hearing was somewhat impaired, but her voice was strong, her movements quick and sure, her manner animated. Scattered about the apartment were curios and *objets d'art* from all over the world; there were several oil paintings on the wall and one, unfinished, on an easel by the big corner window. We talked of many things that evening but mainly of my interest in George W. Cable. Miss Moffat praised his novels and his Open Letter Club and summarized her own connection with Cable's projects. She said she had hardly thought of him since her dismissal from the Home Culture Clubs, for she had spent a very full life after leaving Northampton. She promised to see if she had kept her letters from him and offered to give my research any assistance she could.

At a later interview that spring, I helped Miss Moffat open a large package, untouched for many years, which contained books, clippings, memorabilia, and many letters. In the weeks that followed I went through all this material, taking notes and recording Miss Moffat's explanations and interpolations. Her own interest in this phase of her past was aroused, and at night, with the aid of a magnifying glass, she went through the items I had already taken from the box and studied; nothing in the box was withheld from my examination. Very often her answers to the questions I asked one week were corroborated by correspondence or records I came upon in the next. I was astonished at the apparent accuracy of her memory of events that had occurred fifty or sixty years ago. Only a few of her statements have I discounted for lack of supporting evidence or because they might have had their source in a faulty memory or a natural rancor.

I put the collection in order and was of some help in arranging for its acquisition by Butler Library of Columbia University, though this was accomplished primarily through the efforts of Professors Nicolson and Rusk and the energy and tact of Mr. Roland Baughman, Head of Special Collections. Once or twice I prevailed on Miss Moffat not to destroy correspondence which she thought should not be made available to the public and, so far as I am aware, only one important letter, from a Smith graduate of the class of 1892, has not been preserved. It would have been valuable evidence in support of Adelene Moffat's position in the controversy of 1907.

My acquaintance with Miss Moffat did not come to an end when she disposed of her Cable papers; I continued to correspond and talk with her. On my last interview, in June, 1955, I found her a remarkably active and alert woman, absorbed in her writing and painting. She looked forward to the completion of my research without being aware of the extent to which it involved her own association with Cable. She died on February 10, 1956, without having seen either my notes or the manuscript to which she had made such important contributions. I am grateful to Miss Moffat for sharing with me her knowledge and her memories and for granting me publication rights to her letters to George W. Cable.

These letters *to* Cable, of course, were not in Adelene Moffat's possession. They are part of the very large Cable Collection acquired from the author's family by the

Howard-Tilton Memorial Library of Tulane University. I am indebted to Dr. Garland F. Taylor and his staff for making materials from this collection available to me on microfilm and for a great deal of information. Through the courtesy of Mr. David Randall, formerly head of Scribner's rare book department and now in charge of the Lilly Collection of the University of Indiana, I have had access to the Cable letters in the files of Charles Scribner's Sons. Of crucial importance to my recent research has been the assistance granted by officials of The People's Institute of Northampton. Mrs. Edward T. Heaphy and Smith College Professor Clifford R. Bragdon, acting for the board of trustees, gave me permission to examine all the pertinent documents in the archives of the agency, and Mrs. Alma S. Edwards, Executive Secretary, facilitated my study of those records. Many libraries have been particularly helpful, among them Yale University Library and Northampton's Forbes Library, and so have many librarians, especially Mr. Arna Bontemps, of Fisk University; Miss Clara Mae Brown, of the Joint University Libraries in Nashville; Mrs. Margaret S. Grierson, Archivist of Smith College; Mrs. Jean Blackwell Hutson, of the Schomberg Collection of the New York Public Library; Mrs. Gertrude Morton Parsley, of the Tennessee State Library and Archives; and Mrs. Dorothy B. Porter, Supervisor of the Moorland Foundation of Howard University.

A scholar expects help from institutions, but there is no obligation for individuals to search their memories or dig into family records to satisfy his curiosity. I am, therefore, grateful for the cooperation of members of the Cable family, Miss Moffat's relatives, and various other persons who knew, or knew of, George W. Cable or Adelene Moffat and who have helped me to learn more about them than I could possibly have learned from public records or published works. I can name here only a few of those persons: Mrs. Lucy Leffingwell Cable Biklé, who has granted permission for me to publish the many items from her father's pen which are printed in this book for the first time; Miss Adelene Gilfillan, who has supplied information about her aunt, Adelene Moffat, and her family; Miss Anna Gertrude Brewster, whose encyclopedic and authoritative knowledge of Northampton has been invaluable; Mr. Carl Walz, of Easthampton, who has voluntarily and industriously traced records in Massachusetts which were unavailable to me; Mrs. William E. Martin, who has authorized me to print certain unpublished writing by her father, William M. Baskervill; and Mr. C. N. Langston, who has granted permission for the publication of the letter written by his uncle, James C. Napier.

I have frequently called upon other students of Cable and related matters for information or guidance, and they have responded readily, particularly Professors Arlin Turner and Guy A. Cardwell. Many people have tried to save me from errors of fact or judgment, and Miss Elisabeth L. Shoemaker, of Columbia University Press, has labored to eliminate these and other mistakes from the manuscript.

Under the judicious guidance of Professor Lewis Leary, who succeeded Paul Spencer Wood as my adviser, Professor Robert T. Handy, of Union Theological Seminary, and Professor Richard Chase, I completed a dissertation on George W. Cable in 1956. This book is not that dissertation, for it incorporates the results of two years of further research and has been completely rewritten.

My study at Columbia University was assisted by fellowships from the General Education Board and the John Hay Whitney Foundation. Grants from the Faculty Research Committee of Morgan State College have helped to make the publication of this book possible.

I am indebted to Miss Adelene Gilfillan for the photograph of Adelene Moffat and to The People's Institute for the photograph of a group of sponsors of the Institute, which are reproduced in this book. The photograph of George W. Cable was given to me by Miss Moffat, to whom he had presented it.

PHILIP BUTCHER

Morgan State College
Baltimore, Maryland

Contents

Illustrations

George W. Cable: the Northampton Years

I: "The Faith of Our Fathers"

George W. Cable's brief visit to Fayetteville, Tennessee, in 1887 must have been quite satisfying, for, on successive days, he managed to express himself rather fully in the three areas which most interested him at the time. There was an appreciative audience in Bright Hall for the apostate Southern author's reading from his latest Acadian story, "Grande Pointe," on Friday, June 10, and at least a polite one for his speech, "The Faith of Our Fathers," on Saturday. That politeness he was adroit enough to match by giving extravagant praise for the intelligence of the citizens of the county seat, the grace of the new stone bridge spanning Elk River, and the beauty of the view from the hill north of town. On Sunday, when he reviewed the next week's lesson in the International Sunday School Series, his exposition was regarded, without serious disfavor, as new but not implausible. This attitude was sometimes equally evident at Edwards Congregational Church in Northampton, Massachusetts, where some of the more orthodox took exception to Cable's liberal interpretations of doctrine in his Bible study classes.[1] As his train left Fayetteville he must have felt that his three-day perform-

[1] Biklé, *George W. Cable: His Life and Letters,* pp. 199–200.

ance would enhance his position as one of the most eminent men of letters in America, a renowned reader and lecturer, an advocate of civic reforms, and a Christian gentleman.

Henry James is said to have remarked privately at a later date that Cable suffered badly from an inferiority complex. Other uncharitable observers might have felt he had quite a different psychic problem. In any case, his self-esteem would not have been injured by the account of his visit which appeared in the Fayetteville *Observer* on the following Thursday, June 16, though perhaps he would have failed to appreciate the humor in one news item which the editors chose to treat lightly and aim in his direction. The article reported that a party of thirteen men, chained together, had departed for the coal mines at Tracy City, where they were to work out their crimes by developing the natural resources of the state. Two of the men were white. "Social equality is sometimes enforced," the paper noted.

In "Our Distinguished Visitor" the editors treated Cable and social equality more seriously. Surely it would have pleased him to read that he had "no superior as a lecturer in the United States and not more than one or two equals, if any." His earliest appearances before the public had not been universally acclaimed. Audiences were sometimes unable to hear him because of his squeaky voice, and even after he secured professional instruction in preparation for the lyceum circuits he found it an effort to make himself audible in large halls. With training and practice, Cable made himself an expert reader whose thin renderings of Creole slave songs and dramatic recitations from his fiction contributed much to his literary fame. On the cross-country reading tour he made with Mark Twain in 1884–85, Cable was as much of an attraction and success as his colleague.[2] His press notices were generally favorable, often enthusiastic. When the tour ended Cable went on alone, for, although he was one of the most popular writers of the day, he depended on the lecture platform to provide a considerable part of the income needed to support his large family. In the major cities, however, audiences did not always fill the hall. In 1886 Cable confessed that he was not "the fashion" in Boston, and by March of 1887 he had become convinced that an author's reading from his own pages was no longer a novelty; he declared that his "future platform work must be of a graver sort than story-telling." [3] This resolve would have been strengthened had he known that the Fayetteville paper gave to his recitation from "Grande Pointe" one paragraph of sincere but conventional praise but devoted twice as much space to the issues raised by his speech.

On Saturday night he delivered the lecture prepared for Vanderbilt University—"The Faith of our Fathers." [4] He pictured the South under the old and new regime, and while very many truths were uttered, he made some statements that were not as palatable as they might have been. Yet, whether we approve all he said or not, it must be admitted that the lecture was a very able production.

There are some of the audience who have joined issue with

[2] The tour has aroused much scholarly interest. See Cardwell, *Twins of Genius;* Lorch, "Cable and His Reading Tour with Mark Twain in 1884–1885," *American Literature,* XXIII, 471–86; Ekström, "Extracts from a Diary Kept by Ozias W. Pond during the Clemens-Cable Tour of Readings in 1885," *Archiv für das Studium der neueren Sprachen,* CLXXXVIII, 109–13; and Nye, "Mark Twain in Oberlin," *Ohio State Archæological and Historical Quarterly,* XLVII, 69–73.

[3] Biklé, *George W. Cable: His Life and Letters,* pp. 148–49.

[4] Cable said this was his first lecture given from notes rather than read from a complete manuscript. Turner, *George W. Cable,* p. 251.

Mr. Cable and not only criticise him caustically but, we think, unfairly. In nearly every instance those who are dissatisfied censure him more harshly for what he did not say than what he did; they charge him with the advocacy of social equality, or at least claim the trend of his remarks is in that direction. He emphatically declared himself opposed to this, which he said was a most horrible doctrine that would lead to miscegenation, and cited the cases of San Domingo and Mexico as illustrative of the direful results that attend an amalgamation of races. The social phase, he said, was purely a personal one,—you cannot force yourself on a man to whom your society is unpleasant. We ascribe to Mr. Cable the virtue of conscientiousness; he is honest in his assertions, and does not confine himself to the color line, but says the *lower classes* are denied their civil rights. As we understand it, he wants justice administered to all alike; do not let it become a travesty when the malefactor has stolen millions, and the extremity of the law be visited when the offender has taken a ham to feed his children. Mr. Cable is a humanitarian and at times his zeal leads him too far, and he may become an extremist on this question and thus defeat himself. For reasons that are known only to the Divine Mind, a gulf has been placed between the races which neither sentiment nor philanthropy can bridge. Nature has quarantined the Circassian [sic] race against all others, and the most fearful consequences follow where this is disregarded.

Some residents of Fayetteville evidently felt a need for more reassurance than the newspaper provided. A telegram was sent to Henry W. Grady, editor of the Atlanta *Constitution* and champion of a "New South" more acceptable than that Cable espoused, inviting him to speak in rebuttal. Grady and Cable had published contradictory views in the pages of *Century Magazine* two years earlier,[5] and perhaps

[5] Grady's "In Plain Black and White," *Century Magazine,* XXIX, 907–17, was a reply to Cable's "The Freedman's Case in Equity," which had appeared in the January, 1885, issue.

it was the reaction of Grady's devotees to Cable's speech that led the Nashville *Banner* to report, on June 13, that if Cable should visit Fayetteville again his reception would not be pleasant. The *Observer* denied this and the *Banner* printed a retraction. But in view of the response the Vanderbilt audience made to the same speech, it is unlikely that the *Banner* spoke for all the residents of Fayetteville, or for those of Pulaski, Tennessee, thirty miles away, where the Ku Klux Klan had been organized in December, 1865.

In that unsettled year, young George Washington Cable had returned to his native New Orleans wearing the uniform of a Confederate soldier.

He had been born on October 12, 1844, in a house, once part of a colonial plantation, which fronted on Annunciation Square. He was the fifth child and second son of George Washington Cable and his wife, Rebecca Boardman. The elder George Washington Cable had been born in Virginia, but his parents moved to southern Pennsylvania, where they freed their slaves, and then to Indiana. Rebecca Boardman was born in Indiana. Her parents were descended from New England Puritans. Cable and Miss Boardman were married in Indiana and lived there until the financial crash of 1837, when they moved to New Orleans in search of better prospects. There Cable entered the business of furnishing supplies to river boats. He became part owner of steamboats and other business enterprises, and the family prospered until 1849, when Cable suffered severe business reverses. Plagued by poor health, he was never able to repair his losses, and when he died on February 28, 1859, he left his wife and four children destitute. Young George Cable and a sister, Mary Louise, became the support of the family.

The slight youngster—he was about five feet six inches tall and never weighed more than about one hundred and ten—worked at the task of stamping boxes in a custom warehouse until the approach of the Civil War and the conversion of the warehouse into a bayonet factory. Then he was employed as a grocery clerk and cashier. When New Orleans was captured, his sisters, twenty-two and twenty, were banished to the Confederate lines for refusing to take the oath of allegiance to the Federal government, and Cable, so small that he was regarded as incapable of any military service, was permitted to accompany them. Although he looked much younger, he was almost nineteen when he enlisted in the Confederate cavalry. He served with honor during the war and at its close returned to New Orleans, a paroled prisoner with only useless Confederate money in his pocket.

In the chaotic days that followed he held various jobs for short periods of time: errand boy, clerk, chain carrier on a state surveying expedition along the banks of the Atchafalaya River. Ambitious and alert, Cable became interested in engineering and thought of making it his profession, but in December, 1865, an attack of virulent malarial fever, from which he did not fully recover for two years, forced him to return to New Orleans. Reunited with his mother and sisters, who had made their home in Mississippi since 1863, he turned to clerical work and was soon a trusted accountant for commission merchants. When he was twenty-four he married Louise Stewart Bartlett, a New Orleans girl who was of New England ancestry on both sides of her family, and their first child, Louise, was born in 1870.

In high school Cable had shown considerable ability in mathematics and had written for the school journal. The abrupt termination of his formal education had not put an end to his studies. He read widely and thoughtfully. He revived his old interest in writing, and sometime in 1869 he began to contribute short skits and verses to the New Orleans *Picayune.* The first work that can be established as being from his pen appeared in a column headed "Drop Shot" in the issue of Sunday, February 27, 1870. He continued to do the column for about a year and a half and, for a while, was also a regular reporter for the paper. In these early fugitive pieces Cable revealed the qualities which were to characterize all of his best writing: the didactic impulse, a high moral tone not altogether free of self-righteousness, careful research, logical analysis, penetrating insight into civic problems and the history and politics which shaped them, the reformer's zeal, and a remarkable courage in expressing his convictions in the face of general apathy and outraged opposition. Possibly because an assignment to report a theatrical performance conflicted with his religious scruples, he left the newspaper job to return to the counting room, this time with Wm. C. Black & Co., where he remained for eight years.

But Cable clung to the desire to write; the counting room was not the public arena, and his labors there would not endear him to posterity. In 1871 he tried to obtain book publication for his pieces in the *Picayune;* these would have made a volume of about 120 pages, including 40 pages of verse. The manuscript was rejected, even though Cable offered to defray the cost of publication and asserted, persuasively but it seems inaccurately, that he had been an associate editor of the paper.[6] During 1872, the year in which his second daughter, Mary, was born, he did a few reviews

[6] Letter from Cable, dated October 17, 1871, in the archives of Charles Scribner's Sons.

for the paper, and, at the editor's request, wrote a forthright attack on the Louisiana State Lottery Company and a series of sketches of the principal churches and charities of the city. His studies led Cable to appreciate the literary possibilities inherent in the colorful Crescent City and in the colonial history of Louisiana, and the discovery of the infamous Black Code moved him to write some short stories of old New Orleans. These impressed Edward King of *Scribner's Monthly,* who was on a tour of the South gathering material for the journal's "Great South" papers. King sent two of Cable's stories off to the magazine. The editors did not share his enthusiasm for "Bibi," which Cable later incorporated in *The Grandissimes,* but " 'Sieur George" was accepted in July, 1873, and appeared in the October issue. A second story, "Belles Demoiselles Plantation," was published in the April number of 1874.

Cable was a slow writer and a meticulous craftsman. Though his interest in the cotton business must have been perfunctory, he was a valuable employee who finally became manager of the finances and general affairs of the counting room, private secretary to his employer, and Treasurer's Clerk and Secretary of the Finance Committee of the New Orleans Cotton Exchange. Throughout the years of his residence in New Orleans he continued to be active in civic affairs and various reform movements. Despite his poor health, his arduous counting house duties, his services to the church, and his public-spirited labors for community betterment, Cable found time to write. " 'Tite Poulette" appeared in *Scribner's Monthly* for October, 1874, and "Jean-ah Poquelin" followed in May of the next year. The accuracy of the dialect in the latter story was called into question by the Boston *Literary World.* Cable defended himself in a revealing letter to the editor in which he emphasized that the communication was to be regarded as private and that any reply should be directed to his business address. Evidently he did not want his wife and family to know what he had written. He hoped, he said, to persuade the editor to print something further about the story and to recognize that the statement about the dialect was an injustice. "I assure you that scarce a day has passed since the publication of 'Jean-ah Poquelin' that I am not told by persons who have been accustomed to hear the 'dialect' from their earliest days, and many of whom speak it, that I have rendered it capitally. Though it does not absolutely prove anything I will add that I am a creole myself, living today in sight of the house where I was born." [7] Cable was not a Creole. This letter enjoining a correspondent to secrecy and resorting to a convenient falsification, unimportant in itself, sets a precedent not without significance.

"Madame Délicieuse" was published in *Scribner's Monthly* in August, 1875, a month after a trip to the North had permitted Cable to make the personal acquaintance of his publishers. The magazine printed "Café des Exilés" in March, 1876, and in April "Posson Jone'" appeared in *Appleton's Journal.* In January, 1878, Hjalmar H. Boyesen, author and Cornell University professor, induced the Scribner company to bring out Cable's Creole stories in book form. Boyesen was so impressed by the work of the New Orleans author, with whom he had initiated a correspondence, that he guaranteed Blair Scribner against loss on the volume which, despite Cable's repeated urging, the com-

[7] This letter, quoted in part in Turner, *George W. Cable,* p. 70, is in the Berg Collection of the New York Public Library. When *The Grandissimes* appeared the *Literary World* praised its "inimitable" dialect. *Ibid.,* p. 108.

pany had previously refused to publish. The guarantee proved superfluous, for the collected stories, *Old Creole Days* (1879), attracted favorable comment and more attention than had greeted the tales on their first appearance. Even today, this is the book for which Cable is best known.

Work on Cable's first novel, *The Grandissimes,* was delayed by a severe epidemic of yellow fever which swept New Orleans in October, 1878, taking with it his only son. The first installment of the novel appeared in *Scribner's Monthly* for November, 1879, and book publication followed in 1880. *Madame Delphine,* a long Creole story which ran in *Scribner's Monthly* from May through July, 1881, was issued as a book in that year. Cable had now made his major contributions to American literature, although his last novel was not published until 1918.

It was the family custom to spend the hottest summer months at Ocean Springs, Mississippi, on the shores of the Gulf of Mexico, but in 1881 Mrs. Cable's health, never strong, required a greater change of climate, and Cable took his family to Franconia, New Hampshire, in the White Mountains. Though his wife had qualms about being left with the "Yankees," Cable, who had written Boyesen in 1878, "I yearn toward the North,"[8] felt exhilarated and at home. He went on to New York, where he met William Dean Howells, Mark Twain, Charles Dudley Warner, Harriet Beecher Stowe, and other prominent writers. When his family joined him in New Orleans at the end of the summer he was at work on his second novel, *Dr. Sevier.*

Though Cable had been acclaimed in the North, his re-

[8] Turner, "A Novelist Discovers a Novelist: The Correspondence of H. H. Boyesen and George W. Cable," *Western Humanities Review,* V, 351.

ception in the South had not been uniformly favorable. Creoles violently resented his presentation of their character, patois, and ancestry. Confident that his picture of the Creoles was accurate and just, Cable wrote his publishers that their objections were unimportant because, he said, Creoles did not buy books. Some other Southerners were discerning enough to see that his work rejected traditions they prized and criticized contemporary practices they felt bound to defend, but their views were as yet exceptions to the general sectional approval. In June, 1882, Cable made a commencement address at the University of Mississippi, and in the same month Washington and Lee University conferred on him the degree of Doctor of Letters. Cable's theme was that the literature of the South must be incorporated in that of the nation, and he noted that the South needed readers as well as writers. In tracing the history of the section and analyzing its culture, Cable called slavery a crime and a curse and said that in defending it the South "broke with human progress." [9] The caste system he saw as a perpetuation of the South's error, and he argued for an end to "the stupid wickedness of exalting and abusing our fellow humans class by class and race by race instead of man by man." [10] This address in Mississippi demonstrates Cable's courage beyond question and reveals the extent to which he was out of sympathy with his native section.

He spent September and October of 1882 in New York. From that time on he was often away from his Southern home. He found the North beneficial to his health and his

[9] Turner, "George W. Cable's Revolt Against Literary Sectionalism," *Tulane Studies in English*, V, 20. The article prints Cable's speech from his manuscript.

[10] *Ibid.*, p. 22.

career; he reveled in his visits to New York, where he met the literary celebrities of the day, broadened his vision, and extended his opportunities for making a living from writing and the lecture platform. Through Richard Watson Gilder he met President Daniel Coit Gilman, who invited him to deliver six lectures at The Johns Hopkins University from March 5 to 16, 1883. He was not pleased with his first lecture, "The Necessities from Which Literature Springs," but he improved with each performance and when the series ended he was elated over his success, and touched "to see the brave, learned young fellows full of new life and hope and promise, so handsome & so manly, sitting and catching every word I utter every time I lecture." [11]

The principal uncertainty about Cable's prospects as a lecturer and reader was the power of his speaking voice, which was high and thin, almost falsetto, and had a slightly nasal quality. Previously Cable had experienced difficulty in making himself heard when he spoke before a large audience and now, about to begin a career as a lyceum speaker, he was anxious to allay fears that his voice was not equal to the task. Roswell Smith had arranged for an experimental lecture at Hartford in April, largely under Mark Twain's management. Midway through his series at Johns Hopkins, Cable wrote the following letter to Twain, on March 10, 1883:

My dear Uncle Mark:

It's very, very good of you and the rest to take all this trouble for me, and you must consider me in your hands. I will lecture on "Creole Women" and on such a date as you may choose round about Apl [sic] 3.

I have now delivered my 3'd lecture here and shall give

[11] Biklé, *George W. Cable: His Life and Letters,* p. 92.

the 4th [,] 5th & 6th on the 12th, 14th & 16th. I am proud of my success thus far; the small hall continues to be packed full—aisle and all, and every lecture has been pronounced better than the one before it. My theme was badly chosen. Had my subject been a hit I should have made a ringing success, & even as it is my success is emphatic. Here I'm only half through and Prest. Gilman has engaged me to follow my lecture on the 16th with a reading of selections from my own works on the 18th in the same hall. This was not his own notion only, but came spontaneously and unanticipated from the young university men who have been listening to my lectures. So you see I shall have tried my lecture wings before I get to Hartford.

Immediately after my reading here I shall buckle down to the lecture on "Creole Women" & do nothing else till it's finished.

I wonder how large Unity Hall is. I should only be glad if it held [as] many as 500—Now don't fret—I'm leaving it all to you—but I want you to know some things. Unless a hall is absolutely *bad* for speaking in, I can make 500 hear me as easy as one. Have done it in New Orleans very lately; not the matter I told you of last Jan'y, but another. Of course I know you want the hall to be *full* above all things else. But if you see the fair certainty of gathering four or five hundred, don't be afraid but I'll make them hear. *Ecoutez!* Prest. Gilman tells me that as he passed along the outer corridor of Johns-Hopkins Hall yesterday afternoon, & was going by the closed door of its entrance while I was inside speaking, he asked the janitor why he was sitting with his ear to the key hole. The janitor replied that he was hearing the lecture & added that I spoke so distinctly that he did not lose a single syllable. You see I want you to feel assured about my vocal powers. . . .[12]

Which of the lectures on the relations of literature to modern society this remarkable janitor took such pains to listen to, Cable did not say. About two hundred and fifty people crowded into the hall for the lectures, and their

[12] This letter is in the New York Public Library.

response and that of the press was favorable. The reading from his works was a decided success, and it was this reading, rather than the lecture on "Creole Women," that he gave on April 3 in Hartford. Despite his assertions to Twain that he could make himself heard by a large audience, he took voice training in New York later that month.

In June, Yale awarded him an honorary Master of Arts, and he returned to the South to give a commencement speech, "The Due Restraints and Liberties of Literature," at the University of Louisiana, later named the Tulane University of Louisiana. In this address he ignored the social problems in which he was interested and said that the general function of literature is to entertain. In closing he stated his own practice—and his plight—when he observed that the stroke of the writers' pen "must now and then cross out some notion that some one loves better than truth, and they may from certain quarters even be denounced as turbulent overturners of order, as mischievous innovators and disturbers of the peace." [13]

Cable had come to hold convictions on the Civil War, the Negro, and democratic government which were in contradiction to the tenets of his sectional inheritance and his immediate family environment. Now the cultural influences of the North, the practical necessities of his own position, and the careful logic of his reasoning gradually effected further changes in his opinions and his behavior. Family tradition held that attendance at dramatic performances was a sin, but Cable reasoned that the theater was not morally wrong as an institution. His first public read-

[13] *An Address Delivered by Geo. W. Cable, at the Commencement Exercises of The Academical Department, of the University of Louisiana, June 15th, 1883*, p. 10.

ings from his Creole stories took place in Madison Square Theater. He delighted to hear the finest concerts available in the metropolis, for he loved music. He was introduced to actors and made friends with those who met his now relaxing standards. He relished the social and cultural experiences he enjoyed in New York in the fall of 1883, while he was studying voice and giving public readings. In November, when *Dr. Sevier* began its serial run in the *Century Magazine,* he went to Boston to read from his stories in Chickering Hall and there added more noted people to his growing list of important friends. He remained in the North the whole winter.

On January 21, 1884, he gave a reading in Northampton, Massachusetts. Sidney E. Bridgman, at whose home at 59 Elm Street Cable stayed during this first visit, stressed the attractions of the college town and helped to persuade him that it would be an ideal place of residence.

Cable's first public speech in the South devoted exclusively to the Negro problem was an address made before the Alabama Historical Society after the commencement exercises of the University of Alabama in June, 1884. For the first time, he said, the press found nothing in his remarks to commend. The next month he moved his family to the North in what was to be a permanent change of residence. Roswell Smith, the president of the Century Company and a friend for whom Cable later wrote a memorial volume, found a home for them in Simsbury, Connecticut. It was his wife's poor health, Cable contended, that was primarily responsible for the move, but he recognized that New Orleans was an inconvenient if not impractical place of residence for a writer whose publisher and lecture audience were in the North. Sentiment favored the move, too;

Cable thought of the South as a "literary Sahara" and lamented its uncongenial atmosphere. Of the two books published in 1884, neither *Dr. Sevier,* with its attack on Southern prisons and its conciliatory attitude toward the Civil War, nor *The Creoles of Louisiana,* a version of an earlier study Cable had done for the Tenth Census, was likely to appease his Southern critics.

When Cable was invited to address the annual meeting of the American Social Science Association in Saratoga, New York, on Setember 11, 1884, he chose to expand the remarks he had made at Tuscaloosa, Alabama. This speech, "The Freedman's Case in Equity," was published in the January *Century.* Based on court and prison records Cable had studied in connection with his efforts to reform New Orleans' medieval prison system, the essay urged that full civil rights be extended to the Negro. Even those Southerners who had stood by him in previous controversies now joined in heaping abuse and vilification upon him, charging that he was a traitor and an advocate of a social equality which could only lead to miscegenation. Cable's Creole fiction had been accepted, particularly in the North, primarily as picturesque local color sketches of a unique, exotic people, as romantic glimpses of a decadent past. But his essay brought him to national attention as a social critic and reformer; it revealed that his fiction sprang from a moral rather than an antiquarian interest, drawing its strength from vigorous social analysis rather than charm and indirections of style. In that gilded age of gentility, charm and picturesqueness were welcomed as major virtues; realism and forthright social analysis were not.

The storm of resentment broke when Cable was on his famous reading tour with Mark Twain. Beginning in

November, 1884, they visited eighty-five cities where they gave readings from their works, said Twain, "in the theaters, lecture halls, skating-rinks, jails, and churches of the country." [14] The tour was a financial success and enhanced the reputations of both men, despite some published accounts of strained relations between the "twins of genius." [15] Cable's rigid adherence to Sabbatarian principles brought Twain to hate Sundays and to conclude, in general, that his bearded little colleague was a victim of religiosity. The volatile author of *The Adventures of Huckleberry Finn,* which appeared just as the tour closed, must have been often out of patience with a traveling companion who used no expression stronger than "plague on it!" and that rarely.[16] When the tour ended, Cable continued alone, and for many years his public readings took up a great deal of his time and brought him a major portion of his income.

The house at Simsbury, which was or had been a farm house, did not suit Cable's requirements, and the little town offered poor educational prospects for the four girls and the boy, William, who was born there in 1885. The search for a more suitable residence was rewarded when the family moved into Red House, Paradise Road, Northampton, shortly before the publication of *The Silent South* (1885), a collection of articles on the Negro and the convict lease system.

During his service as a Confederate soldier, Cable spent much of his leisure in Bible study. He seems to have engaged

[14] *Mark Twain's Autobiography,* ed. Paine, I, 57. At one time Cable was reluctant to give readings in churches.

[15] Cardwell, "Mark Twain's 'Row' with George Cable," *Modern Language Quarterly,* XIII, 363–71.

[16] Dennis, *The Tail of the Comet,* p. 74.

in Sunday School work and taught Bible classes very soon after the war ended. For fifteen years he and his wife were active in church work in New Orleans, and he became a deacon of the Prytania Street Presbyterian Church in 1882. In Simsbury, where there was no Presbyterian church, he allied himself with the Congregationalists, and on moving to Northampton he became active with the Edwards Congregational Church, where he soon organized a Bible study class. Cable's theological views became increasingly liberal, and when he was away from home he attended services conducted by various denominations. Often he attended Bible classes in the cities he visited and sometimes, as in Fayetteville in the summer of 1887, he conducted them himself.

The furor that had raged about Cable's espousal of Negro rights and his aspersions on the justice of the Confederate cause had subsided little at that time, although in the previous year he had published nothing but some articles on the songs and dances of Creole slaves and two Acadian stories, from which he was reading on the tour that brought him to Nashville. There he could count on a hearty welcome from Vanderbilt's William M. Baskervill, an authority on the literature of the South, who had said in a lecture at Tulane University on January 11, 1887, that although Cable had been condemned "because the sentiment underlying his art was not in accord with our own," future historians of American literature would pronounce him "the best literary artist and the greatest literary genuis," except Poe, whom the South had produced up to that time.[17]

[17] Manuscript, "Southern Literature," pp. 45–46, in the William M. Baskervill Collection, Joint University Libraries, Nashville, Tennessee.

Baskervill had written an article about Cable in the *Vanderbilt Observer* when resentment over "The Freedman's Case in Equity" was at its height. He quoted some of the praise which had been bestowed on Cable's fiction and a description, taken from George E. Waring's *Century* article, of the man himself. " 'Personally, Mr. Cable is a small, slight, fragile-looking man, forty years old. He is erect, bright and frank, with a strong head and a refined, gentle face. His hair and beard are dark, and his large hazel eyes are expressive, happily more often of merriment than of sadness, though they are capable of becoming sad eyes too.' "[18]

The commencement program at Vanderbilt lasted several days and there were a number of speakers. The address Cable delivered to the literary society on June 14 was never published, but it is possible to get an adequate idea of what he said from two contemporary though somewhat conflicting accounts. The *Christian Advocate,* general organ of the Methodist Episcopal Church, South, regarded the speech as an affront.

As it was a purely literary festivity, there was a fresh surprise when Mr. Cable took the race question as the subject of his address. That large audience, composed of the most cultured elements of Nashville society, besides not a few of the representative men of the Southern Methodist Church who were in attendance upon the Commencement exercises of the University, listened with politeness and patience to his remarkable address. A remarkable address it was—remarkable in the choice of his topic, remarkable in what he felt called upon to say, remarkable in his apparent obliviousness to existing facts, remarkable in the assumption of the speaker that the great problem at which he glanced could be brought nearer to a solution by the use of such an occasion for such a purpose.

[18] "George W. Cable," *Vanderbilt Observer,* VI, 9.

His manner was admirable, his style was characteristically brilliant. But his logic was as peculiar as his language was fine. He contended with an earnestness that was almost pathetic for the equal political rights of the Negro, which are now guaranteed by Federal and State constitutions, and which nobody denies. He distinctly affirmed the inferiority of the Negro race, and then, while disclaiming the notion of social equality, argued on a line that if it did not mean that, seemed to us to mean nothing at all. He laid down political axioms that nobody would question, and then made deductions whose relevancy might be apparent to a genius or a poet, but were [sic] not visible to the common sense of the men and women who sat and listened with mingled astonishment, delight, and disapproval—astonishment at the logic, delight at the crisp and brilliant style, and disapproval of the taste that selected such an occasion for such an utterance.[19]

The *Vanderbilt Observer* gave a more temperate reaction and a more detailed report of the address. Here is the full account:

When the author of "Dr. Sevier" made his appearance in the Vanderbilt chapel Tuesday evening, he found a vast and expectant audience already assembled there. When he was introduced and advanced to the front of the platform, he was greeted with rounds of applause. His voice trembled a little at first, but he gradually warmed with his subject, and his embarrassment passed away. Then, indeed, we felt that he was speaking to us "eye to eye, as friend speaketh unto friend." We had hoped to hear him speak on a literary subject, and our heart sank as soon as we divined what we were going to hear. Mr. Cable began with telling us about his recent trip through the South, of her beautiful harvests, and of the unparalleled material and intellectual development which he had witnessed. He then spoke of patriotism, of patriotism in its primitive state, and of patriotism developed, resting upon broad and eternal principles.

[19] "Mr. George W. Cable at Vanderbilt University," *Christian Advocate,* XLVII, 1.

After discussing the importance of patriotism, the speaker passed to the statement that the majority must rule. The elevation of the masses depends upon the will of the majority fervently appealed to.

The fear that the supremacy of the masses would be used for the overthrow of political order and for the subversion of private society—and now Mr. Cable had reached the acme of his argument—was utterly groundless.

The speaker next discussed a few points of the social problem, already familiar to readers of the "Silent South." Social equality was only a fool's dream, and everything must be done for the elevation of the masses in order that all may be elevated. When we wish to raise a house, we do not put a rope around the chimney and pull, but we put screws beneath the sills and elevate it from the bottom. It is by free education that the masses must be elevated, and the negro must have perfect personal freedom.

And now a few words about the address: This was Mr. Cable's sole opportunity to address the South from the platform of its leading institution, yet, he evidently sacrificed the desire of making a fine impression upon his audience by means of a literary address to the voice of duty—to a duty that would very probably make him unpopular with the greater part of his hearers. If ever we had any doubt of Mr. Cable's sincerity, that doubt was utterly removed that night, for earnestness and a deep love for his fellow men shone forth from his eyes, and manifested themselves in every tone of his voice. Whatever may be said about the inappropriateness of this subject for a commencement address, the truth of what Mr. Cable said is beyond dispute, and he uttered not one word that need wound the heart of a true son of the South.[20]

One journal which gave Cable's address unmitigated praise was the *Fisk Herald,* a monthly published by the literary societies of Nashville's Fisk University. This organ of the Negro institution, which had been founded by Gen-

[20] "G. W. Cable," *Vanderbilt Observer,* IX, 13–14.

eral Clinton B. Fisk and developed under the auspices of the American Missionary Association, was jubilant that the noted author it had praised so often had advocated education for the masses and, in the heart of the South, had boldly argued for the freedman. In an interview, Cable was asked by the *Herald* whether the Negro was given his full civil rights. "Why, of course he is not; did you ever see one who said he was?" said the visiting novelist. "I believe in full and equal and impersonal civil liberty to the blacks and whites alike." [21]

The *Herald* said that the address was the act of a moral hero. And so it was. Thomas Sancton, a modern liberal whose experiences as a native of New Orleans and a Louisiana journalist contribute to his appreciation of Cable's achievement, has praised Cable for his courage and intelligence, his brilliant and broad-minded protests against segregation. When in 1883 the Supreme Court invalidated the Civil Rights Act, a consolidation of several bills intended to assure the freedman his full rights as a citizen, it made possible the establishment of segregation in all public life and led to the "separate but equal" subterfuge which was not repudiated by the Court until its historic decision on the school segregation cases in May, 1954. Sancton says Cable's "realization of the true issues of democracy, religion, and humanity involved in segregation is all the more remarkable for having been achieved in the Reconstruction South." [22] Cable's adoption of the role of the devil's advocate at such a time as the 1880s is almost astounding. He was aware that his could not be a popular

[21] "Cable at Vanderbilt," July, 1887. Other articles applauding Cable appeared in the issues for February, March, and May, 1885.

[22] "A Note on Cable and His Times," *Survey Graphic*, XXXVI, 28.

cause. The North was indifferent to the plight of the Negro and the poor white; it had surrendered the problem to the South for solution, and Cable understood that the majority in the New South proposed to let time provide a solution, so long as it did so in accordance with the South's material interests and caste traditions. Charles W. Chesnutt, the Negro novelist whose relations with Cable will be discussed later, said of this period:

> At the North, a new Pharaoh had risen, who knew not Israel, —a new generation, who knew little of the fierce passions which played around the negro in a past epoch, and derived their opinions of him from the "coon song" and the police reports. Those of his old friends who survived were disappointed that he had not flown with clipped wings; that he had not in one generation of limited opportunity attained the level of the whites. The whole race question seemed to have reached a sort of *impasse,* a blind alley, of which no one could see the outlet. The negro had become a target at which any one might try a shot. Schoolboys gravely debated the question as to whether or not the negro should exercise the franchise. The pessimist gave him up in despair; while the optimist, smilingly confident that everything would come out all right in the end, also turned aside and went his buoyant way to more pleasing themes.[23]

Yet Cable wrapped himself in the martyr's gown reserved for leaders of lost causes and suffered himself to be dubbed the champion of Negro rights. But the essays which earned him that title single out the Negro only as the man farthest down; they are also devoted to the cause of poor whites, of any Americans exploited by unjust social traditions and an increasingly industrialized economy. Cable said he never spoke for one race or one section alone, and his record

[23] *The Marrow of Tradition,* pp. 238–39.

bears him out. The following correspondence, published in the *Wisconsin State Journal* of January 28, 1885, when Cable and Twain were on their tour, is an example of the esteem in which he was held by Negroes for his work in their behalf; more important, it is evidence of his freedom from the extremes of the zealot.

Madison, Jan. 21.—Dear Mr. Cable: I do not apologize for addressing you thus, because you must feel that the stand you have taken for justice to my people has turned the heart of humanity toward you in admiration for your bravery, in love for your kindness. Hundreds of men like myself are living in this rigorous climate because of the unfair treatment you so eloquently set forth in your article ["The Freedman's Case in Equity"] in last month's *Century* magazine, which is our portion at home. You, sir, have raised a hope in our bosoms that our old neighbors and friends are at last allowing their own hearts to speak for us, and that we will soon see the dawn of a brighter day for our country and our children.

Sir, if you are not inundated with grateful letters from colored people, it is not because of any lack of a keen sense of appreciation, but alas! so few of us *can* let you know how we feel toward you; accept this, dear sir, as the thanks of the colored people of this city, who are only sorry that they have no more able representative than your humble servant. Arthur B. Lee.

Madison, Wis., Jan. 28.—*Mr. Arthur B. Lee*—My dear sir: I thank you most heartily for your letter of 21st inst., received only last night. It is a comfort and a reward to me. I am proud and grateful to say that I have many such from colored men, and also from white men, both north and south.

I am tempted to take the liberty of saying that men of color who can write such letters as these, ought to write to and for the public; and especially to add that in my belief nothing will work more powerfully for the *special* interests of the colored people than for such men to make themselves felt in terse, brief, pointed utterances upon current topics of *general* public interest,—upon interests common to all. This will be to utilize that 'touch of nature' that 'makes the whole world akin.'

When colored men get to writing for white men's newspapers from the standpoint of common citizenship and mutual interests, then we shall see not one or two or half a dozen white men writing in behalf of freedmen's rights, but whole communities yielding those rights.

In short, let all colored men patiently, persistently and with all possible intellectual skill ignore their African origin and do, say and seek everything purely, only and entirely as American citizens, equally interested with all other American citizens in *all* the rights of *all*. I do not, by any means, imply that they should overlook colored men's interests and rights, but that the part of wisdom is to let the greater—at least the larger—include the less. Let colored men show such sagacious, active interest in the rights and interests of all men, that all men, shall gradually be won to regard them as valuable accessions to the community, and most valuable when most free.

Pardon me if my deep interest in the advancement of colored men has led me to speak too freely, and believe me

Yours truly, G. W. Cable [24]

The consistency of Cable's position is shown in an exchange of letters that took place with another colored correspondent some years later. Cable wrote in support of civil rights for the Negro to persons who were planning a new publication, probably the *Woman's Era,* official organ of the National Federation of Afro-American Women. On May 18, Mrs. Josephine St. P. Ruffin replied.[25] Born in Boston in 1842, Mrs. Ruffin was a prominent clubwoman and the wife of George L. Ruffin, a freeborn Virginia Negro

[24] Reprinted in Lorch, "Cable and His Reading Tour with Mark Twain in 1884–1885," *American Literature,* XXIII, 485–86.

[25] This letter is in the Cable Collection at Tulane University. Unless otherwise specified, all letters *to* Cable which I quote or to which I refer in this book are in this collection.

who, on taking up residence in Boston, served in the Massachusetts House, belonged to the city Common Council, and, as judge of the Municipal Court of Charleston District, was the first Negro judge in the state. She asked Cable to supply a new date for his letter and any alterations he might wish; it was her plan to publish the letter in a journal in which her group had become interested. Cable's response, dated May 20, 1891, was entirely in accord with what he had written to Lee six years earlier. He was not an advocate of special privilege for the Negro, and he insisted on emphasizing the freedman's responsibilities, even while pleading that he be granted his rights.

Miss Josephine St. P. Ruffin:

Your letter of the 18th instant has just reached me. I hear with satisfaction of the project you write of. For while it is made more avowedly in the interest of one race in our nation, I have no doubt that the plan is not to limit it to race-interests as such, but only, at the least, as they are part of all mankind's interests and of this whole nation's interests in particular; and without the acceptance of arbitrary race lines and distinctions in any public relations. The Negro race needs, even more than others, to embrace and cultivate partnership in every national & local interest and measure of true progress, sometimes seemingly to the postponement of its own rightful claims. We can often float our stranded ship sooner by putting part of our freight into other vessels than by trying to dig from under her the sands which every breaker brings back again.

With all my heart I wish you Godspeed, confident that your aim is to strike hands with every good cause.

Yours truly

G. W. Cable [26]

If the reception of his commencement address at Vanderbilt was less approving than he might have hoped, Cable

[26] This letter is in the Ruffin Papers in the Moorland Collection at Howard University.

was supported by his confidence that his was a good cause, and he encountered there some enlightened men with whom he could join hands. He and Baskervill found themselves in fundamental agreement; later they collaborated in the work of the Open Letter Club, a project by which Cable undertook to mold the New South into a democratic South. And his respect for Vanderbilt was not appreciably diminished. Late in December, 1887, he wrote in its praise to Richard Watson Gilder and urged that the editor accept an invitation to speak at the university. "I count it one of the chief centers of new, strong light in the true new south—the south of reformed thought and civil order." [27]

In his Nashville speech Cable courageously condemned in the South the exploitation of its disfranchised minority. Efforts to book readings for him in other cities on this southern trip had been largely unsuccessful, and he needed the income such readings would provide, but in order to adhere to principle he sacrificed the opportunity to retreat from his stand as a severe critic of his native section. This even his opponents grudgingly admitted. The chilly reactions of the audiences at Fayetteville and Vanderbilt did not shake his convictions or disturb his equanimity, though the latter was to be sorely tried when he returned to Nashville two years later.

[27] This letter is in the Joint University Libraries, Nashville, Tennessee.

II: Creole Days

At the time when he had the temerity to address Tennesseans on the faith of their fathers, the works which established George W. Cable as a significant American author and a controversial public figure were already in print. Any study of his role as a social critic must depend in large measure upon a careful analysis of the stories, novels, and other writing that flowed from his pen for forty years, particularly upon the books he produced when he believed, as he did most firmly at the outset of his career, that literature should be based on fact, should present truth, and should be an instrument for good. His were the instincts of the reformer, and his manner was moralizing and didactic as well as quaint and sentimental. His treatment of ante bellum Louisiana cannot be dismissed as mere local color; it is also sociological diagnosis which interprets and criticizes, not simply to expose past evils but to arouse public pressure for the amelioration of present ills. It springs from careful research and thoughtful observation of a Creole culture with which Cable was not really in sympathy; it is directed at the traditions and practices of a contemporary South which he felt was not yet a democratic society adhering to principles of "reformed thought and civil order." Picturesque his work was, but it was not therefore lacking in realism. For its sound social criticism, and for its realistic picture of the Negro, it requires close attention here as a necessary preliminary to the study of Cable's later efforts to serve as the conscience of the nation and a public benefactor.

Old Creole Days, which brought him his first fame, is still his best-known work. The original edition of 1879 contained his first seven stories, but in the edition of 1883 and later printings "Madame Delphine" was often added.[1] Arranged chronologically according to the period with which they deal, the tales trace the social history of New Orleans and its environs. Cable knew exactly to which year of the city's history each story related.[2]

"Jean-ah Poquelin" is set in the New Orleans of 1805, two years after the Louisiana Purchase, "when the newly established American Government was the most hateful thing in Louisiana." [3] Jean Marie Poquelin, an ex-smuggler and slave trader, is suspected of having murdered his younger brother, Jacques. He leads a hermit-like existence on an old estate fallen into decay and he resists all the city's efforts to clear the swamp on his property so that a road may pass through. A mob gathers one night to annoy the unpopular Creole who is halting the march of progress. When it reaches the "haunted" house it finds his slave hauling a coffin—for Jean has just died—followed by the living remains of Jacques, a leper. The ghastly figures disappear in

[1] My citations are from The Heritage Press edition (1943). This includes "Père Raphaël," which first appeared in *Century Magazine* in 1901, and reprints Lafcadio Hearn's essay "The Scenes of Cable's Romances," and a revised version of Edward Larocque Tinker's "Cable and the Creoles."

[2] Biklé, *George W. Cable: His Life and Letters,* p. 58.

[3] *Old Creole Days,* p. 1.

the swamp in the direction of leper's land and are seen no more. This slight narrative is hardly more than a framework for Cable's portrait of a culture in a state of transition, the decadent Creole society—"still kicking at such vile innovations as the trial by jury, American dances, anti-smuggling laws, and the printing of the Governor's proclamation in English" [4]—being overwhelmed by aggressive, industrious aliens with a new set of values. Cable evidences the local colorist's interest in exotic characters and dialects, but there is also the objective realism of the social scientist depicting the history of an epoch.

A romantic story of New Orleans in 1810, " 'Tite Poulette" introduces several plot devices of which Cable made later and more extensive use. Poulette is the pretty daughter of Zalli (Madame John), a quadroon who was once the mistress of a white man. Kristian Koppig, a Dutchman and a stranger to the South, who lives across the street from the quadroons, falls in love with Poulette against his will. He proposes to her, only to have her refuse him because the law prohibits their marriage. Zalli clears away that obstacle by swearing that Poulette is not her child but the daughter of Spanish parents who entrusted the infant girl to her keeping just before they died.

Cable points out that the penury of the quadroon women, despite their struggles to achieve respectability and a little security, must be laid at the door of the white women who are their natural competitors and enemies; the quadroons are ever beaten back "by the steady detestation of their imperious patronesses." [5] Lamenting their unfortunate plight, Madame John says to her beautiful

[4] *Ibid.*

[5] *Ibid.*, p. 27.

daughter, "There is no place in this world for us poor women. I wish that we were either white or black!" [6]

The use of an "alien," like Kristian Koppig, as hero is a common device in Cable's fiction. Often the hero is a man estranged by national or sectional origin from the culture in which he functions, or somehow out of sympathy with it. There is every reason to suppose that this approach was adopted as an aid in describing the locale—it is common in the literature of local color—but perhaps it is also an unconscious reflection of Cable's own position in his native city. As a Protestant American, he was in a sense a "foreigner" to the Creoles, and his lack of sympathy for Bourbon traditions, discernible in even his early fugitive writing, soon made him an alien to the South's political principles. Kristian Koppig may be taken for Cable himself: Cable the outsider, the man of Christian principle and practice, the poor clerk, the Puritan in a sinful land where the laws condone and the customs perpetuate iniquities.

The description of Zalli reveals Cable's sympathy for the quadroon caste and foreshadows the glamorous stereotype of later historical novels. His use of the quadroon balls, affairs at which Creole gentlemen contracted alliances with beautiful young colored women reared to be their mistresses, did nothing to endear him to his Creole contemporaries, though it has put a hundred romancers in his debt.

"Posson Jone'," one of Cable's rare attempts at humor, was a favorite story with the author, and many years after it was written he was still giving readings from it. Dialect and deviations from the accepted norm are always the basis for Cable's humor, a humor which is condescending and

[6] *Ibid.*, p. 29.

mildly disapproving. The involved tale of the New Orleans of 1815 concerns the attempts of Jules St.-Ange, an irresponsible young Creole much addicted to gambling, to relieve a giant American minister from the backwoods of Florida of a large roll of bills belonging to his church. The story displays Cable's talent for rendering varied dialects with fidelity, and his range of character types, but it is the panorama of fabulous New Orleans—the atmosphere—which dominates the narrative. Cable had difficulty in securing publication for this story because of its uncomplimentary picture of the clergyman, whose adherence to Sabbatarian practices was almost as inconvenient to Jules as Cable's was to Mark Twain.

If in "'Tite Poulette" Cable is merely exploiting the sentimental possibilities of a unique situation, in "Madame Delphine," set in the New Orleans of 1821–22, he seems to be consciously crusading. The two stories have much in common; in each a supposed octoroon marries a white man after her mother denies relationship to the girl and produces "evidence" that the young woman is really white. But in "Madame Delphine" the reader knows that the girl is colored, despite her mother's protestations.[7]

Madame Delphine Carraze, "a small, rather tired-looking, dark quadroone of very good features and a gentle thoughtfulness of expression,"[8] manages to support herself and her pretty daughter, Olive, on the small income from property left her by her white American "husband." Olive has

[7] Cable said, in the preface to an 1895 edition of *Old Creole Days,* that he received a letter from an anoymous quadroon urging him to change the story he had told in "'Tite Poulette" to reveal that the mother lied in order to make her daughter's marriage possible. Turner, *George W. Cable,* p. 105.

[8] *Old Creole Days,* p. 97.

just returned to her mother after spending most of her seventeen years with her father's relatives. On the voyage to New Orleans, her ship had been stopped by pirates captained by the famous Ursin Lemaitre, who was so affected by Olive's delicate beauty that he spared the ship in exchange for her Bible. Later, unknown to Olive or her mother, Lemaitre, converted by this experience, returns to the city and sets himself up quietly as a benevolent banker. Madame Delphine is so impressed by his kindness that she secures his services as guardian for Olive in the event of her own death. Lemaitre, constantly wandering about the city in an aimless search for the girl with whom he has fallen in love, accidentally discovers that she is the quadroon's daughter. After promising to find the girl a white husband and thus assure her safety, he calls at the home of the mother and daughter and immediately becomes engaged to Olive, who has loved him all the time. Lemaitre's friends threaten to reveal his identity and whereabouts to the federal officers who are seeking him, unless he will agree to break the engagement. Madame Delphine overcomes all objections to the union by producing pictures of Olive's father and the white woman whom she identifies as the girl's real mother, and she signs an affadavit declaring that Olive is white. The marriage takes place, but Madame Dalphine confesses to her priest, the sympathetic Père Jerome, that she has lied. Olive is her own child. Ill since her renunciation of her daughter, Madame Delphine dies in the confessional.

This story is probably Cable's most thorough analysis and revelation in fiction of the plight of the quadroon. It has more particularized characterization than " 'Tite Poulette," and it exploits more effectively the odd history of New

Orleans. There is romance—traceable mainly to the sweep of the large canvas which is the scene—rather than merely sentimental melodrama. Here is Cable at the height of his powers, using a style perfectly suited to evoke a brilliant, exotic past and, without being obtrusively didactic, to strike at the pretensions and injustices of a decadent culture.

In building his scene, Cable gives a leisurely description of New Orleans quadroons which is worthy of quotation in its entirety.

During the first quarter of the present century, the free quadroon caste of New Orleans was in its golden age. Earlier generations, sprung, upon the one hand, from the merry gallants of a French colonial military service which had grown gross by affiliation with Spanish-American frontier life, and, upon the other hand, from comely Ethiopians culled out of the less Negroidal types of African live goods, and bought at the ship's side with vestiges of quills and cowries and copper wire still in their headdresses—these earlier generations, with scars of battle or private rencontre still on the fathers, and of servitude on the manumitted mothers, afforded a mere hint of the splendor that was to result from a survival of the fairest through seventy-five years devoted to the elimination of the black pigment and the cultivation of hyperion excellence and nymphean grace and beauty. Nor, if we turn to the present, is the evidence much stronger which is offered by the *gens de couleur* whom you may see in the quadroon quarter this afternoon, with "Ichabod" legible on their murky foreheads through a vain smearing of toilet powder, dragging their chairs down to the narrow gateway of their close-fenced gardens, and staring shrinkingly at you as you pass, like a nest of yellow kittens.

But as the present century was in its second and third decades, the *quadroones* (for we must contrive a feminine spelling to define the strict limits of the caste as then established) came forth in splendor. Old travelers spare no terms to tell their praises, their faultlessness of feature, their perfection of form, their varied styles of beauty—for there were even pure Caucasian blondes among them—their fascinating manners, their sparkling vivacity, their chaste and pretty wit, their grace in the dance, their modest propriety, their taste and elegance in dress. In the gentlest and most poetic sense they are indeed the sirens of this land, where it seemed "always afternoon"—a momentary triumph of an Arcadian over a Christian civilization, so beautiful and so seductive that it became the subject of special chapters by writers of the day more original than correct as social philosophers.

The balls that were got up for them by the male *sang-pur* were to that day what the carnival is to the present. Society balls given the same nights proved failures through the coincidence. The magnates of government—municipal, state, federal—those of the army, of the learned professions and of the clubs—in short, the white male aristocracy in everything save the ecclesiastical desk—were there. Tickets were high-priced to insure the exclusion of the vulgar. No distinguished stranger was allowed to miss them. They were beautiful! They were clad in silken extenuations from the throat to the feet, and wore, withal, a pathos in their charm that gave them a family likeness to innocence.[9]

Cable manipulates his characters and plot deftly, telling the story with unhurried care. The glamorous backdrop of early Louisiana history is more than a setting; it is the real strength of the tale. There are melodramatic lapses—lapses which were counted as virtues in an age of sentiment and gentility—such as the scene in which Lemaitre is led to cash a counterfeit note for Delphine as a device to establish his kindliness. Coincidence is strained when he discovers Olive's identity without disclosing his own. There is patent foreshadowing when the reader learns that none of Lemaitre's family "ever kept the laws of any government or creed."[10] Delphine's death is contrived and un-

[9] *Ibid.*, pp. 96–97. [10] *Ibid.*, p. 98.

convincing. But the story avoids the clumsiness of "'Tite Poulette," which Lafcadio Hearn regarded as the poorest of Cable's Creole tales,[11] and it does not dodge the social issues it raises. Epitomizing both his strengths and weaknesses, it is perfectly characteristic of Cable's early work.

Père Jerome, the figure around whom the action revolves and through whose eyes it is interpreted, is the author's *raisonneur;* it is through him that Cable condemns the caste system of old New Orleans and, by implication, of the South of his own day. When Madame Delphine first takes her troubles to Père Jerome and speaks of her love for Olive's father, the priest consoles her. "If your love was pure and lawful I am sure your angel guardian smiled upon you; and if it was not, I cannot say you have nothing to answer for, and yet I think God may have said: 'She is a poor quadroone; all the rights of her womanhood trampled in the mire, sin made easy to her—almost compulsory—charge it to account of whom it may concern.'"[12] The priest asks if Olive looks like her mother. "Oh, thank God, no! you would never believe she was my daughter; she is white and beautiful!" He replies, with an insight one might expect of the woman herself, "You thank God for that which is your main difficulty, Madame Delphine."[13]

Cable heightens Olive's tragedy by making her the traditionally beautiful young heroine of all romances. Thus he offended Creoles who were quick to recognize that the practice of depicting such women of mixed blood as virtuous and beautiful was a device for criticizing the society that exploited them.

[11] See Hearn's letter to H. E. Krehbiel in 1883. Bisland, *The Life and Letters of Lafcadio Hearn,* I, 289.

[12] *Old Creole Days,* p. 110. [13] *Ibid.,* p. 111.

She was just passing seventeen—that beautiful year when the heart of the maiden still beats quickly with the surprise of her new dominion, while with gentle dignity her brow accepts the holy coronation of womanhood. The forehead and temples beneath her loosely bound hair were fair without paleness, and meek without languor. She had the soft, lack-lustre beauty of the South; no ruddiness of coral, no waxen white, no pink of shell; no heavenly blue in the glance, but a face that seemed, in all its other beauties, only a tender accompaniment for the large, brown, melting eyes, where the openness of child-nature mingled dreamily with the sweet mysteries of maiden thought. We say no color of shell on face or throat; but this was no deficiency, that which took its place being the warm, transparent tint of sculptured ivory.[14]

While he does not stress them, Cable recognizes, here and elsewhere, the shortcomings of the quadroon caste. Delphine's prejudices, molded by the society of which she is a victim, are apparent when she resents Lemaitre's offer to provide Olive with a husband until he explains that he means a white gentleman. But Delphine is not naïve and does not accept supinely the statutes which stigmatize and oppress her caste. When she tells Père Jerome that she has engaged her daughter to Lemaitre in defiance of the law against mixed marriages, she rages against that law, supposedly designed to keep the races apart.

"Separate! No–o–o! They do not want to keep us separated; no, no! But they *do* want to keep us despised!" She laid her hand on her heart and frowned upward with physical pain. "But, very well! from which race do they want to keep my daughter separate? She is seven parts white! The law did not stop her from being that; and now, when she wants to be a white man's good and honest wife, shall that law stop her? Oh, no!" She rose up. "No; I will tell you what that law is made for. It

[14] *Ibid.*, p. 121.

is made to—punish—my—child—for—not—choosing—her—father! Père Jerome—my God, what a law!" [15]

That Delphine—and Cable—conceive of marriage to a white man as the only real solution to Olive's problem is evidence of the pervasive strength of the caste tradition. This, however, detracts but little from the force of the story's social criticism.

Cable finds quadroon and octoroon women attractive, often beautiful, and depicts their plight as tragic; the men, always of a character similar to that of the more ignoble Creoles, are objects of his scorn or, at best, pity. In this respect, Cable adopts Creole and majority attitudes. By invariably coupling octoroon women and white men he suggests the pattern, historically correct but not inviolable, which later romances have made a cliché.

"Belles Demoiselles Plantation" is of interest for its admission of the fact of Creole-Indian miscegenation and its suggestion that the barriers between the various races were little observed in the Louisiana of 1820. The opening paragraphs, which impute moral laxity and an obscure origin to one of the great Creole families, did not endear Cable to his neighbors of French or Spanish descent.

The original grantee was Count ———, assume the name to be De Charleu; the old Creoles never forgive a public mention. He was the French king's commissary. One day, called to France to explain the lucky accident of the commissariat having burned down with the account-books inside, he left his wife, a Choctaw Comptesse, behind.

Arrived at court, his excuses were accepted, and that tract granted him where afterwards stood Belles Demoiselles Plantation. A man cannot remember every thing! In a fit of forgetfulness he married a French gentlewoman, rich and beautiful, and "brought her out." However, "All's well that ends well"; a famine

[15] *Ibid.*, p. 134.

had been in the colony, and the Choctaw Comptesse had starved, leaving nought but a half-caste orphan family lurking on the edge of the settlement, bearing our French gentlewoman's own new name, and being mentioned in Monsieur's will.[16]

Creoles could not pardon Cable for saying that a Creole will not "go back on the ties of blood, no matter what sort of knots those ties may be."[17]

"Madame Délicieuse" and "Café des Exilés" are condescending romances which pretend to condone in Creoles qualities which would be shortcomings in other people. Creole principles need not be constructed in "the austere Anglo-Saxon style," Cable says, since the lattice of the confessional is always at hand.[18] " 'Sieur George," Cable's first published story, is more directly related to the author's penchant for social criticism. Its moral springs specifically from his study of the Louisiana Lottery Company, but incidental comments ridicule the foibles of the Creoles and their "doubtful purity of blood."[19]

Before *Old Creole Days* was published, Cable had begun work on his first novel. Later he said of it:

It was impossible that a novel written by me then should escape being a study of the fierce struggle going on around me, regarded in the light of past history—those beginnings—which had so differentiated Louisiana from the American scheme of public society. I meant to make "The Grandissimes" as truly a political work as it has ever been called. . . . I wrote as near to truth and justice as I knew how, upon questions I saw must be settled by calm debate and cannot be settled by force or silence.[20]

[16] *Ibid.*, p. 147. [17] *Ibid.*, p. 150.

[18] *Ibid.* ("Madame Délicieuse"), p. 167.

[19] *Ibid.*, p. 211. For Cable's attacks on the lottery company and other early reform efforts see Turner, "George W. Cable's Beginnings as a Reformer," *Journal of Southern History*, XVII, 136–61.

[20] Biklé, *George W. Cable: His Life and Letters*, p. 55.

When Boyesen saw the work in outline he predicted that it would be "a novel in which the struggling forces of opposing civilizations crystalize & in which they find their enduring monument." [21] The book is a realistic portrait of a state of society—New Orleans in 1804—and is powerful social criticism.

The main plot is a conventional romantic love story with local color treatment; this is an expression of one aspect of Cable's character and is what his publishers wanted.[22] Joseph Frowenfeld, a young apothecary of German extraction, falls in love with Clotilde Nancanou, the last of the De Grapions. Honoré Grandissime, merchant, loves Clotilde's widowed mother, Aurora. The pairs of lovers are kept apart by their social positions—Frowenfeld is an "alien" and the Nancanous are impoverished—and by an ancient feud. Years before, Agricola Fusilier of the proud Grandissime clan killed Aurora's husband in a duel after winning all his property at the gambling table. Honoré's decision to make restitution, at considerable loss to himself, and a reconciliation of the families arranged by Honoré's sister after Agricola's death enable the couples to marry.

It is the minor plots which extend the scope of the novel and give it significance. One of these, a version of the rejected "Bibi" which Cable said he wrote in sheer indignation over his discovery of the Black Code, is the story of Bras-Coupé. In his reading in the colonial history of Louisiana, Cable found accounts of a tribe of Negroes who resorted to self-mutilitation rather than accept slavery.

[21] *Ibid.*, p. 56.

[22] Throughout his career Cable's work was much affected by the supervision of his publishers, whose efforts were directed toward reducing the social criticism and increasing the romantic charm. On the editing of *The Grandissimes* see Turner, *George W. Cable*, pp. 95–98.

Bras-Coupé, dead more than eight years before the main events of the novel take place, was a Jaloff prince before he was enslaved in a tribal war, brought to America, and sold to Agricola Fusilier who resold him to Don José Martinez. Having accepted slavery as his fate, Bras-Coupé, whose name is translated as "the Arm Cut Off," has not resigned himself to the indignity of work. When a slave driver explains to him by signs that work is expected of him, he kills the driver, tosses another Negro into the branches of a willow, throws a black woman, Clemence, into a draining-ditch, and bounds for freedom. A ball from the overseer's pistol brings him down. Impressed by the giant Negro's regal bearing, the Spaniard orders the overseer to get an interpreter and arrive at an understanding with the slave. Agricola volunteers the services of Palmyre, a quadroon maid to his niece. On sight of the beautiful colored woman, Bras-Coupé's spirit is broken by desire and he consents to work as a driver of other slaves on condition that Palmyre be given him as a wife. She protests, for she is secretly and hopelessly in love with Honoré Grandissime, but Agricola Fusilier maliciously agrees to the arrangement.

The wedding of Bras-Coupé and Palmyre is held at the same time as that of Palmyre's mistress, Honoré's sister, and Don José, a distant cousin of the De Grapions. At the banquet which follows, Bras-Coupé tastes wine for the first time, and with a drunken demand for more, he claps his fellow bridegroom on the shoulder. The outraged white man lifts his hand, but before he can strike he is felled by the slave's fist.

Dolorous stroke!—for the dealer of it. Given, apparently to him—poor, tipsy savage—in self-defence, punishable, in a white offender, by a small fine or a few days' imprisonment, it assured

Bras-Coupé the death of a felon; such was the old *Code Noir*. (We have a *Code Noir* now, but the new one is a mental reservation, not an enactment.) [23]

But Bras-Coupé escapes the fury of the mob by fleeing to the swamp. When finally he leaves his hiding place to join the dancers in the Place Congo he is taken by the police. Under the Black Code, established by the French and continued in force by the Spaniards, his punishment for striking a white man is death, but the master spares his life and contents himself with the "lesser" punishment decreed for a slave who twice runs away to freedom. Bras-Coupé is branded on both shoulders with the *fleur de lis*, his ears are cut off, and he is hamstrung. Then he is strapped down and lashed. "And yet not a sound came from the mutilated but unconquered African to annoy the ear of the sleeping city." [24]

This summary does not do justice to the story of Bras-Coupé, with its revelation of Creole superstition and promiscuity, its biting commentary on the viciousness of slavery as a system that ignores the fact that God "made men's skins of different colors, but all blood of one," [25] and its sharp delineation of a wide range of characters. In Bras-Coupé himself, Cable has brought to life a well-realized individual who is also a symbol of a type of Negro who did exist—the man who refused to adapt himself to the status of a slave.

After Bras-Coupé's death, Palmyre is given her freedom. She is a woman "of superb stature and poise, severely handsome features, clear, tawny skin and large, passionate

[23] *The Grandissimes* (1898), p. 235. In the first edition (1880) there was excessive dialect. The work was revised in 1883 to eliminate some of this, especially in Honoré's speeches to Frowenfeld.

[24] *Ibid.*, p. 249. [25] *Ibid.*, p. 219.

black eyes." [26] Her life is dominated by her hatred of slavery and a fierce determination to kill Agricola Fusilier. She stabs him, but he recovers. She then turns to voodoo, but the old man's death is finally accomplished by a passive, ineffectual man from whom Palmyre might have expected little direct assistance.

There are two Honoré Grandissimes, half-brothers. One, for whom Palmyre holds an unrequited passion all her life, is the active head of the aristocratic Creole family; the other, a "free man of color," is a successful real estate broker. Although they have been educated together in Paris as boys, they have had little contact in their adult life in New Orleans. When he returns from France the colored man falls in love with Palmyre and offers to buy her so that he may free her and make her his wife. Agricola Fusilier tells him that the quadroon is the wife of Bras-Coupé, that his request is impudent, and promises, "if ever you bring your Parisian airs and self-sufficient face on a level with mine again, h-I will slap it." [27] Agricola carries out this threat when the "f.m.c." presumptuously attends a quadroon ball.

Frowenfeld, whose identification with Kristian Koppig of "'Tite Poulette" and with Cable himself is obvious,[28] cannot understand why the colored man accepts his outcast position so passively.

"It seems to me," said Frowenfeld, "that you—your class—the free quadroons—are the saddest slaves of all. Your men, for a

[26] *Ibid.*, p. 71. [27] *Ibid.*, p. 242.

[28] The earliest of Cable's paternal ancestors to settle in America was evidently Jacob Kobell of Wurtemberg, Germany, who arrived in the early eighteenth century. His son changed the name to Kable, which spelling was kept by one branch of the family. See Turner, *George W. Cable*, p. 4*n*.

little property, and your women, for a little amorous attention, let themselves be shorn even of the virtue of discontent, and for a paltry bait of sham freedom have consented to endure a tyrannous contumely which flattens them into the dirt like grass under a slab." [29]

The colored man admits the justice of this indictment but protests that his broken heart (because of Palmyre's refusal to marry him) and his good judgment prevent him from acting; he says he has not the ability to be a Toussaint L'Ouverture.

"You entirely misunderstand me," said Frowenfeld in quick response. "I have no stronger belief than my disbelief in insurrection. I believe that to every desirable end there are two roads, the way of strife and the way of peace. I can imagine a man in your place, going about among his people, stirring up their minds to a noble discontent, laying out his means, sparingly here and bountifully there, as in each case might seem wisest, for their enlightenment, their moral elevation, their training in skilled work; going, too, among the men of the prouder caste, among such as have a spirit of fairness, and seeking to prevail with them for a public recognition of the rights of all; using all his cunning to show them the double damage of all oppression, both great and petty———" [30]

Thus Cable expresses his philosophy of the action necessary to combat, not slavery, but discrimination and segregation. It was the course of action he followed personally in his advocacy of civil rights for the Negro.

The father of the two Honoré Grandissimes has bequeathed the bulk of his fortune to the elder of his sons, the colored man, and has left the other a mere competence. When the white man decides to repay the family's indebtedness to the Nancanous, he considers a proposition made by his richer namesake. The quadroon offers to invest all

[29] *The Grandissimes,* p. 255. [30] *Ibid.,* p. 256.

his capital in the family mercantile house on condition that he be made a full partner. The enlightened white man is glad to accept the proposal, without which he could not make restitution to the Nancanous, and he regards the condition as just. But though his kinsmen admit that the colored man's money has saved them from ruin, they are infuriated by the idea of a partnership. Agricola leads a mob to lynch the presumptuous quadroon, who goes into hiding. Later the two men meet in Frowenfeld's pharmacy. Agricola, demanding that the quadroon be ejected, strikes him with his staff, and the mulatto takes the revenge he and Palmyre have so long desired. He stabs Agricola fatally and walks away unmolested. He flees with Palmyre to France, where he commits suicide when she persists in her refusal to marry him.

Though they are "tragic quadroons" to the end, Palmyre and the "f.m.c." are departures from the stereotype in that their tragedy is that of unrequited love rather than mixed racial inheritance.[31] Neither for "a little property" nor for "amorous attention" have they permitted themselves to be shorn of "the virtue of discontent." Palmyre is by far the stronger character, for she is the very spirit of resentment and revolt. Her militant disregard for the caste philosophy of Creole and mulatto society and her recognition of the essential unity of interest between the free quadroon and the black slave represent a social consciousness ahead of her time and give her a stature above that of Cable's other women of mixed blood, whose concern is solely for their personal fortunes and their own caste.

Probably the most genuine and moving figure in the

[31] See Brown, *The Negro in American Fiction,* pp. 66–67, and "Negro Character as Seen by White Authors," *Journal of Negro Education,* II, 192–96.

novel is the old black woman, Clemence, the *marchande des calas* who dispenses a droll, biting wisdom as she sells her rice croquettes and ginger cakes. She cannot quite conceal beneath her playful manner the fact that she has thought carefully about her condition of life and that the spirit of rebellion burns in her as fiercely as in Palmyre. The violent end that Clemence meets is largely the result of the indiscretions that flow from her sharp tongue. When she is told that the slaves are the happiest people under the sun, she denies it indignantly.

"Oh, . . . white folks is werry kine. Dey wants us to b'lieb we happy—dey *wants to b'lieb* we is. W'y, you know, dey 'bleeged to b'lieb it—fo' dey own cyumfut. 'Tis de sem weh wid de preache's; dey buil' we ow own sep'ate meet'n-houses; dey b'leebs us lak it de bess, an' dey *knows* dey lak it de bess."

The laugh at this was mostly her own. It is not a laughable sight to see the comfortable fractions of Christian communities everywhere striving, with sincere, pious, well-meant, criminal benevolence, to make their poor brethren contented with the ditch.[32]

The men of the Grandissime clan, with the exception of Honoré and Agricola, assemble to mete out punishment to the old black woman when she confesses that, acting as Palmyre's agent, she put voodoo fetishes on Agricola's pillow. The quadroon has fled the country and is out of reach; Clemence must bear the full brunt of their vengeance. She pleads for her life, for she recognizes that she is in danger of more than a whipping.

" 'Tain' no use to hang me; you gwan to kyetch Palmyre yit; *li courri dans marais;* she is in de swamp yeh, sum'ers; but as concernin' me, you'd oughteh jis gimme fawty an' lemme go.

[32] *The Grandissimes,* p. 330.

You mus'n' b'lieve all dis-yeh nonsense 'bout insurrectionin'; all fool-nigga talk. W'at we want to be insurrectionin' faw? We de happies' people in de God's worl'!" [33]

When the noose is dropped over her head Clemence is eloquent even in her terror.

"Ah! no, mawsteh, you cyan' do dat! It's ag'in' de law! I's 'bleeged to have my trial, yit. Oh, no, no! Oh, good God, no! Even if I is a nigga! You cyan' jis' murdeh me hyeh in de woods! . . . You ain' got no mo' biznis to do me so 'an if I was a white 'oman!" [34]

They draw her up, but some of the men dissent. One of them lets the struggling woman down and loosens the noose.

"Let her go!"

"Let her go!" said Jean-Baptiste Grandissime; "give her a run for life. Old woman rise up. We propose to let you go. Can you run? Never mind, we shall see. Achille, put her upon her feet. Now, old woman, run!"

She walked rapidly, but with unsteady feet, toward the fields.

"Run! If you don't run I will shoot you this minute!"

She ran.

"Faster!"

She ran faster.

"Run!"

"Run!"

"Run, Clemence! Ha, ha, ha!" It was so funny to see her scuttling and tripping and stumbling. *"Courri! courri, Clemence! c'est pou' to vie!* ha, ha, ha———"

A pistol-shot rang out close behind Raoul's ear; it was never told who fired it. The negress leaped into the air and fell at full length to the ground, stone dead.[35]

[33] *Ibid.*, pp. 425–26. Cable remarks that bitter, persecuted Palmyre belongs "to what we used to call 'the happiest people under the sun.' We ought to stop saying that." *Ibid.*, p. 173.

[34] *Ibid.*, p. 426.

[35] *Ibid.*, pp. 427–28.

That Cable—and his editors and public—delighted in the picturesque cannot be denied, but in *The Grandissimes* the romantic and picturesque are used merely as sugar coating for the social critic's bitter pill. Cable has intentionally invested Bras-Coupé with qualities that give him heroic proportions and make him significant as well as unique. Even the quadroons are more than stereotypes, for their problem is not that of mixed inheritance, with the white blood supposedly arousing aspirations which the baser Negro blood inevitably frustrates; it is that of caste. They do not long to be white; they long to be really free. And Cable tells the story of Clemence—not a pretty young quadroon but an old black woman—with an artistic insight and power later realists might imitate but not excel.

The Creoles of Louisiana (1884) should be studied in connection with the author's early fiction. Except for the Civil War and Reconstruction, here omitted, the history is a summary of all that Cable wrote in his fiction about the subject on which his literary reputation is based.[36]

Cable's disregard for the approval of the Creoles is shown in this reference to their ancestry:

> There is no need to distinguish between the higher and humbler grades of those from whom they sprang. A few settlers only were persons of rank and station. Many were the children of the casket-girls, and many were of such stock as society pronounces less than nothing. . . .[37]

[36] Cable was one of the twelve members who incorporated the Louisiana Historical Society in 1877 (it had been organized about 1836) and as late as 1888 his name was still on the roll. Willink, "The Louisiana Historical Society Fifty Years Ago," *Louisiana Historical Quarterly*, VII, 667–71. Cable's history and his fiction were sometimes considered unparalleled attacks on the Creoles, but all his unfavorable observations had first been made by other writers, some of whom were Creoles.

[37] *The Creoles of Louisiana*, p. 42.

Cable's preference for Creole women is evident in his evaluation of Creole character:

The women were fair, symmetrical, with pleasing features, lively, expressive eyes, well-rounded throats, and superb hair; vivacious, decorous, exceedingly tasteful in dress, adorning themselves with superior effect in draperies of muslin enriched with embroideries and much garniture of lace, but with a more moderate display of jewels, which indicated a community of limited wealth. They were much superior to the men in quickness of wit, and excelled them in amiability and in many other good qualities. The more pronounced faults of the men were generally those moral provincialisms which travellers recount with undue impatience. They are said to have been coarse, boastful, vain; and they were, also, deficient in energy and application, without well-directed ambition, unskilful in handicraft—doubtless through negligence only —and totally wanting in that community feeling which begets the study of reciprocal rights and obligations, and reveals the individual's advantage in the promotion of the common interest. Hence, the Creoles were fonder of pleasant fictions regarding the salubrity, beauty, good order, and advantages of their town, than of measures to justify their assumptions. With African slavery they were, of course, licentious, and they were always ready for the duelling-ground; yet it need not seem surprising that a people so beset by evil influences from every direction were generally unconscious of a reprehensible state of affairs, and preserved their self-respect and a proud belief in their moral excellence.[38]

The assertion that Cable "conveyed to Eastern readers the idea that the Creoles have a strain of negro blood" [39] may have been based on this history and such other nonfiction as his article, "New Orleans," in the *Encyclopaedia Britannica* (1884).

The Creoles of New Orleans and the surrounding delta are a handsome, graceful, intelligent race, of a decidedly Gallic type; though softened in features, speech, and carriage, and somewhat

[38] *Ibid.*, pp. 139–40.

[39] DeMenil, *The Literature of the Louisiana Territory*, p. 217.

relaxed in physical and mental energies by the enervating influences that blow from the West Indies and the Spanish Main. Their better class does not offer to the eye that unpleasant evidence of gross admixture of races which distinguishes those Latin-American communities around the borders of the adjacent seas; and the name they have borrowed from those regions does not necessarily imply, *any more than it excludes,* a departure from a pure double line of descent.[40]

While *The Creoles of Louisiana* gives sympathetic attention to the role of the Negro soldiers in the early wars and to the labors of the field hands and artisans, it does not ignore the ignorance of the blacks or the caste reasoning of the quadroons. But Cable understands the extenuating circumstances involved. He says in "New Orleans":

The coloured population, not withstanding the presence among it of that noted quadroon class which has enjoyed a certain legal freedom for many generations, has not greatly improved since the date of emancipation. A conventional system of caste cuts them off from the stimulating hope of attaining social rank and confines them closely to servile employments.[41]

The "legal freedom" the quadroon caste had experienced for many generations was little more than a fiction.

A poor freedom it was, indeed: to have f.m.c. or f.w.c. tacked in small letters upon one's name perforce and by law, that all might know that the bearer was not a real free man or free woman but only a free man (or woman) of color,—a title that could not be indicated by capital initials; to be the unlawful mates of luxurious bachelors, and take their pay in muslins, embroideries, prunella, and good living, taking with them the loathing of honest women and the salacious derision of the blackamoor; . . . to fall heir to property by sufferance, not by law; to be taxed for public

[40] *Encyclopaedia Britannica* (Ninth Edition), XVII, 404. Italics mine.

[41] *Ibid.*, p. 405.

education and not allowed to give that education to one's own children; to be shut out of all occupations that the master class could reconcile with the vague title of gentleman; to live in the knowledge that the law pronounced "death or imprisonment at hard labor for life" against whoever would be guilty of "writing, printing, publishing, or distributing anything having a tendency to create discontent among the free colored population": that it threatened death against whosoever should utter such things in private conversations. . . .[42]

But however much Cable bemoaned the status of the quadroon, he knew that the position of the slave field hand was far worse. "Even the requirement of the law was only that he should not have less than a barrel of corn—nothing else,—a month, nor get more than thirty lashes in twenty-four hours."[43]

Cable evidently believed that his portrait of Creole dialect, manners, psychology, character, history, and culture was accurate. But his claim for the kindly intent of his work is hard to support. The charm of his Creole characters is generally superficial and they are slyly ridiculed. Creole shortcomings are magnified and criticized and used to support generalizations which a sensitive minority could not but regard as malicious misrepresentation. Cable's picture of the Creole suffers from limitations imposed by his background and his personality. His attitude toward the Negro, the object rather than the perpetrator of injustice, is far more generous, and he is particularly indulgent with the quadroon, whose guilt must be charged to society.

The success of *Old Creole Days* undoubtedly pleased Cable, but it was not a success which seemed to guarantee the serious gratitude of his contemporaries or of posterity.

[42] "Creole Slave Songs," *Century Magazine,* XXXI, 811.

[43] "The Dance in Place Congo," *Century Magazine,* XXXI, 522.

The stories did not satisfy his humanitarian instincts—though they reveal them—and even *The Grandissimes,* in which his equalitarian idealism is more evident, gives only indirect expression of the talent for social analysis and the zeal for civic reform which dominated George W. Cable in the 1880s. Yet these two books have proved to be the lasting monument he sought. Never again did he blend quite so effectively romance and realism, sentiment and social purpose, the opposing forces in his own complex personality that drove him for years to divide his time and efforts between story telling and civic service.

III: Into the Main Current

In his address on literature in the Southern states, delivered at the commencement program of the University of Mississippi in June, 1882, Cable lamented the failure of Southern authors to enter the main current of American thought. Approving the use of native subjects, he urged that the resulting literature be written "to and for the whole nation." [1] At this time he was at work on his second novel, *Dr. Sevier,*[2] and was endeavoring to practice what he preached.

This novel is evidence of the broadening of Cable's horizon and his further defection from the political traditions of the South. For the first time he is not writing about old Creole days. Only incidental use is made of the quadroon caste and the single important Creole character merely serves, as a sort of trademark, to placate a publisher and readers who expected the author to continue to treat material with which he had had notable success. The emphasis

[1] Turner, "George W. Cable's Revolt Against Literary Sectionalism," *Tulane Studies in English,* V, 19.

[2] I have a letter from Cable to James R. Osgood, dated April 4, 1882, in which he says he has completed the equivalent of about 225 pages. Osgood published the first edition of *Dr. Sevier* in 1884. Editions after 1887 were published by Scribner's. My citations are from the edition of 1910.

is on Americans and on Italian, German, and Irish immigrants. Interest is centered on the problem of making a plain living in various small occupations rather than on the decay of an aristocratic society. Here the crusade is not against a dead issue—slavery—but against the South's substandard prisons and asylums. As usual, Cable's writing in this instance parallels his civic activities; *Dr. Sevier* is an outgrowth of his labors in New Orleans for prison and asylum reform, a work which began when he was made grand jury secretary in April, 1881.[3] With characteristic thoroughness, he made a point of studying prisons and asylums in other cities and, once convinced of the need for reforming the medieval institutions of the Crescent City, he headed civic committees and wielded a vigorous pen in an effort to stir the community to action. *Dr. Sevier* is a product of his research and indignation as much as of his creative imagination. As in *The Grandissimes,* the sentimental story is little more than a basis for Cable's message.

The plot follows very closely that of a story told him by his friend and family physician, Dr. D. Warren Brickell, who served as the model for Dr. Sevier. Cable said he related the story he had heard from Dr. Brickell to his father-in-law, whose tears convinced him of its appeal.[4] The novel covers the years between 1856 and the fall of New Orleans in 1862. John Richling, a Kentucky aristocrat who is estranged from his family, brings his Milwaukee bride, Mary, to the Southern city. When Dr. Sevier (who is not a Creole) is called to treat the young woman for an

[3] Turner, "George W. Cable's Beginnings as a Reformer," *Journal of Southern History,* XVII, 147.

[4] *Ibid.,* p. 143, and Ekström, *George Washington Cable: A Study of His Early Life and Work,* pp. 105–7.

illness, her resemblance to his dead wife and John's nobility of character enlist the doctor's interest. John searches for work without success and the young people sink into extreme poverty. Mary's next illness takes her to a charity hospital, where later John becomes a patient. Despite strong indications of the approach of the Civil War—a street vendor selling campaign medals for Breckenridge and Lane is nearly lynched because a Lincoln medal has accidentally been included in his wares—John is persuaded to send Mary to her parents in the North, where a daughter is born to her. Dr. Sevier gets John a job with a German baker, and the young man does so well that the business is left in his charge after the owner's death. When John again becomes sick, his illness aggravated by a humiliating experience in the local prison, he sends for Mary, who has been trapped in the North by the war. She and the baby make their way through the lines and arrive at John's bedside shortly before he dies.

Cable wrote three drafts of this book before he was satisfied with it and before it met the approval of the publishers of *Century Magazine,* in which it appeared as a serial. Richard Watson Gilder objected that in the first version of the novel, tentatively titled *Bread,* Cable had turned his mind so completely to philanthropical work that he had lost his sense of art. On February 20, 1882, Gilder protested that "the characters are dragged from misery to misery in order that the writer can preach his theories through them."[5] His restraining hand induced Cable to eliminate advocacy of specific reforms and to tone down the didacticism which sprang from his character and pur-

[5] Ekström, *George Washington Cable: A Study of His Early Life and Work,* p. 88.

pose.[6] But, as was inevitable at this stage of Cable's career, the final version mixes elements of the reform tract and the sentimental romance.

In deserting the scene that had made him famous and attempting a broader picture, Cable reveals the limitations of his artistry. The quaint charm of his style is effective when applied to ante bellum Creoles but is inappropriate and inadequate for the more robust material he attempts to treat in *Dr. Sevier.* What his erstwhile friend Charles Gayarré called his "lofty tone of moral and intellectual superiority"[7] is all too evident, and his inability to create a hero who is noble and yet artistically satisfying is strikingly illustrated in the unconvincing John Richling, who refuses to borrow even to keep his beloved wife from starving. As in Cable's other fiction, the best realized characters are the minor figures—the Creole Narcisse, the Italian Ristofalo, the Irish Kate Riley, and Madame Zenobia, the middle-aged quadroon who nurses Mary in her first illness and John in his last.

Zenobia is a far cry from the glamorous quadroons of Cable's stories of an earlier New Orleans. The explanation lies in Cable's insistence upon historical accuracy. The caste arose and flourished largely as a result of the influx of quadroon women in 1809, "refugees from Cuba, Guadeloupe, and other islands where the war against Napoleon exposed them to Spanish and British aggression."[8] By 1856

[6] Turner, "George W. Cable, Novelist and Reformer," *South Atlantic Quarterly,* XLVIII, 541. For a study of one instance of Gilder's use of the editorial blue pencil see Scott, "The *Century Magazine* Edits *Huckleberry Finn,* 1884–1885," *American Literature,* XXVII, 356–62.

[7] "Mr. Cable's 'Freedman's Case in Equity,'" *The Louisiana Book: Selections from the Literature of the State,* ed. by M'Caleb, p. 199.

[8] Cable, "Creole Slave Songs," *Century Magazine,* XXXI, 811.

the character and status of the quadroon had changed. "Difference was made between virtue and vice, and the famous quadroon balls were shunned by those who aspired to respectability, whether their whiteness was nature or only toilet powder."[9] For a while the Richlings are Zenobia's tenants, because the most economical, "respectable and comfortable rented rooms of which the city could boast were those *chambres garnies* in Customhouse and Bienville streets, kept by worthy free or freed mulatto or quadroon women."[10] Madame Zenobia is not concerned when the Civil War breaks out. She says, "What I got to do wid Union? Nuttin' do wid Union—nuttin' do wid Conféderacie!"[11] But the black man who helps Mary, her infant daughter, and the Union spy who is their guide to get through the army lines is not so unaware of where his interests lie, for he makes them promise to take him through to the Yankees when they come back.

Cable avoids any discussion of the Civil War until late in the novel, when he describes a parade of Union soldiers in New York City. He calls them saviors of the Union and asserts that their cause is just. "Lo, now, since twenty-five years have passed, we of the South can say it!"[12] This proof of emancipation from the traditional convictions of his former neighbors was a defection amounting to treason. His right to speak for the South, of which he was no longer a resident, was heatedly denied. His parents had owned slaves when he was a child, and as a youth he had cheered for Jefferson Davis, but as a Confederate veteran he had studied the issues of the great conflict in which he had fought and his reluctant conclusion was that both secession

[9] *Dr. Sevier,* p. 17. [10] *Ibid.* [11] *Ibid.,* p. 463.
[12] *Ibid.,* p. 377.

and slavery were wrong in principle. This was not a view which the South could accept. Cable's open letter in *Century* for November, 1884, in which he defended his position, did little to restore him to favor.

Cable inveighs against prison abuses in that portion of *Dr. Sevier* concerned with John's arrest for vagrancy and his stay in the Parish Prison, which needs no minute description, the author says, for "it may be seen there still." [13] But he was not content to let his assault rest with the novel, weakened as it was by the caution of his publishers. He had discovered that parish jails were less in need of reform than were the management of prisoners under the convict lease system of the state penitentiaries and the Southern practice of denying the freedman justice in court and the rights of a citizen in civil life. These, he must have recognized, could not be attacked effectively in his fiction. He made them the subjects of essays which infuriated the South and made him not only a controversial figure but, in Southern eyes, a notorious renegade.

Cable abhorred the convict lease system, by which convicts were leased to private contractors for work outside penitentiary walls, as "the worst prison system in Christendom, a system that cannot be reconciled with the public honor, dignity or welfare." [14] He believed that it existed in the twelve Southern states only "because the people do not know what they are tolerating" [15] and he undertook to provide them with that information in an address on September 26, 1883, before the meeting of the National Con-

[13] *Ibid.*, p. 215.

[14] "The Convict Lease System in the Southern States," *The Silent South*, p. 157.

[15] *Ibid.*, p. 178.

ference of Charities in Louisville. The speech, published in *Century* the following February, foreshadowed his later essays and further demonstrated his emancipation from a preoccupation with the interests and traditions of his own section. The theory that society should make its convicts pay for the expense of their incarceration Cable regarded as unjust and unwise. His carefully detailed analysis reveals the abuses of the system, worse in Louisiana than elsewhere; it urges that attention be given to rehabilitation as well as punishment and demands that the lease contracts be ended at once.

Cable had considered including in his lecture at Louisville some reference to the fact that among the various inequities of treatment accorded prisoners in the South the grossest was that from which the Negro suffered, simply because he was a Negro. Instead he wrote this indictment out in full in "The Freedman's Case in Equity," which he read before the American Social Science Association meeting at Saratoga, September 11, 1884, and published in *Century Magazine* in January, 1885.[16]

In his introduction, Cable observes that the presence of the Negro constitutes the nation's greatest social problem and he traces the history of slavery. While both North and South were responsible for slavery, the South, where it became an essential institution, undertook to rationalize and justify it. "Hence, our Southern forefathers, shedding their blood, or ready to shed it, for this principle [liberty], yet proposing in equal good conscience to continue holding the American black man and mulatto and quadroon in slavery, had to anchor that conscience, their conduct, and their laws

[16] Turner, "George W. Cable's Beginnings as a Reformer," *Journal of Southern History,* XVII, 160–61.

in the conviction that the man of African tincture was, not by his master's arbitrary assertion merely, but by nature and unalterably, an alien." [17] They abandoned reason for a convenient assumption.

They therefore spoke much of the negro's contentment with that servile condition for which nature had designed him. Yet there was no escaping the knowledge that we dared not trust the slave caste with any power that could be withheld from them. So the perpetual alien was made also a perpetual menial, and the belief became fixed that this, too, was nature's decree, not ours.[18]

Cable asserts that the Negro is no longer a slave, but is far from free. The letter of the law makes him a citizen, but "there is scarcely one public relation of life in the South where he is not arbitrarily and unlawfully compelled to hold toward the white man the attitude of an alien, a menial, and a probable reprobate, by reason of his race and color." [19] This, says Cable, is systematic oppression.

Examine it. It proffers to the freedman a certain security of life and property, and then holds the respect of the community, that dearest of earthly boons, beyond his attainment. It gives him certain guarantees against thieves and robbers, and then holds him under the unearned contumely of the mass of good men and women. It acknowledges in constitutions and statutes his title to an American freedom and aspirations, and then in daily practice heaps upon him in every public place the most odious distinctions, without giving ear to the humblest plea concerning mental or moral character. It spurns his ambition, tramples upon his languishing self-respect, and indignantly refuses to let him either buy with money, or earn by any excellence of inner life or outward behavior, the most momentary immunity from these public indignities even for his wife and daughters.[20]

[17] "The Freedman's Case in Equity," *The Silent South,* p. 8.
[18] *Ibid.,* p. 9. [19] *Ibid.,* pp. 16–17. [20] *Ibid.,* p. 17.

Rejecting the doctrine of gradualism, Cable gives a brilliant plea for extending to the freedman the full civil rights to which the citizen is entitled, in accordance with both constitutional and moral law. He disapproves Southern conventions, theories of states' rights, and laissez-faire concepts, where these conflict with the principles of the Declaration of Independence.[21]

That the Negro was not accorded justice in Southern courts, which impaneled juries excluding black men, was clear to Cable from his study of the region's prisons, even after he took into account the probability that the number of Negro criminals would exceed their proportion of the population.

> Yet, when the actual numbers confront us, our speculations are stopped with a rude shock; for what is to account for the fact that in 1881 there were committed to the State prison at Columbia, South Carolina, 406 colored persons and but 25 whites? The proportion of blacks sentenced to the whole black population was one to every 1488; that of the whites to the white population was but one to every 15,644.[22]

South Carolina was not unique; in Georgia there were 115 whites and 1,071 Negroes in the penitentiary. The fact that the South often yielded "to the tremendous temptation to hustle the misbehaving black man into the State prison"[23] was bad enough, Cable remarks, but "what shall we say of the records of lynch law?"[24]

Cable's Jeffersonian faith in the perfectibility of man led him to conclude that there were moral and intellectual

[21] Doherty, "Voices of Protest from the New South," *Mississippi Valley Historical Review*, XLII, 54.

[22] "The Freedman's Case in Equity," *The Silent South*, p. 32.

[23] *Ibid.*, p. 31.

[24] *Ibid.*, p. 32.

forces in the South which would assert themselves and right the injustices he deplored. He did not recognize how far in advance of his times he was; he could not know that his comments would be quoted half a century later by liberal social thinkers struggling against the injustices he fought in the 1880s and early 1890s. While he may have anticipated an unfriendly Southern reaction to his essay, he scarcely expected the torrent of abuse which was showered upon him even by friends who had aided his attempts at local reform in New Orleans. However, if he was disappointed and hurt, he was not deterred.

He persisted in the belief that he was not alone. He said that when he spoke in the South the silent, established leaders of the community often quietly endorsed his opinions. He supposed he was a leader whose followers, once convinced of the logic of his opinions and the justice of his cause, merely needed to be prodded to make them rally to his standard. No doubt there were enlightened Southerners who privately shared Cable's views, admired his courage, and wished him well. Booker T. Washington said in a letter, dated December 21, 1885, that there were many in the South who thought as Cable did but had not the integrity to announce their sentiments.[25] In defense of his previous essay and as spokesman for this better, silent South, he published in *Century Magazine* for September, 1885, an extension of his arguments and a refutation of the damning charge that he endorsed social equality. This article, "The Silent South," denies that "in these United States there is any room for any one class of citizens to fasten arbitrarily upon any other class of citizens a *civil status* from which no

[25] Butcher, "George W. Cable and Booker T. Washington," *Journal of Negro Education*, XVII, 463.

merit of intelligence, virtue, or possessions can earn extrication."[26] Cable says, "The domination of one fixed class by another without its consent, is Asiatic."[27]

Cable says that his opponents insist that neither race wants the extension of civil rights to the freedman, but he notes that they offer no evidence that Negroes support their contention while he has received from colored writers many testimonials of their gratitude for his appeals in their behalf. To whites who say that character, intelligence, and property have the right to rule, he replies that these belong preeminently but not exclusively to the white race.

> It is widely admitted that we are vastly the superior race in everything—as a race. But is every colored man inferior to every white man in character, intelligence, and property? Is there no "responsible and steadfast element" at all among a people who furnish 16,000 school-teachers and are assessed for $91,000,000 worth of taxable property? Are there no poor and irresponsible whites? So, the color line and the line of character, intelligence, and property frequently cross each other.[28]

Slavery is gone, he says, now let civil caste be ended. "This done, the words North and South shall mean no more than East or West, signifying only directions and regions, and not antipodal ideas of right and government; and though each of us shall love his own State with ardor, the finest word to our ear as citizens shall be America."[29]

When these three essays were published in 1885 as *The Silent South,* George W. Cable and his family were settled in Northampton. For the moment he withdrew from the controversy over civil rights. But he had not ceased to be

[26] *The Silent South,* p. 54. [27] *Ibid.,* p. 55. [28] *Ibid.,* p. 79.

[29] *Ibid.,* p. 108. For Cable's answer to the charge that he attacked the shortcomings of the South and apologized for those of the North, see his letter, "Is It Sectional or National?" *Century Magazine,* XXXII, 963.

a social critic; he merely turned once again to fiction as a means of expression. And his next major work showed an extension of his humanitarian sympathies to another under-privileged minority, the Louisiana Acadians.[30]

These descendants of the Nova Scotians who had been exiled from their homes in 1755 first interested Cable when he worked with a surveying expedition along the banks of the Atchefalaya River shortly after the Civil War. Having planned to include an account of these unique people in his report on New Orleans for the Tenth Census, he returned to the Acadian country in the autumn of 1880, and his careful notes served later as the basis for *Bonaventure.*[31] The three tales of which this "prose pastoral of Acadian Louisiana" is composed are related in having a common setting and some characters, Bonaventure in particular, who appear in each.

"Carancro," the first of the stories, appeared in *Century* in January and February, 1887. Bonaventure, an orphaned

[30] In one version of "My Politics," an essay which he intended to use as a preface to the 1889 edition of *The Silent South* but which he was prevailed upon to withhold from publication during his lifetime, Cable quotes a church manuscript he wrote in 1881 in which he groups Chinese, Indians, Irish, and Negroes as the Samaritans—i.e., mongrel, inferior races—of Louisiana at that time and urges that brotherhood be extended to them all. Cable, "My Politics," in *The Negro Question: A Selection of Writings on Civil Rights in the South,* ed. by Turner, p. 15.

[31] Scribner's published the original edition of the book in 1888. According to Ekström ("The Cable-Howells Correspondence," *Studia Neophilologica,* XXII, 58–59), Cable and William Dean Howells became interested in "a publishing scheme for an International Association of Newspapers and Authors." Charles Scribner advised against the plan, and Cable wrote to him, May 31, 1900, implying acceptance of his view; the letter is in the Scribner archives. Nevertheless, an edition of *Bonaventure* was published by the Association in 1901.

Creole, is adopted by Acadians and grows up as one of them. An unrequited love affair leads him to dedicate himself to the service of others; like John Richling, he is too noble a hero to be appealing. In "Grande Pointe," which the magazine published the next month, the sober young man becomes a school teacher in an Acadian settlement north of New Orleans. Cable's picture of his enthusiastic struggles to teach his peasant charges a language, English, which he has not mastered himself, is weakened by the patronizing humor and an affected style, but it is redeemed by its stress on the fundamental integrity of the people and by evidences of its sympathetic intent.[32] "Au Large," an involved and stylized romance, is interesting for its depiction of the Americanization of alert and aspiring Acadians. It began its magazine run in November, 1887, too late to permit its inclusion among Cable's readings on the tour that took him to Nashville in June.

He returned to Tennessee later that summer to visit a mountain resort community established by a temperance lecturer, John Moffat,[33] whose life provided the author with some of the central episodes of his next novel. Moffat was born in Glasgow, Scotland, on November 9, 1828, but the family moved to Canada when he was a child. The father disappeared three years later, leaving the mother to care for

[32] For Cable's announced Acadian sympathies, see the newspaper interview reprinted in Lorch, "Cable and His Reading Tour with Mark Twain in 1884–1885," *American Literature,* XXIII, 481.

[33] My information on John Moffat has been assembled from members of his family and from a number of other sources, often conflicting. See Purnell, *John Gamp: or Coves and Cliffs of the Cumberlands;* Bratton, *An Apostle of Reality: The Life and Thought of the Reverend William Porcher DuBose; Life and Lectures of Rev. John Moffat,* ed. by Abernethy; and Moffat, *Our Nation's Peril and the Way to Escape.*

three small children. At seven, John was adopted by a Canadian family. He left home at fourteen to work and study and within four years had earned a first-class certificate as an English teacher. During the years when he was working his way through college he helped support his mother and the other two children, and he continued to do so until he married Lydia Landon. She had been born in Canada, July 4, 1829, but was of American parentage. In 1858, when Professor Moffat became absorbed in temperance work and toured the United States as lecturer and editor of a temperance magazine, the family consisted of two sons, Henry and John, and a daughter Jane, who was called Jennie. Mary Adelene was born in Cincinnati in May, 1862; another daughter, Lilian, was born in Canada the next year.[34] Bothered by poor health, John Moffat retired from the lecture platform in 1869. But his retirement, which proved to be temporary, did not make him inactive. In 1871 he found the healthy environment he wanted on the top of Cumberland Mountain in Tennessee, a hundred miles southeast of Nashville. Impressed by the possibility of establishing a summer resort on the plateau, he bought a tract of land extending from bluff to bluff.

At that time there was an interest in many parts of the South in attracting immigrant labor, generally as an aid to industrialization. Tennessee considered persuading Swiss immigrants to settle in the state to help develop its resources. John Moffat became division manager for the Tennessee Immigration, Labor and Real Estate Association in

[34] Adelene Moffat sometimes used her first initial, and she signed some of the letters she wrote for the Open Letter Club "M. A. Moffat." Lilian's name appears in some records and correspondence as "Lillian." Jennie Moffat Weir signed her letters to Cable "J. Weir."

1872. There was some opposition to the program because it was feared the immigrants might ultimately become a burden to the state, but there were prominent men supporting the project and later some individual immigrants did settle around Franklin and other counties. Governor James D. Porter appointed Moffat Commissioner of Immigration for Middle Tennessee in 1875.

Besides temperance and immigration, "Colonel" Moffat was concerned with education and the special educational problems of the South. Sometime in 1872 or early 1873, Mrs. Mary Louise Yerger and Mrs. Harriet B. Kells, who considered Jackson, Mississippi, too ridden with malaria and yellow fever for them to continue their school for girls there, inspected the Cumberland plateau as a possible site to which to move their institution. The ladies rejected an offer made by officials of the Tennessee Coal and Railroad Company of five hundred acres of land near Tracy City, where the company had its mines, and free lumber for the school buildings, but were pleased to accept fifty acres from John Moffat. His youngest daughter said he also constructed the first building for the school, which was called Fairmount, and gave the founders twenty years to pay for it, with no interest charged for the first five years. (Perhaps one reason for his philanthropy was the fact that state law prohibited the sale of alcoholic beverages within four miles of a school.) Fairmount opened with ten pupils on April 9, 1873. Dr. William Porcher DuBose was chaplain; he served in the same capacity at Sewanee's University of the South, about six miles away.[35]

[35] Mahoney, "Ladies in the Making," Nashville *Tennessean*, November 13, 1949. Mrs. Yerger married Dr. DuBose in 1879. Miss Susan Peronneau DuBose, his elder daughter, became principal of Fair-

In 1875 the Tennessee legislature established a bureau of immigration and John Moffat was named commissioner. One of his major ambitions at this time was to establish a collegiate and normal institute. It was intended to be nonsectarian (the University of the South and Fairmount were under Episcopal auspices). Moffat Institute was chartered in 1877. There were financial difficulties, and Professor Moffat returned to the lecture platform to raise funds. Whatever success he met with, it does not appear that the school ever came into existence. Whether at this time or later, Moffat suffered very serious financial reverses. Family tradition says that he was swindled out of some of his property by a partner and nearly ruined when it was discovered that he had given guaranty deeds for land that was not legally his. From 1878 to 1880 temperance work kept him in Washington, D.C., and in Chester County, Pennsylvania, where he lectured and edited a temperance monthly, the *Monitor*. During these years his daughter Adelene was a third- and fourth-year student in the Ladies' Course at York Collegiate Institute, York, Pennsylvania.

Evidently Professor Moffat was a man of high moral character, benevolent and upright. He never lost his concern for religion or his interest in developing the spiritual, intellectual, and material resources of his settlement. In 1882 a convention anxious to establish an assembly for summer schools and for special instruction in Bible study

---

mount in 1894. According to a diary kept by C. B. Roote, who was headmaster of Northampton High School for many years, Miss DuBose, accompanied by Mrs. Jennie Weir, visited the high school in 1898. From 1895 to 1898, Roote and his wife were boarders at Adelene Moffat's home.

met at Tullahoma, Tennessee, and sent out a committee to choose an appropriate site. Moffat, one of the delegates, persuaded the group to visit his community on Cumberland Mountain.

At Cowan the committee was handsomely entertained by Mrs. Bouchez in her log-cabin home down under the hills, near the station. A narrow-guage railroad conveyed the body to Moffitt [sic] Station, where, under a brush arbor, the conclave met; and after visiting all points of interest, considering every item of advantage to the Assembly, which was enhanced by Professor Moffitt's brilliant Scotch eloquence, this choice location upon the Cumberland Mountain was made, the present site for the Amphitheater selected, and the rude structure put up at once from material at hand. The name "Monteagle Sunday School Assembly" was then adopted.[36]

The name of the village, which consisted of a hotel, a few houses, and the railroad station, was changed from Moffat to Monteagle. John Moffat died there on Christmas day, 1886.

The Monteagle Sunday School Assembly became a Southern Chautauqua.[37] Some of the professors from Sewanee lectured there, and many notable singers and

[36] Purnell, *John Gamp: or Coves and Cliffs of the Cumberlands*, p. 350. Purnell says here that the name was based on the supposition that eagles once inhabited the area. Rather it was chosen because Moffat wanted to honor his Canadian friend, Lord Mounteagle. The present spelling is a corruption. According to Moffat family tradition, Moffat gave one hundred acres to the Assembly, but Dr. Lilian W. Johnson wrote me, on May 9, 1953, that the Assembly bought the land. Dr. Johnson donated the land for the present Highlander Folk School at Monteagle.

[37] For a short, colorful account of the Chautauquas of the time, see Boyesen, "The Chautauqua Movement," *Cosmopolitan*, XIX, 147–58.

speakers appeared on the programs. When Cable spoke on "The Faith of Our Fathers" at Nashville, Monteagle was preparing for the fifth session of the Assembly, which was to be held from July 6 to September 7. Construction was being rushed on the cottages—the number was doubled—in order to provide for the anticipated increase in attendance.[38] There were plans for an "educational week, Sunday-school Congress, Sunday-school Normal, Children's Meetings, Temperance Week, and many musical attractions" and nineteen different "schools" were to be conducted, with stress placed on the training of teachers. The July, 1887, issue of the *Chautauquan,* a monthly magazine published by the Chautauqua Literary and Scientific Circle, announced details. Speakers for the program included Baskervill, Cable, and other prominent Southerners.

When Cable arrived at Monteagle, he met John Moffat's family, who were charmed by his personality, pleased with his piety, and impressed by his fame. He singled out Adelene, a serious, pretty young woman of twenty-five, several inches taller than he. Seven months after her father's death, she was still wearing mourning. Cable found that her views on religion and the problems of the day were, like her father's, in accord with his own.

On August 3, Cable delivered the lecture which he had prepared for the occasion, a lecture which became part of his platform repertoire. "Cobwebs in the Church" protested religious formalism and urged a liberal interpretation of doctrine.[39] Adelene, who was a talented amateur artist, drew a design for the lecture program, for which Cable wrote her a brief note of thanks:

[38] *Chautauquan,* VIII, 45.
[39] Turner, *George W. Cable,* pp. 263, 275, 279.

Monteagle
Aug 3, 1887

Miss Adelene Moffat:

I feel constrained by my sense of appreciation to thank you in this form for the pretty device executed on your programme of today. May the web of your life's experience be, like it, only a few slender threads of darkness on the broad white field of a pure and happy nature and fate.

Yours truly

G. W. Cable[40]

Thus began a correspondence that extended over nearly twenty years and an association that was one of the most important experiences of Cable's long life.

[40] All the letters *from* Cable *to* Adelene Moffat which I quote or to which I refer are in the Cable Collection at Columbia University. They were acquired from Miss Moffat, together with other Cable memorabilia, in 1950.

IV: Home Culture

Adelene Moffat met Cable when he was at the height of his fame as a public figure. He was, of course, still primarily a literary personage; he continued to write books for another thirty years and he remained very active as a lyceum reader. But he thought of himself as a man with many public responsibilities, gifted with an insight into the political, social, and moral problems of the period and obligated to guide his fellow citizens toward solutions. His religious interests found partial expression in his Bible class work in Boston and Northampton and in the series of articles which culminated in *The Busy Man's Bible* in 1891. He fancied the role of lay prophet, and the vain self-righteousness revealed in some of his letters of this time seems to spring from a desire to prove that he was on good terms with God. Adelene Moffat did not think him vain and she found his piety admirable because of the good works that accompanied it. She was an intense young woman who had much of the sense of public service and social responsibility characteristic of the father she admired so deeply and something of the spiritual emphasis which had induced her mother to become a Christian Science practitioner. She wanted to become an artist and hoped to go to Europe to study, but she had no money to finance professional training, and her ambitions seemed unattainable. She had had two years' experience as a teacher and was committed to spend the school year of 1887–88 in Cynthiana, Kentucky, but she did not look forward to her job in the bluegrass country with elation.

She and Cable had been favorably impressed with one another on their brief meeting at Monteagle and were even more pleased as their correspondence developed. The relationship was less important to the author than to the young woman; it sustained her at a trying time. She had read and admired his books; she was soon convinced that his was a noble soul. Here was an eminent man whose opinions on matters of religion and conduct and politics she shared, whose advice was inspiring and comforting, whose friendly offers of help must have seemed to open the way to a promised land. Her long, intimate letters to him expressing her admiration for his work and his character must have been adequate compensation for the efforts he exerted in her behalf, particularly since those efforts also served to further the projects he was developing at the time.

Cable's second letter to his new acquaintance was written on August 6, 1887, the day after his return to Northampton. The occasion was his promise to send her a scrap of manuscript, which he enclosed.

I have been telling Mrs. Cable about you and making her want to know you. You are much like a cousin—a Canadian cousin of Scotch descent, too, as it happens, whom she loved most of all her kindred beyond her home circle & whom she has lost.

I find that I did not gather from anything you said where you will be and what doing this fall and next winter and spring. As to summer I dare say you will be at Monteagle when I return there as the management says I must. But I count on being in Tennessee before that; in the winter or spring at Chattanooga,

Nashville, Columbia, Knoxville, &c &c chance may bring us together at some short turn and we may make wider & deeper an acquaintance & a friendship that already is one of my treasures.

I wonder why I did not talk to you about coming East at some time or another; art ought to draw you to Boston. Is there no likelihood of this? I have friends there to whom both Mrs. Cable & I would be ever so glad to introduce you; those whom you would like. I wish it might be my honor as it would be my pleasure to be somehow a helping hand to you.

In his postscript he said: "Mrs. Cable insists on my sending this picture. I can some day replace it for a better."

His letter of August 22 included a long, sanctimonious recapitulation of his Bible lesson—"my church class, not my large opera-house class"—and a rather surprising prediction.

I feel the confidence almost of knowledge, that we are both fitted and destined to be a noble stimulation to each other, an enlargement of each other's higher parts and thus of our higher conceptions and powers. If this is a mistake we may as well find it out early, and we may as well find out early if it is a fact. The very differences between us, of place and of years, the differences fit us to be useful friends to one another in spiritual things. So whenever you feel like writing about your art or even your personal affairs be assured I shall be more than glad of every line you may choose in your caprice to give me.

Again there was a postscript. "There! I got so interested in my own sermon as to forget to say we want your picture—Mrs. Cable and I." The young woman's long reply, dated September 5, 1887, spoke of his genius and "the unusual sweetness" of his nature and thanked him for the sermon. She said, "I shall always be a better woman, more steadfast in purpose, less frivolous in thought, and therefore a

ADELENE MOFFAT

happier one for the flash of recognition that has passed between us."

To the young teacher in Cynthiana, Cable wrote on October 13, 1887, that he was sending proof and books—*The Roman Emperors in Marble* and *Antique Statues*—and he gave her the itinerary of his current platform appearances. The egotistical epistle is interesting for the details it supplies about Cable's activities and for its reference to a project which was to be the core of his long association with Adelene Moffat.

See how busy I am: on the 15th I shall meet my Boston Bible Class in Tremont Temple. Last Saturday it numbered 2500. On Sunday, 16, my Northampton church class of 100. On the 17th I give "Cobwebs" before the Congregl Club of New York City. 18th back in Northampton to first general meeting of my "Home Culture Clubs." On the 19th Portland, Maine, before a large audience. 20th Lynn, Mass. 21st probably guest of the Tavern Club, Boston, of which Howells is president. 22 & 23, Bible Classes in Boston & Northampton. 24th Everett House, Union Square, New York City, on the way to Washington Pennsylva, via Pittsburg to read before a large Teachers Institute. 26th New York City again, visiting my publishers &c, 27 Brattleboro, Vermont. 28 Lecture, "Cobwebs," Tremont Temple, Boston. And so on.

This is going to be the greatest year of my life thus far.

About a year earlier the first of the clubs to which Cable refers had developed as an outgrowth of a little reading circle which met in the home of Miss Carrie Lincoln on King Street in Northampton.[1] The original idea was much like that of various home study programs that were in

[1] "George W. Cable: Our Fellow Citizen," an unpublished paper by Anna Gertrude Brewster, delivered before a meeting of the Northampton Historical Society, *ca.* 1929.

vogue.[2] A few people who were interested in books gathered at a private home and read aloud from a selected work. The announced object was not social service but entertainment, fellowship, and instruction that would contribute to a revival of "culture" in the home and its spread to homes previously little acquainted with it. But early in its history the project began to function as something other than a reading circle, quite outside the private home. Probably the first public program was one held in mid-May, 1887, in Grand Army Hall, now Memorial Hall.[3] It included a piano duet, a zither and guitar number, and two vocal solos—"The Bedouin Love Song" and "Florian's Song." The feature of the evening was a lecture, "Pond Life," illustrated with the stereoptican, by John H. Pillsbury, Smith professor of biology. In its dependence on the cooperation of Smith College personnel, this initial program set a pattern which was to be followed in later years.

At the end of 1886 there were four clubs; by January 10, 1888, when a mass meeting was held in the Northampton Opera House, there were fourteen clubs and 102 members. That evening the building was crowded with club members, their friends, and members of the public who had been invited by card. Northampton's *Daily Herald*, which on the next day gave a full account of the proceedings, re-

[2] Cable had met the head of the Women's Society for the Promotion of Culture at Home in 1881 and was acquainted with the details of several similar programs. Turner, *George W. Cable*, p. 280. See also the *Chautauquan*. It had required readings, study hints, an adult education approach, a tone of uplift, and a tabulation of pages read at various meetings.

[3] The printed program gives the date as Thursday, May 19, but the printed announcement and admission card is for Wednesday, May 18. Both are in the Smith College archives.

garded the large audience as evidence of the community's social and intellectual progress. After a band overture, Cable expressed his pleasure over the growth of the clubs. He said they were conceived on the idea that we need and can be useful to one another and that their object was not to encourage members to read much but to read well, to digest and assimilate; but it is evident that he was more concerned about the number of clubs, members, and pages read than about the quality of the reading. He asserted that the clubs were intended to cut across social lines and to fill with pleasure and profit hours that might otherwise be wasted in idleness or spent outside the home. Mayor Hill and President Seelye of Smith College spoke on the contribution the clubs could make in inspiring the residents of Northampton and helping to break down the many barriers that separated them from one another.

It is not clear, however, quite how the clubs, supposedly designed to contribute to the education and social culture of working men and women, could accomplish the objectives suggested for them. Cable's article in *Century* for August, 1888, treats the project as a benevolent scheme for the elevation of the masses, but the outline of the enterprise is exceedingly vague and the tone of the essay decidedly condescending. Some of the social theories Cable advances are sound enough—e.g., "Now in our country the idea of classes differing from one another in their rights is intolerable to the very ground principles of the nation's structure" [4]—but it is not apparent that the Home Culture Clubs implemented these theories. Cable's articles on education, the race problem, and prison reform are logical,

[4] "Home Culture Clubs," *Century Magazine*, XXXVI, 501.

direct, detailed, and forceful. This essay on the Northampton experiment is defensive and apologetic; it is more circuitous than the most mannered of his stories.

> The experiment has been cautiously made. . . . Proposals to start clubs in many towns far apart from one another have been held in suspense, and the venture until very lately has been intentionally and entirely confined to one place, the town of Northampton, Massachusetts. Here there have been started, one by one, from time to time during the year 1887 and the winter and spring of 1888, twenty home culture clubs. Eighteen still exist, and the only two that have disbanded have done so for reason of changes beyond control, and not for lack of interest or from any discovered fault in the scheme. Many thousands of pages of standard literature have been read and heard around the evening lamp, or in "collateral readings," by those with whom reading had been no habit. Two other clubs have lately been admitted, though meeting in distant towns. The total membership is at present one hundred and forty-four, and the aggregate number of pages read weekly averages about eighteen thousand.[5]

A tabulated report of the combined reading of the various groups for the week ending Saturday, April 21, 1888, accompanies the article. The two clubs located outside Northampton—one in Parkville, Missouri, and the other in Baltimore, Maryland—had made no report for the week. Cable's statement of the total number of pages read is somewhat misleading; it is obtained by multiplying the number of pages read at each meeting by the number of members present. The reading ranged from about twenty to forty pages and it was the "collateral reading," done outside of meetings, which swelled the total. From the nature of the collateral works, and of some of the club selections themselves, it seems unlikely that much of the reading was

[5] *Ibid.*, p. 506.

being done by persons "with whom reading had been no habit."

A printed prospectus which was prepared about this time offers some additional information on the objectives and program of the groups. It announces that the clubs are intended for anyone too tired after work to read or study alone.

They are for such persons as this who, still, are not content to let their minds go totally neglected, but are willing to give one regular hour a week to some profitable pursuit with four or five others in a small fireside circle. They are for those who have more or less self-culture, and who are looking for some practicable way to share their advantages with those who have fewer. Such persons can give and get much benefit by assuming the secretaryship of a small group of persons who need only contact of some mind better trained, in order to hold together for the accomplishment of some definite self-improvement.[6]

The subject for study or reading was chosen by each club, the only restriction being that meetings should not be held merely for visiting or "sociality." There were no dues; each club contributed what it chose to defray the trivial expenses of the central organization. There were no rules, but it was suggested that meetings be held at the homes of members in regular rotation and that care should be exercised by each group "to avoid long meetings, late hours, the habitual serving of refreshments, and whatever else might divert it from its true purpose." Each week the club secretary filled in a simple report on a printed postal card and mailed it to the general secretary, whose consolidated reports kept the individual clubs informed of the activities of the whole organization. Membership in a club involved

[6] A copy of the circular is in the Cable Collection at Columbia University.

no preparation, no addition to one's daily cares, says the circular. "A lawyer, or a mechanic who has to work from dawn to dark, may belong to a Home Culture Club and get and give much pleasure and profit without any appreciable loss of indoor or outdoor recreation. The work can be taken up or laid down at will; there are no pledges and no penalties."

Someone, however, must be responsible for establishing each reading circle, and it is to prospective leaders that the circular is really addressed. "If you can take the leadership of a club, seek out a few persons *singly* and *personally,* who by reason of any drawback have had fewer advantages than you. Persuade them to join with you in some agreeable pursuit; be prepared to suggest several such pursuits from which they may choose the one which suits the whole group best. Two are enough to constitute a club; any number may belong; but five or six are best." And it is suggested that two persons, already friends, might well undertake the direction of a club together.

So loose a confederation, so tenuous a scheme for social betterment, probably required and received little attention from Cable during its early months of operation. His letters to Adelene Moffat in Kentucky make few references to the Home Culture Clubs, though they have much to say about his concern for the Negro. His young correspondent, who never forgot the lynching she had seen when she was a girl, shared her father's distaste for race prejudice and applauded Cable's advocacy of the rights of the colored citizen. The hostile reaction to his address at the Vanderbilt commencement had not disturbed his confidence in his convictions or lessened his courage in expounding them, and when the London *Contemporary Review* invited him to write a paper on the race problem he undertook to revise that speech to suit it to the different audience it would reach. He wanted an American audience, too, for it was American public opinion he wished to influence, and so it was arranged that the Chicago *Inter-Ocean* and the New York *Tribune* should print the article simultaneously with its London appearance. The first draft of "The Negro Problem in the United States" was completed in September, 1887, and the essay was published the following March. Reprinted as a pamphlet, *The Negro Question,* it was distributed in the South by the American Missionary Association and later was included in the book of the same name, Cable's second volume of collected articles on this subject.

The research and correspondence in which Cable engaged in preparing the essay helped him to buttress his original arguments, and he produced a brilliant plea for civil rights for the Negro, brilliant because it is based upon an incisive analysis of the position of the Negro in American culture and of the political tenets upon which democratic government rests. Cable censures the Supreme Court, "the inner citadel of our government's strong conservatism,"[7] for having invalidated the Civil Rights Act in 1883. Separate accommodations, he says, cannot be equal: "as if a permanent ignominious distinction on account of ancestry, made in public, by strangers and in the enjoyment of common public rights were not an insult or an injury unless joined to some bodily discomfort."[8] He surveys the history of the problem—slavery, secession, war, emancipation, Reconstruction, and the New South with its industrial growth and its white supremacy. He presents the inconsistencies of segregation in neighboring areas, notes the achievement

[7] *The Negro Question,* p. 5. [8] *Ibid.,* pp. 10–11.

of the freedmen, and urges adequate public education for the whole nation. Through education the North can Americanize its twenty million immigrants; the South has an advantage in that its masses are wholly American in their cultural and political traditions and have proved their loyalty to their heritage.[9] But with their participation in the democracy restricted to such a degree that they are "subjects and not citizens, peasants instead of freemen," Negroes "are learning one of the worst lessons class rule can teach them—exclusive, even morbid, pre-occupation in their rights as a class, and inattention to the general affairs of their communities, their States and the Nation." [10]

On the day his essay appeared in the newspapers, March 4, 1888, Cable wrote Adelene Moffat, "Tonight I shall

[9] In his famous address at the Atlanta Exposition, in September, 1895, Booker T. Washington used much the same argument in opposing the use of immigrant labor in the South and urging employment of the 8,000,000 freedmen who constituted the native labor supply.

[10] *The Negro Question,* pp. 50–51. Invariably Cable objected to advocacy of the rights of any special group at the expense of the rights of others. His acquaintance with Negro leaders and organizations was evidently extensive and no doubt made him aware of their natural preoccupation with their special problems. Yet Cable did not adopt the paternal view that the race problem could be solved without their help. In the Cable Collection at Tulane University there is a long letter Cable wrote to A. K. Smiley, March 21, 1890, accepting an invitation to attend the Lake Mohonk Conference on the Negro Question. Cable urged that some Negro leaders be invited and mentioned specifically Booker T. Washington; Prof. William S. Scarbrough, classical scholar and author of a widely used textbook, *First Lessons in Greek;* J. W. Cromwell, "foremost statistician of the Negro race's industrial progress"; and Rev. B. T. Tanner, "able editor of the [African Methodist Episcopal] Quarterly Review." The Mohonk Conference was held after the appearance of Cable's essay. No Negroes were present.

speak, with Phillips Brooks & others, in the new Old South Church [Boston] in behalf of southern educational missions, a grateful task." As their correspondence had developed over the months, Adelene Moffat's admiration for the crusading author had grown with every new evidence of his idealism, and her sympathy for his causes and her alert understanding of the public issues which engaged his attention strengthened the bond between them. The idea took shape that in the East she could be useful to his work while she studied art formally; until now her mother had been her only art teacher. Cable asked her what she could expect to earn during the summer and told her to hold on to what money she had. "Save it. You will want it; for you are going to come to New England."[11] On March 4, he devoted much of his letter to details of a loan which would enable the young woman to spend the next year studying art in New York. When her work at Cynthiana ended, she returned to Monteagle where she stayed for a few weeks to help her sister Lilian prepare for her September marriage to William J. Gilfillan. At the end of June, Adelene arrived in Northampton.

At that time the Cables occupied two houses in the college town. Cable had first visited Northampton when he read there in January, 1884, at a time when he was seeking a permanent home in the North.[12] Northampton appealed to him because it was accessible to both New York and Boston, to publishers and lecture audiences. An important attraction was Smith College, which offered free tuition to the daughters of local residents. In September, 1885, the

[11] Undated letter, presumably written in the winter or early spring of 1888.

[12] Turner, *George W. Cable,* p. 223.

novelist moved his wife and children into a brick home, 61 Paradise Road, in the vicinity of the college grounds. Red House was on a rise beside a woodland and offered a charming view of the blue Holyoke range. Two years later Cable's mother, his sister Mary Louise, and his widowed sister Antoinette Cable Cox with her three children left New Orleans and rented a home in Northampton, a mansion known as the Whitcomb House, at the corner of Park and Elm streets. Cable was responsible for this second household, too, and he sometimes worried because, as he wrote his mother in 1888, he had "nine children to think about, not one of whom has a clearly indicated future." [13] Smith College girls boarded at this second Cable residence, managed by Mary Louise, and Adelene Moffat and some of her relatives stayed there at times, but during her first summer in Northampton, Miss Moffat lived at Red House.

There was more than enough to keep her busy. She said that during her early days in Northampton she often helped Mrs. Cable, who never seemed really well, to care for her brood of children. Cable's gentle, attractive wife, whom everyone loved, made the young woman from Tennessee feel welcome and at home. Adelene Moffat functioned as Cable's personal secretary and probably she assumed at once direct responsibility for the Home Culture Clubs. On May 1, about two months before she reached Northampton, club headquarters had been established in two rooms over McCallum's department store at 152 Main Street. These rooms, one of which was reserved for ladies, were open from six to ten each night. Cable solicited the support

[13] Biklé, *George W. Cable: His Life and Letters,* p. 205. The total was increased the next year when Cable's last child, Dorothea, was born.

of local residents to pay the four hundred dollar rental and to stock the shelves with books and magazines.[14]

This was the first step away from Cable's original concept, the first move toward the Home Culture Clubs' later status as a quasi-municipal agency serving and supported by the community. Cable evidently supposed that anyone, however uneducated, could benefit from membership in his reading circles, but Northampton was a factory town and many of its mill workers, drawn from a dozen different nationalities, could not speak English. The poorer people were unable to participate in the clubs so long as there was any demand that their homes be used for meetings. Initially Cable's project did not contribute to the Americanization of the immigrants, and it had no appeal, no consequential benefits, for most of the people who worked long hours in the mills or in the homes of the well-to-do.[15] His theory that the clubs would cut across class lines, without disturbing "necessary social distinctions and divergencies,"[16] was visionary. Occasionally the ladies of Elm Street attended

[14] Turner, *George W. Cable,* p. 283.

[15] In "Home Culture Clubs," *Century Magazine,* XXXVI, 497–507, Cable says that many class distinctions are desirable but that class status should be a matter of the inherent worth of the individual; it should not be subject to chances of fortune or government control. He considers the masses, however uninspired and unintelligent, only partly to blame for their plight; society is also responsible. This is consistent with his position on segregation, to which he objects elsewhere because the system takes no account of individual differences among Negroes and whites. On page 499 of the *Century* article, Cable scorns "pride of place, of purse, of blood, of mind, and that worst pride of all, the pride of morals." His patronizing tone and later developments in his career suggest that, in varying degrees, he was guilty of them all.

[16] Biklé, *George W. Cable: His Life and Letters,* p. 189. In the letter cited here Cable refers to the club work as "Home Extension."

club meetings in the homes of humbler people, but they did not arrange for the visits to be returned. Once the reading room was open and had proved its usefulness, it was inevitable that the enterprise would take a direction contrary to its title and to the original intent of its founder. Inspired by Toynbee Hall in London's East End, which several American social workers had studied, the settlement house movement was getting under way at this time. Northampton needed a settlement house and, although Cable repeatedly denied for twenty years that there was any connection between that uplift movement and the work he was sponsoring,[17] the Home Culture Clubs soon came to fill that need.

Active as he was in local affairs, Cable's absorbing interest during these years was in what he took to be the nation's most pressing problem, the place of the Negro in American life and, particularly, in a new, industrialized South. Sometime in the spring of 1888, he conceived the idea of organizing a group of influential men for public discussion of problems pertaining to the South. He hoped that by dispassionate debate and wide distribution of the views of these men he could influence public opinion in the direction of his own reasoned and enlightened convictions. Adelene Moffat approved his plans and helped them to mature. When the summer ended and Cable began to pay installments on the $600 he had promised to lend her, the young woman moved to 25 West 45th Street in New York City and began her studies at the Art Students' League. Art was her main reason for coming east, but it was not an exclusive interest. The excitement of being in New York and the pressure of her studies did not prevent

[17] "The Home-Culture Clubs," *World's Work,* XII, 8111.

her from giving important assistance to Cable's civic crusade as the year progressed.

Henry W. Grady had called the famous oratorical speech he delivered before the New England Society in New York on December 21, 1886, "The New South," a title which was in wide use as a popular label for a movement in Southern thought.[18] Cable considered calling his organization the New South Clubs, but in December of 1888 he settled upon the Open Letter Club when his New York protégée agreed that it was a better name. An article in the *Forum* for October, 1888, stimulated his plans. "Race Antagonism," by Louisiana's Senator James B. Eustis, aroused heated controversy, and Cable was invited by the editors to reply. The result was "A Simpler Southern Question," published in December. In it Cable reviewed recent and contradictory papers by several Southern spokesmen and invited further discussion.

That winter the Open Letter Club was set up with headquarters in Nashville, conducted by Professor Baskervill, and in New York, and much of the work fell on Adelene Moffat as the New York secretary. Some two dozen prominent men were induced to join in the scheme, and many others scattered about the country, particularly in the South, read the manuscripts and reprints sent to them by the club and contributed facts and opinions to the discussions.[19] There was correspondence and research for the New York secretary to attend to, and a great deal of "leg

[18] In his commencement address at the University of Mississippi in June, 1882, Cable objected to the term, already in vogue, and proposed instead "the No South." Turner, "George W. Cable's Revolt Against Literary Sectionalism," *Tulane Studies in English,* V, 21.

[19] Turner, *George W. Cable,* p. 264.

work" was involved in submitting to periodicals the essays Cable forwarded to her from various members.

His prediction, "It may or may not be a momentous year for the Negro, but it is going to be very full of hard work for you in his behalf," was fulfilled.[20] Seven hundred copies of *The Negro Question* had been sent to people whose names Cable had assembled, and the names of others interested in receiving such matter had been sent to Baskervill. The mailing list was large enough to justify three thousand reprints of the article written by Atticus G. Haygood, president of Emory College, for the *Independent* of November 8, in which he replied to Senator Eustis, and in January Adelene Moffat and Mary Louise Cable were kept busy wrapping and mailing the pamphlets. Cable considered having club members take special Southern problems, such as the crop-lien laws which exploited tenant farmers or particular legal subterfuges which disfranchised the Negro, and he labored to get the contributions he wanted and to put them in print. A symposium from the club appeared in the *Independent* of February 21, 1889. These articles, together with three others, were published as a pamphlet, *Shall the Negro Be Educated or Suppressed?* and given a wide circulation.

Efforts to induce the collaborators to submit the manuscripts Cable wanted were often unsuccessful, and the New York secretary tried her hand, with his guidance, at filling the need. In reference to an article on which she was at work, he wrote her on March 20, 1889:

> One point I would particularly desire to see you make more strong and clear. That in one question of civil manners we are ahead of Europe & G Britain; for it is the just boast of America that here a man's public rank, has less power to make or mar

[20] Letter dated January 25, 1889.

his private social fortunes than in any other country. And *yet,* in relation to one class of people, only, in America, & they the class which Nature has already hopelessly differentiated, from the rest, we have an abject fear that their enjoyment of common public rights—the rights of their civility—which only the most glaring public incivility can deny them, will bring them tumbling into the lap of a horror-stricken private society.

He advised her to submit the finished paper for publication; she did get it accepted but it never appeared in print. This minor disappointment and all the hard work her thankless position demanded did not quench her enthusiasm for the project. Sixty years later, proud of her part in it, she still regarded it as George W. Cable's most genuinely philanthropic and unselfish undertaking.

Adelene Moffat returned to Massachusetts when her year of study at the Art Students' League came to an end in the summer of 1889. Efforts to obtain a suitable teaching position had failed, and her benefactor insisted that he needed her help in Northampton. Cable had enjoyed a relatively prosperous year [21] and had made sundry loans to the young woman. When they straightened their accounts on September 1, she paid him the full amount of the interest, $30, but remained in his debt to the extent of $532.[22] On September 24, he wrote the following agreement.

Miss Adelene Moffat:

I will pay you $850 for the year from Sep. 1st '89 to Aug. 31, 1890, all your time (in ordinary hours of work) to be mine.

As far as in my judgment is best for all interests I will sell back to you at double this rate such time as you find it profitable to use in art work either painting or teaching & its kindred pursuits.

G. W. Cable

[21] See his letter to Adelene Moffat, April 11, 1889.

[22] See MS, "The Home Culture Clubs, In Account with Adelene Moffat," in the Cable Collection at Columbia University.

She took up her duties that fall with no feeling that she was being exploited, but rather with a sense of being at home and occupied in a work deserving her best efforts because of its inherent possibilities for helping the community and because of her continuing admiration for its sponsor. She had not given up hope of a career as a professional artist, but for the moment she felt that it was career enough if she could make life a little less difficult for other people.

Her work with the Open Letter Club was now mainly correspondence. After a topic for discussion was chosen, interested members would write comments, possibly even short essays, about it. These were duplicated on sheets with wide margins and circulated among the participants, who were urged to reply in the margin or to develop their views as separate articles designed for publication. But most of Adelene Moffat's labor, and an increasing proportion of Cable's, was spent on the Home Culture Clubs. These were growing and she helped to strengthen and spread them. Before 1889 had ended there were thirty units with a membership of nearly two hundred people, and Cable was confident that it was time to extend the movement. "What is good and practicable for Northampton," he felt, "is good and practicable for a thousand other towns. There are thousands of good people, young and old, male and female, who want to give some effort of their own to the betterment of others less fortunate than they, yet have no fortune to bequeath, nor any consciousness of large executive capacities calling them to the prosecution of large benevolent schemes."[23] Just such a person was the young general secretary of the Home Culture Clubs, who brought to her

[23] Biklé, *George W. Cable: His Life and Letters,* p. 189.

work energy, imagination, and a sympathetic understanding of people of all classes.

Clubs were not easy to organize or to keep in operation.[24] People who expressed an interest in the idea often lost enthusiasm before organization could be accomplished. One obstacle was the natural reluctance of those who read poorly to reveal their incapacity by attempting to read aloud to even a small and friendly audience. The general secretary found it advisable to attend the first meeting of all new clubs, to take part in the reading herself, and to make enough obvious blunders in doing so to put the members at ease and give them confidence in their own ability to perform satisfactorily. She found much prompting of the club leaders and secretaries necessary, and she learned to exercise tact and ingenuity in dealing with club members. The job was wearing but not unrewarding, and she was soon dedicated to what she and Cable came to call "the blessed work."

[24] Cable wrote Adelene Moffat on May 20, 1892, "Better say Club No. ——— adjourned; don't say disbanded. You will see the difference."

v: Open Letters

Adelene Moffat became Cable's assistant and colleague only because the man whom the author wanted to hire as his secretary rejected the post. That man was Charles W. Chesnutt, a Negro writer who came to Cable's attention through the pages of the *Atlantic Monthly.* Born in Cleveland on June 20, 1858, Chesnutt had been reared in North Carolina, where he taught school for a time, married, and became principal of the State Normal School at Fayetteville. He was an ambitious man and, like ambitious young Cable, he yearned for the North. They were somewhat alike in temperament, too; the wish Chesnutt expressed at seventeen that, when he came to die, he might be "regretted and remembered with love and respect" [1] parallels the pious hope George W. Cable announced in 1866, in a letter to his mother: "May the world regret me when I die!" [2] Chesnutt taught himself stenography, moved his family to Cleveland, and worked as a stenographer while he read law. He had a passion for literature, a creative bent, and a strong sense of social and civic responsibility. Deploring the picture of Negro life being circulated in even the best

[1] Chesnutt, *Charles Waddell Chesnutt: Pioneer of the Color Line,* p. 12.

[2] Biklé, *George W. Cable: His Life and Letters,* p. 31.

periodicals, he proposed to use his talent to modify the stereotypes which were developing and thus to oppose the spread of segregation and prejudice.

Much as Cable had done earlier in New Orleans, Chesnutt wrote in what time he could spare from his business and gradually came to hope that literature would become his profession. Although he had sold a few pieces to the McClure Syndicate and minor weeklies, his literary career really began in 1887, when the *Atlantic Monthly* accepted "The Goophered Grapevine." This tale is in the local color tradition and to a casual reader may seem merely an imitation of Joel Chandler Harris, but Uncle Julius, Chesnutt's narrator for this and the other stories of *The Conjur Woman* (1899), differs from Uncle Remus in his devotion to his own interests and his determination to get the best of his white folks. A second story, "Po' Sandy," appeared in the *Atlantic* in May, 1888, and led to a correspondence between Chesnutt and Cable. That winter Chesnutt sent Cable his article, "An Inside View of the Negro Question." Cable suggested changes in the manuscript and a new title, "The Negro's Answer to the Negro Question." [3] The revised article, Cable wrote to Adelene Moffat on February 7, 1889, was "a noble paper."

A few weeks later Chesnutt sent Cable a long letter detailing his financial position, experience, and ambitions, and appealing for information about any employment which would give him enough free time so that he could devote himself to literature.[4] At the moment Cable was badly

[3] Letter, January 30, 1889. Cable's letters to Chesnutt are in the Charles W. Chesnutt Collection at Fisk University.

[4] Chesnutt, *Charles Waddell Chesnutt: Pioneer of the Color Line*, pp. 44–46.

in need of someone with just the character and training the Negro writer seemed to have in abundance. Adelene Moffat was serving as New York secretary of the Open Letter Club and Baskervill was filling the same capacity in the less active Nashville headquarters, but there was pressing work to be done in Northampton in connection with the Home Culture Clubs, the Bible classes, and the controversial essays on the Negro which Cable was preparing. His reply to Chesnutt's inquiry was to suggest that he visit Northampton on his next trip east and have a personal talk. When Chesnutt arrived in the college town his first task was to take down in shorthand Cable's Bible talk, "Blind Bartemus," which was printed in full in the Northampton *Daily Herald*, March 18, 1889.[5] On the same day, Cable wrote Adelene Moffat that Chesnutt's first work was satisfactory.

He told her on March 25 that his new secretary was "a treasure," but he had scant hopes of retaining him. His fears were justified; on April 1 Chesnutt was back in Cleveland, where Cable wrote to announce plans for a western tour from April 24 through May 9: "My charge is $100, but for this trip, and where a town is really too small to pay that, I can make a reduction if you will put them in correspondence with me." Somewhere the plans went awry, for Cable did not make the western trip until October. That Chesnutt had not yet announced a course of action is clear from Cable's letter of April 13, asking the Negro writer what salary he would accept to come to Northamp-

[5] A clipping of this article in the Cable Collection at Columbia University bears this comment in longhand: "Shorthand report by Chas. W. Chesnutt." See Cable's letters to Adelene Moffat, April 1 and 22, 1889.

ton as his secretary. Chesnutt replied, on May 3, that his business arrangements in Cleveland now promised to leave him some time for writing and that to accept the twelve or fifteen hundred dollars a year Cable might be able to pay him would cut his income in half and require a sacrifice he could not ask his family to make.[6]

Disappointed, Cable wrote Adelene Moffat three days later: "Chesnutt has declined my sec't'y-ship. What shall I do? We must talk it over. Meantime think about it. I may have to have you." On May 13, he wrote to ask her to go to the office of the *North American Review,* get Chesnutt's article if they did not intend to publish it, "and carry it to the Independent office & offer it there, in my name, for sale and publication."[7] The *Independent* printed the article, "What Is a White Man?" on May 30, 1889. In his capacity as literary mentor, Cable offered advice that day which was not in accord with his own practice. "I take the liberty to say out of an unfortunate experience, speaking as one artist in fiction to another—don't found fiction on fact. Go by the other side. Found your fiction on truth, but keep away from actual occurrences of historical value." The letter was dictated to Adelene Moffat, who had begun her long career as secretary to Cable's enterprises only a few days before. When he wrote on June 12, to comment on Chesnutt's article in the *Independent,* Cable called to his attention the similarity in attitude and subject matter which related the two writers and said that all of his own earlier stories about quadroons really asked "What is a

[6] Chesnutt, *Charles Waddell Chesnutt: Pioneer of the Color Line,* pp. 46–47.

[7] Cable had offered the article to *Century,* but Gilder rejected it. See Gilder's letter to Cable, March 13, 1889.

white man?" and "What is a white woman?" In closing, he added that he thought the time was ripe for the Open Letter Club "to get important cooperation from such men as you, Col. Williams and other men classed by the 'all-pervading all-conquering Anglo-Saxon race' as aliens."

George Washington Williams, the Negro historian, had begun a correspondence with Cable in November of 1888, when he was told by Major James B. Pond that Cable wanted to meet him.[8] A mysterious figure of commanding appearance, Williams was then in Worcester, Massachusetts, where he was doing research. He had published two commendable volumes on the history of the Negro in America, and an address to the World Federation of Missions in London, "The Drink Traffic in the Congo," had brought him a measure of fame.[9] Cable met Williams in January, 1889, and was favorably impressed. He wrote Adelene Moffat, on January 9, that the colored scholar "joins the [Open Letter] Club with ardor," but, although Williams did write to suggest that his oration, "The Constitutional Results of the War of Rebellion," be distributed through the club, and though each writer respected the achievement of the other, nothing came of their brief association. Soon Williams went abroad to study the liquor traffic in the Belgian Congo. He died in England in August, 1891.

Chesnutt, the only Negro member of the Open Letter Club,[10] continued to provide Cable with information, and Cable maintained his role as literary adviser. Adelene Moffat wrote to Chesnutt on Open Letter Club business on

[8] Letter to Cable, November 5, 1888.

[9] Franklin, "George Washington Williams, Historian," *Journal of Negro History*, XXXI, 60–90.

[10] Evidently, at least one of the other members was not aware that Chesnutt was colored. Turner, *George W. Cable*, p. 270.

September 16, and Cable sent a long letter to him a few days later. Chesnutt's letter to Adelene Moffat, November 13, 1889, suggests the degree to which Cable's many correspondents furnished him with points of view and factual details which he wove into the articles on Negro rights he was preparing at the time. It reveals, too, the scope of Chesnutt's knowledge, the extent to which he and his white colleague were in agreement on the issues of the day, and the didactic bent which later led him to make his own novels more social studies than romances and to spend much of his time writing essays and delivering speeches in an effort to elevate the status of his people.[11]

The direction in which Chesnutt's writing was going was apparent in "Rena Walden," a short story which he sent to Cable for criticism. Cable's reply of September 25, 1889, indicates the meticulous care he gave to his own writing. He must have felt especially qualified to exercise editorial judgment on this story of North Carolina Negroes who, like Chesnutt and Cable's own octoroons, were fair enough to pass for white. Chesnutt followed his friend's advice. He made a revision which Cable read in the Chesnutts' new home on Brenton Street when he visited Cleveland early in November on the western tour he had originally expected to make the previous April. Cable stayed to tea, and Chesnutt let his children sit up beyond their usual bedtime, while he and his distinguished friend discussed the story and talked of the many matters in which they were interested.[12]

[11] Chesnutt, *Charles Waddell Chesnutt: Pioneer of the Color Line,* pp. 50–54.

[12] *Ibid.,* p. 50. See also Biklé, *George W. Cable: His Life and Letters,* p. 207.

In dining with the Negro family, Cable gave further evidence of emancipation from his native tradition. Since his Vanderbilt address in 1887, he had continued to attack Southern mistreatment of the Negro and the poor white and to offer bold proposals for the extension of civil rights and educational opportunities to all Americans. His essay in the *Congregationalist* for September 26, 1889, "Congregational Unity in Georgia," urged an end to segregation in that sect. *Strange True Stories of Louisiana,* which had begun its serial run in *Century,* reverted to the ante bellum scenes of his early literary successes and, like them, contained strong and now unmistakable censure of the indolence, immorality, and cruelty which Cable saw as causes of the death of the old South and malignant, congenital ailments of the new.

His tour carried him to Nashville, where he gave a reading from his works at Ward's Seminary on December 2 [13] and, probably earlier in the day, spoke informally at Fisk University. The Negro students assembled in the chapel of Livingstone Hall and a few white visitors heard him introduced by President Cravath as a famous writer and philanthropist, endeared to all by his love of liberty. Evidently Cable had not planned to speak; his short address, reported in full by the *Fisk Herald* of that month, was disorganized and the opening sentences were particularly clumsy and vain. After a fumbling beginning, he struck out at those who feared foreign immigration and who felt that the lower element in society constituted a threat to the safety of the country. "You who are favored in this University, should see that your people are trained in the largest love of liberty." He said he enjoyed hearing the

[13] Nashville *Banner,* December 3, 1889.

students sing "The Battle Hymn of the Republic," and he went out of his way to praise Julia Ward Howe, but otherwise there was little in his remarks to offend the South. The offense came when he visited the home of James C. Napier, a prominent Nashville Negro to whom Cable had been introduced by a letter from Charles F. Smith, a Vanderbilt professor and a member of the Open Letter Club. Cable was in search of information, and Smith believed Napier was the best man to supply it.[14] Born in Nashville in 1845, Napier had been educated at Wilberforce, Oberlin, and Howard University's School of Law, and he owned an enviable reputation in his city as a lawyer, statesman, educator, and banker. His wife, Nettie Langston Napier, was the daughter of John M. Langston, the first colored member of the United States Congress and later Minister to Haiti. Napier was twice offered consular positions abroad and was Registrar of the Treasury during President Taft's administration. When he died in 1940, he was a member and vice president of the board of trustees of the Jeanes Fund and a trustee of both Howard and Fisk.[15]

The Nashville *Banner* for December 3, 1889, merely reported, without comment, that Cable "was entertained" at the Napier residence and there met a number of colored people, and it did not later join in the attack on the author, though it remarked with satisfaction on December 10 that Henry W. Grady had gone to Boston to speak on the race problem: "He will probably give the Bostonians ideas which Mr. Cable has omitted to elucidate in his Boston

[14] Smith's letter of introduction is in the Napier Collection at Fisk University.

[15] "James C. Napier," *Howard University Bulletin,* XX, 13. See also Sykes, "James Carroll Napier," *Negro History Bulletin,* V, 114, and the Nashville *Tennessean,* April 22, 1940.

Bible class."[16] The attack came from the Nashville *American,* beginning with an editorial on December 6.

> Mr. George W. Cable, just before his departure for the East, was entertained by J. C. Napier, colored, where he spent a most agreeable evening in the society of our colored elite. Mr. Cable has often urged social equality of the races, and we are glad to see him following his own advice on the subject. . . . We do not mean to say that Cable lowered himself by accepting the hospitalities of Mr. Napier, colored; on the contrary we think he found his proper level. . . . Mr. Cable is a Southern man who has turned renegade with an eye to Yankee taste and Yankee money, and . . . it is money in his pocket to slander the people among whom he was born.[17]

This was followed four days later by a charge that Cable's action had insulted Baskervill and his other Nashville friends. One of these, who signed himself merely "Tennesseean," explained and defended Cable's action at length and said, "I think I am not mistaken in recalling the names of several prominent citizens of Nashville among those of the guests at the wedding reception of this same Napier, some time since."[18] From Nashville Cable had gone to Monteagle, where he talked with Adelene Moffat's sister, Mrs. Jennie Weir, and made notes for the Reconstruction novel he was planning. Clippings from the Nashville newspapers, including the editorial reply to the "Tennesseean" which the *American* printed on December 22, were awaiting him when he returned to Northampton. Cable wrote the *American* to defend himself, and the newspaper reluctantly published the letter on December 31, accompanying

[16] Cable had ceased to conduct the Bible study class in Boston in November, 1888. Turner, *George W. Cable,* p. 274.

[17] *Ibid.,* p. 268.

[18] A typed copy of this letter, with corrections in longhand, is in the Cable Collection at Columbia University.

it with an editorial rebuttal. A second letter from Cable appeared on January 12. Angered by the paper's charges that he was a "renegade," a "traitor," and a "defamer of the South," and by such phrases as "the slime of the serpent" and "the stench of the gutter," Cable said he did not retract one word he had ever written or spoken about any phase of the race problem, but he vigorously denied that he had ever advocated any forced social mingling of the races. Any gathering of colored people provided ample proof, he said, that the blood of the two races is already mingled, and "not one in a thousand owes his or her mixture of blood to anyone suspected of advocating 'social equality.'"

As to the actual occurrence at Nashville it was this: I called on a colored lawyer of Nashville to submit to him and some other colored men of that city a plan to engage them in a calm, friendly, public, written and printed discussion of our southern problem with a view to its progressive reduction to a peaceable and equitable solution acceptable to both races. I preferred to meet them in some small public room, say the waiting room of some hotel. But remembering that three summers ago a deputation of professional colored men, calling at my hotel in Richmond to pay me a simple brief visit of public respect, were forbidden to sit down anywhere in the hotel, I accepted the offer of the lawyer's parlor. I was asked if a few wives and daughters of the men I expected to meet might be included in the group long enough to shake hands with me and thank me for what they were pleased to call my services to their race—although no public word or act of mine has ever been intended for the good of one race only. I consented on condition that nothing like a reception should take up any large portion of the time. There was no dinner party. From the time of my arrival until the last guest except myself was gone there was no eating or drinking nor any show of things to eat or drink. When all were gone, I, seeing that my host and hostess were in a dilemma between asking a white man to sit at their board and sending him away supperless, said bluntly I had not eaten. We broke bread together.[19] Was I wrong in that? To anyone who answers yes, I can only reply, Shame on you! Shame on you!!

The *American* had said that Cable's published work proved he deserved the South's resentment. Denying this, Cable challenged the paper to prove the statement and enclosed written permission from his publisher for the newspaper to print anything it chose except fragments of paragraphs. He sent another letter on January 16, which the *American* published on February 9. He insisted that many Southerners secretly felt just as he did and that pages 58, 72, and 89 of *The Silent South,* which the editors had specifically denounced but had not printed, did not warrant Southern resentment.

Whether the animosity against Cable was justified or not, it did exist. A convenient target for it was Professor Baskervill who, as Cable's host and the Nashville secretary of the Open Letter Club, was doubly vulnerable. A wrenched right arm resulting from a fall in the gymnasium was troubling him, and he was busy preparing etymologies for the *Century Dictionary* and one of a series of articles for *Chautauquan,* but on January 8 he took time to send Cable a long letter. "Yes," he wrote, "you did raise Cain! and for several days I had to bear the brunt of the attack. Our friend [Charles F.] Smith did not say 'us' but 'you' all that time." He spoke of the narrowness of the two young editors of the *American,*

[19] A month before the Napier episode, Cable had had tea with the Chesnutts in Cleveland. It seems that on more than one occasion visiting Negroes dined at the Cable residence in Northampton. Booker T. Washington was one who did so (Butcher, "George W. Cable and Booker T. Washington," *Journal of Negro Education,* XVII, 462), and Chesnutt and Wallace A. Battle were probably others.

who had been glad to grasp the opportunity Cable had given them by eating with the Napiers.

Now, as for that matter I wish to say a few words—not on the question of conscience or principle. That concerns you alone. But as a question of expediency I think you made a mistake in "breaking bread" with the Napiers. The bugbear used to frighten the southerner is social equality and this act came near enough to suit the purposes of our young editors and all who think like them. If you had not eaten with the Napiers, you could have come here & filled a house. Now your coming would be the signal for a personal attack on you in every newspaper in the city, and all manner of false representations and malicious and lying charges would be made against you. One lady had the impudence to ask me whether I would entertain you at my house again. I asked her, "Why not?" &c. I think she was anxious to get off the street-car before she reached home. A gentleman told me that an old Confederate soldier sent me word by him that if I ever invited Cable here again he and about three hundred other old soldiers would duck me. I told him to say to that old soldier that all fools were not dead yet. Some of . . . the newspapers made direct and open attacks on the University & some of the American staff wished to do the same, but the Managing Editor would not permit it. But these are mere side issues. My opinion in regard to the Negro question is that it is difficult enough in itself and that we must not handicap it with social equality or with any actions that can be so construed. But this is a matter of private judgment with me. I abhor miscegenation, for it would be a degradation of our race without any great resultant good to the other race. And while I know that no act, speech, deed or word of yours tends in *that* direction; still your enemies can claim, as they now do, that you have all along taught social equality; and the prejudices of the thinking people joined to the ignorance of the unthinking united in accepting & believing this false statement and hence in aggravating the real trouble—the solution of the Negro problem.[20]

[20] Cable replied that he was sorry for the inconvenience he had caused Baskervill but said he was glad the incident was a matter of public record. Turner, *George W. Cable,* p. 271.

Pressed though he was by various personal difficulties, Baskervill promised to try to send a short paper on another matter for the Open Letter Club later in the week.

To judge from his letter of January 10, 1890, Napier was much less perturbed about the *cause célèbre* than were the other principals.

Mr. George W. Cable,
Northampton, Mass.
My dear Sir:

Your letter of December 31st last was duly received. Immediately upon its receipt I forwarded you the American from December 27th to that date. Since I have seen nothing in regard to the matter of which you spoke, except your note I have wondered whether you desired all the papers containing references to yourself since you left Nashville. So, if you wish them of an earlier date than I have already sent please let me know and I'll forward them to you at once.

I have looked with some anxiety, since the receipt of your letter, for your communication in the "American" but it has not thus far appeared. I suppose it has been suppressed.

I cannot find words to express to you my deep regret at the onslaught made upon you by the "American" on account of your visit to my house. Although they have tried time and time again to induce me to say something in regard to the matter I have studiously refrained because I have thought, and told them, that it was none of their business.

I hope to be able to write you more at length at another time.

Very truly yours &c.,

J. C. Napier

In the issue for February, 1890, the *Fisk Herald*, torn between conflicting loyalties, found it necessary to censure its former idol.

We read Mr. G. W. Cable's letter to the Daily American, justifying his recent action in Nashville, with some disappointment. The letter seems to lack Mr. Cable's usual courage and boldness. It appears to aim more at soothing the wrath and revilings of the American than anything else.

The value of Mr. Cable's heroic fight for human rights cannot be over estimated. . . . In his contest for right and justice, Mr. Cable has probably done more, in recent years, than any other man in placing the grievances of the Negro before the people, and in every colored man's breast there burns a deep feeling of gratitude and thankfulness. That Mr. Cable deserves the highest esteem and veneration of every Negro, in fact of the oppressed everywhere, is unquestioned. But, while Mr. Cable's letter is in the main true, it is rather a weak statement of the case. . . .

The *Vanderbilt Observer,* which had remarked only about a year earlier that anyone who read Cable's works with an unprejudiced mind would be a pleased and better man,[21] had a change of heart too, evidently because it came in for a share of the abuse aimed at the author by the press and the public. The issue of February, 1890, quoted a ludicrous misstatement which had appeared in the New York *World* to the effect that Cable had been the guest of one of the colored professors of Vanderbilt University. The *Observer* used this as a point of departure for critical comments on the North's pretensions to culture and its theories of Southern ignorance. It turned its ire on Cable in passing.

We have said that we were surprised that the New York *World* should make such a blunder as to tell its readers that the professors of Vanderbilt University were colored men, but viewing the blunder from another stand-point it is not a matter of the greatest surprise after all. However ignorant the *World* might have been concerning Vanderbilt University it well knew the cause which Mr. Cable appears to champion and it also well knew that upon more than one occasion that gentleman's name had been connected with the University.

Consequently being well informed as to Mr. Cable's partiality

[21] *Vanderbilt Observer,* XI, 44.

toward the colored race and knowing nothing of Vanderbilt except that its relations with Mr. Cable had been mentioned by Southern papers in a somewhat unfavorable manner it was but natural for the *World* to suppose that Mr. Cable was mixing with the society which he seems to prefer, while he was being entertained upon the Vanderbilt campus.[22]

A few months after the Cable-Napier incident, the Open Letter Club died quietly, a casualty of this battle of Nashville. Cable felt that the South could not take its rightful place in the American democracy unless its material development was accompanied by adherence to principles of law and justice and that no solution to the Negro problem could be achieved without objective study and unemotional, nonpartisan public discussion. The Open Letter Club was intended as a forum for such discussion; Baskervill called it "a medium for the interchange of information of every sort and from every direction, valuable to the moral, intellectual and material interests of the South."[23] But the North, on the whole, was apathetic to the race problem and the South considered that by imposing white supremacy it had found a satisfactory solution.

It is difficult now to trace the history of the Open Letter Club or to credit it with positive results of a beneficial kind. Undoubtedly it aroused or encouraged consideration of a serious issue which otherwise might not have had real study and debate. It disseminated a good deal of information, especially that favorable to the Negro, which otherwise might not have come to the attention of the public. But despite the disguise provided by New York and Nashville headquarters and notwithstanding Cable's adoption of a relatively inconspicuous role, his connection with the project

[22] *Vanderbilt Observer,* XII, 8–9.
[23] *Shall the Negro be Educated or Suppressed?* Preface.

was apparent. He had cautioned against newspaper publicity, anticipating that "a howl of denunciation" would come from "the most peppery ones," [24] and his fears were justified. Once Cable was known to be the directing intelligence of the enterprise, the weight of public disapproval directed against the author made it impolitic for Southern liberals to continue to collaborate with him, and put an end to any possibility that the organization might beneficially affect the status of the Negro or the policies of the South. The failure of the scheme is hardly to its discredit; it simply could not stem the tide of public feeling which inexorably overwhelmed the liberalism and high-principled logic in which it was conceived. Throughout the South the Negro was being disfranchised by law and subterfuge, and the segregation formerly confined to that section was winning approval and imitation in the North. Perhaps the only contribution the club made was to establish, historically, the existence of a small, cautious, disorganized, and nearly silent minority in both the North and the South inclined to favor an extension of civil rights to the nation's largest group of submerged and exploited citizens.

Cable was wounded by the Nashville episode, but he was not put out of action. He continued to believe that the Negro deserved a chance, not a place, in American society, and for two more years this conviction found expression in his articles and platform appearances in the North. And when his Reconstruction novel, *John March, Southerner,* appeared in 1894, its principal scene, "the State of Dixie," bore a remarkable resemblance to Tennessee.

[24] Letter to Adelene Moffat, February 1, 1889.

VI: Facts and Fiction

One of Adelene Moffat's early tasks in Northampton was to take to a photographer the old manuscripts about ante bellum Louisiana Cable had collected.[1] Pictures of these documents served as illustrations for his *Strange True Stories of Louisiana*, which ran in *Century Magazine* from November, 1888, through October, 1889, and appeared in book form in the latter year. These true stories, which the author edited and composed from pages of history and travel, law reports, court records, old manuscripts, letters, and oral tradition, are as surely indicative of his artistic ability and his social philosophy as are his political essays, his novels, or the famous short stories.

That many of Cable's incidents, scenes, and whole plots can be traced to true narratives and that his characters were often based on recognizable human counterparts caused some critics to decry his lack of originality. Cable did not have a fertile imagination; his work is not characterized by inventiveness. He acknowledged that it was his custom to use models for his characters, but he said that he composed his fictional personalities very carefully, taking some qualities from one person of his acquaintance and adding traits

[1] Letter from Adelene Moffat to Cable, September 15, 1888.

from other people he knew and read about.[2] He confessed to "a keen preference for true stories of actual occurrence," [3] and he said, "It is the facts in the fiction,—not mixed with it, as some boor may mix sand with sugar, but the facts *in* the fiction, as our life is in our blood,—it is this that holds our interest." [4]

Yet he was aware that the truth of a story is not alone sufficient to justify it as art, and in the introductory essay, in which he explains how he came into possession of the stories and vouches for their authenticity, Cable is careful to stress the role of the editor. "The relations and experiences of real men and women rarely fall in such symmetrical order as to make an artistic whole. Until they have had such treatment as we give stone in a quarry or gems in the rough [true stories] seldom group themselves with that harmony of values and brilliant unity of interest that result when art comes in—not so much to transcend nature as to make nature transcend herself." [5] Aside from heightening the artistic value of the true stories in his collection, Cable's practice of editing his material and relating the narratives in his customary manner makes it possible to consider certain of them as instances of his social criticism.

"The Adventures of Françoise and Suzanne," is a redaction of an account, reputedly written in 1822, of events that took place in 1795. Pierre Bossier, a planter much interested in travel, decides to make a pleasure trip into the Louisiana hinterland with a group of poor families migrating in search

[2] "After-Thoughts of a Story-Teller," *North American Review*, CLVIII, 16–23.

[3] *The Amateur Garden*, p. 1.

[4] "The Speculations of a Story-Teller," *Atlantic Monthly*, LXXVIII, 96.

[5] *Strange True Stories of Louisiana*, p. 1.

of prosperity. He takes his daughters, Françoise and Suzanne, with him. The other members of the party are an Italian, Mario Carlo, and his colored wife and children; Joseph Carpentier and his wife, both French; and the Irish John Gordon and his wife and son. Mario is already familiar with the prairie of Attakapas; his description of its wealth of game and fertile land spurs the others into migrating, and his flatboat is used for the trip.

In a passage which is in Cable's words, not those of Françoise's manuscript, the Italian accounts for his family.

> Mario told his story of love and alliance with one as fair of face as he, and whom only cruel law forbade him to call wife and compelled him to buy his children; and told the story so well that at its close the father of Françoise silently grasped the narrator's hand, and Carpentier, reaching across the table where they sat, gave his, saying:
>
> "You are an honest man, Monsieur Carlo."
>
> "Will your wife think so?" asked the Italian.
>
> "My wife comes from a country where there are no prejudices of race." [6]

The colored woman and her children are not despised servants. She and the Irish woman share the menial tasks, and the oddly assorted members of the party function almost as one family during the trip. When disaster befalls the flatboat, the travelers scatter in accord with their varied purposes, but Mario reaches his promised land and settles his family on his "principality."

"Salome Müller, the White Slave" is the story of a girl who is mistaken for an octoroon and enslaved. The subject obviously intrigued Cable; he tells the story in his own intrusive way and infuses it with the same propaganda against slavery and caste which is so evident in his fiction.

[6] *Ibid.*, p. 42.

A group of German immigrants sails to New Orleans in 1818. Among them are redemptioners who pay for their passage by working as bond slaves after their arrival in the new country, and others are unjustly forced into the same service. Salome Müller, a "pretty, black-eyed, olive-skinned" little girl, is taken into service in Attakapas, and relatives lose sight of her for many years. When they finally locate her, Salome, now a slave and the mother of three children, supposes herself to be "a yellow girl" named Mary.

But the relatives are certain of her real identity and instigate a legal battle to secure her freedom. Her owner, John F. Miller, admits the probability that she is white and entitled to her release, but he protests that he has paid his money for her. Witnesses at the trial testify that Miller has other slaves even fairer than Salome. "Whether he had any better right to own the several other slaves whiter than this one whom those same witnesses of his were forward to state he owned and had owned, no one seems to have inquired." [7] Nor was it remarkable at that time, Cable says, that this man was a gentleman and his wife a woman noted for her good works.

One point, in view of current beliefs to-day [1889] compels attention. One of Miller's witnesses was being cross-examined. Being asked if, should he see the slave woman among white ladies, he would not think her white, he replied:

"I cannot say. There are in New Orleans many white persons of dark complexion and many colored persons of light complexion." The question followed.

"What is there in the features of a colored person that designates them [sic] to be such?"

"I cannot say. Persons who live in countries where there are many colored persons acquire an instinctive means of judging that cannot be well explained."

[7] *Ibid.*, p. 177.

And yet neither this man's "instinct" nor that of any one else, either during the whole trial or during twenty years' previous knowledge of the plaintiff, was of the least value to determine whether this poor slave was entirely white or of mixed blood.[8]

When the trial first comes to court, general public sympathy is with Salome. "It rested not on the 'hardship, cruelty, and oppression' she had suffered for twenty years, but only on the fact, which she might yet fail to prove, that she had suffered these things without having that tincture of African race which, be it ever so faint, would entirely justify, alike in the law and in the popular mind, treatment otherwise counted hard, cruel, oppressive, and worthy of the public indignation."[9]

A birthmark, a skillful lawyer, and a Virginia precedent induce the court to declare Salome free. But the innocent ex-slave, like a seduced woman, cannot altogether live down her past, and years pass before she settles into a comfortable, respected life.

"The 'Haunted House' in Royal Street" is really two true stories in one. The first part of the tale concerns the house in the days before the Civil War when it was an aristocratic Creole residence; the second pertains to its use as a school during Reconstruction and the years immediately afterward.

Madame Lalaurie, who buys the house in 1831, is such an established figure in Creole society that rumors of horrible mistreatment of her slaves are long ignored. An investigation of the suicide of an eight-year-old slave, whom she had been seen to pursue with a cowhide whip before the child flung herself off the roof of the house, results in

[8] *Ibid.*, pp. 177–78.

[9] *Ibid.*, p. 170. Cable made later use of the experience of Salome Müller. *The Flower of the Chapdelaines* (1918) includes the story of Fortune, a white girl who is illegally enslaved.

the woman's conviction for cruelty. Her slaves are taken from her; but they are bought by her relatives and sold back to her without public protest. An old Negro cook, chained in the kitchen, sets fire to the house, and when the blaze is put out and the building searched, the slaves are found chained, mutilated, and tortured. The insane mistress flees to a waiting ship. From that time on the deserted house bears the reputation of being haunted by the ghosts of the tormented Negroes.[10]

It remains empty until just after the Civil War.

> The era of political reconstruction came. The victorious power decreed that they who had once been master and slave should enter into political partnership on terms of civil equality. The slaves grasped the boon; but the masters, trained for generations in the conviction that public safety and private purity were possible only by the subjection of the black race under the white, loathed civil equality as but another name for private companionship, and spurned, as dishonor and destruction in one, the restoration of their sovereignty at the price of political copartnership with the groveling race they had bought and sold and subjected easily to the leash and lash.[11]

As a result, Cable says, the Reconstruction government of New Orleans was dominated by corruption and misrule.

> And yet when history's calm summing-up and final judgment comes, there must this be pointed out, which was very hard to see through the dust and smoke of those days: that while plunder and fraud ran riot, yet no serious attempt was ever made by the freedman or his allies to establish any un-American principle of government, and for nothing else was he more fiercely, bloodily

[10] Cable's main source for this story of Madame Lalaurie was Martineau, *Retrospect of Western Travel,* I, 263–67. For a contrary version, see Street, "This Haunted House Has Only Happy Ghosts," *American,* CIV, 16, 17, 118, 121, 124, 126.

[11] *Strange True Stories of Louisiana,* p. 219.

opposed than for measures approved by the world's best thought and in full harmony with the national scheme of order.[12]

During Reconstruction the house was used as a public school and for several years was the only one attended by both white and colored girls. It became an issue in the struggle between the Radicals and the Democrats, who proposed to evict the Negroes. In December, 1874, the students were assembled and told to answer to the roll by a band of White Leaguers, who, a few months earler, had beaten the city police in an infantry and artillery battle in the center of New Orleans.

As each name was called its young bearer rose and confronted her inquisitors. And the inquisitors began to blunder. Accusations were met with denials and withdrawn with apologies. Sometimes it was truth, and sometimes pure arrogance and falsehood, that triumphed over these champions of instinctive racial antagonism. One dark girl shot up haughtily at the call of her name—

"I am of Indian blood, and can prove it!"

"You will not be disturbed."

"Coralie ———," the principal next called. A thin girl of mixed blood and freckled face rose and said:

"My mother is white." [13]

"Step aside!" commanded the White Leaguer.

"But by the law the color follows the mother, and so *I* am white."

"Step aside!" cried the man, in a fury. (In truth there was no such law.)

"Octavie ———."

[12] *Ibid.*, p. 220. For a brief statement of a later view of Reconstruction which is akin to Cable's, see Simkins, "New Viewpoints of Southern Reconstruction," *Journal of Southern History*, V, 49–61.

[13] Cable was enough of a realist to acknowledge in this dialogue that quadroons and octoroons were not invariably the offspring of white fathers and colored mothers, although this was a tenet of the literary tradition to which his fiction contributed.

A pretty, Oriental looking girl rises, silent, pale, but self-controlled.

"Are you colored?"

"Yes; I am colored." She moves aside.

"Marie O———."

A girl very fair, but with crinkling hair and other signs of negro extraction, stands up and says:

"I am the sister of the Hon. ———," naming a high Democratic official, "and I shall not leave this school."

"You may remain; your case will be investigated."

"Eugénie ———."

A modest girl, visibly of mixed race, rises, weeping silently.

"Step aside."

"Marcelline V———."

A bold-eyed girl of much African blood stands up and answers:

"I am not colored! We are Spanish, and *my brother will call on you and prove it.*" She is allowed to stay.[14]

A sympathetic teacher who knows the family history of one girl is relieved that she escapes detection, for the girl is engaged to a white gentleman who does not know she is colored.

"Her mother—she is dead now—was a beautiful quadroon. A German sea-captain loved her. The law stood between them. He opened a vein in his arm, forced in some of her blood, went to court, swore he had African blood, got his license, and married her."[15]

[14] *Strange True Stories of Louisiana,* pp. 227–28.

[15] *Ibid.,* p. 230. While the girls who are expelled are colored, the reader is encouraged to infer that some of those who are allowed to remain are hardly less so. What Cable at least implies here and elsewhere is that some persons of Negro ancestry succeeded, both before and after the Civil War, in gaining permanent acceptance as whites. This is, of course, historically true. Cable's treatment of this fact of American life was an important reason for Creole and Southern resentment of his work.

Cable feigns disinterest in the propaganda value of this narrative. He says he writes "to tell a true story, and not to plead one cause or another. Whatever the story pleads, let it plead." [16] Such patent dissembling does not lessen the force of the tale or discredit Cable's long interest in equal education for all. Years earlier, on September 26, 1875, he had written a letter to the New Orleans *Bulletin* in which he condemned the mob action of the White Leaguers in evicting the colored girls from this school. He signed it "A Southern White Man," but, he said, he gave his name to the editor, who published the letter accompanied by a long rebuttal. Both the *Bulletin* and the *Picayune* refused to print Cable's second letter on the subject.[17] His story of the haunted house gave him, belatedly, the last word. It is an eloquent plea for his cause.

"Attalie Brouillard," a slight story of quadroon intrigue, suggests that Cable's sacrificial dedication to that cause and, perhaps, his powers as a serious creative artist were on the decline. This is the one story in the collection which he wrote rather than edited; significantly, it omits social criticism. Cable carefully assigns the role of Attalie's "protector" to an Englishman, and he makes the villain a wily free man of color.[18] The characters are mere puppets, and the spurious

[16] *Ibid.*, p. 222.

[17] Biklé, *George W. Cable: His Life and Letters,* p. 158; Turner, *George W. Cable,* pp. 75–78; and Cable, *The Negro Question: A Selection of Writings on Civil Rights in the South,* ed. by Turner, pp. 8–9, 12–13, 26–33.

[18] Cable's heroine is not individualized and has few of the attractions of the quadroons of *Old Creole Days.* Attalie is "a worthy woman; youngish, honest, rather handsome . . . with good manners. . . ." But Camille Ducour, the *male* quadroon, is "narrow-chested, round-shouldered, his complexion a dull clay color spattered with large red freckles, his eyes small, gray, and close together, his hair not long or

plot, the truth of which is supported only by tradition, does not deserve the attention he gives it. This is romance, not social criticism, and it is undistinguished fiction.

The last story in the volume, "War Diary of a Union Woman in the South," Cable had bought from Mrs. Dora Richards Miller, a New Orleans school teacher who had been a Northern sympathizer during the war. By careful editing, of which he was quite proud, he reduced the length of the manuscript by nine thousand words before putting it in print.[19] In his account of how these true stories came into his hands, Cable acknowledged that this particular manuscript was one that publishers would be unlikely to decline. "I bought it for my little museum of true stories, at a price beyond what I believe any magazine would have paid—an amount that must have filled the widow's heart with joy, but as certainly was not beyond its worth to me." [20] Certainly the manuscript he obtained from Mrs. Miller must have repaid his investment of time and money. The first part of the diary, an account of the siege of Vicksburg, originally appeared in *Century* for September, 1885, and the other section was published in the magazine in October, 1889. The complete narrative, "War Diary of a Union Woman in the South," was included in *Strange True Stories of Louisiana* and in *Famous Adventures and Prison Escapes of the Civil War*, an anthology published in London in 1894 and re-issued in American editions in 1898 and 1915. Mrs. Miller's

---

bushy, but dense, crinkled, and hesitating between a dull yellow and a hot red; his clothes his own and his linen last week's." *Strange True Stories of Louisiana*, pp. 234–35.

[19] See his letter to Clarence Clough Buel, July 3, 1889, printed in Russell, "George Washington Cable Papers in Duke University Library," Duke University *Library Notes*, No. 25, pp. 6–7.

[20] *Strange True Stories of Louisiana*, p. 18.

New Orleans school was the one invaded by the White Leaguers, and some of the strengths and insights of Cable's account may have been derived from her version of the incident. Another manuscript which Cable bought from her, after she had been unable to get it accepted for publication, was an account of a Santa Cruz insurrection she had witnessed as a child in 1848. This he edited and published as "A West Indian Slave Insurrection" in *Scribner's*, December, 1892; he used it again in *The Flower of the Chapdelaines* (1918) as "The Holy Cross," and this time the narrator is a little girl named Dora.

During the years of their friendship, Cable paid Mrs. Miller to do research and served as her literary mentor, advising her on her writing and aiding her efforts to break into print.[21] She was evidently content with the relationship until the magazine appearance of "A West Indian Slave Insurrection." Piqued that Cable failed to name her as the author of the original document, she protested in the New Orleans *Times-Democrat*. Cable was in rather a difficult position from which to answer her charges and those which appeared in other journals. On the one hand, in order to stress their authenticity, he wanted to minimize the editing he had done on the true stories; on the other hand he wished to make it clear that they were products of his talent as a creative artist and to claim them as companion pieces

[21] See Turner, *George W. Cable,* pp. 240–42. Without assurance that it is supported by evidence other than Cable's own testimony, I hesitate to accept the view that no discredit attaches to Cable in this controversy with Mrs. Miller. Cable did serve as literary adviser and agent to a number of aspiring writers, whose admiration and dependence upon him appealed to his vanity, and he did so without remuneration. He was generous in many ways with both time and money, but his arrangements with Adelene Moffat suggest that he could also drive a hard bargain.

to his earlier writing. He replied in a letter in the *Critic*, February 4, 1893, stating that he had done extensive work on Mrs. Miller's manuscripts, that he had announced himself as editor rather than author, and that he had paid for the stories. Mrs. Miller's response in the *Critic* of March 18, 1893, reiterated her version of the dispute and damaged Cable's reputation for integrity by quoting passages from his letters to her which seemed clearly to refute all that he had said publicly in his defense. Cable did not reply.

Throughout most of the story about the slave uprising, the author's sympathy seems about equally divided between the owners and the slaves. At the conclusion he takes a stand reminiscent of Emerson's "Boston Hymn." He says that the Danish government was justified in not paying the planters when it put an emancipation proclamation into effect after quelling the uprising, for "if the ex-master ought to be paid for his slave, then much more should the ex-slave recover back pay for his labor." [22]

During the years when he collected and edited these true stories, Cable's absorbing interest was not in slavery and ante bellum Louisiana but in the post-Reconstruction New South. His next book, *The Negro Question* (1890), was a collection of his essays on the race problem written in connection with his sponsorship of the Open Letter Club. These essays concentrate on the denial of civil rights and adequate public education to the Negro, but they also pay attention to other groups which suffer the same injustices.

The Negro Question states Cable's conviction that the solution to the Southern—and national—problem was to accord civil rights to the colored citizen and to provide

[22] *Scribner's Magazine*, XII, 720.

public education for all. This view was not unique; Walter Hines Page, another white Southern liberal, and T. T. Fortune, a leading Negro journalist with whom Cable was acquainted, held similar opinions.[23] Cable was not so naïve or idealistic as to suppose that education would solve the problem all by itself: "I do not consider the education of the lower masses in the South a cure for all the ills of Southern society, but I fail to see how they can be cured without it, and I fail to see any excellence in the policy that is content to withhold it." [24] He knew that the freedmen held no monopoly on ignorance—"Whatever we say with regard to illiteracy of blacks in the South applies to the illiteracy of whites also" [25]—and hence it was not blacks alone who must be educated.

Cable consistently invited Negroes to participate in the solution of the race problem. He felt that only through their own struggles to obtain civil rights could they prove that they deserved them. He spoke to colored audiences on several occasions and was interested in the national organizations Negroes were attempting to establish.[26] "What Shall the Negro Do?" was first presented as an address on April 13, 1888, before a league of colored men in Boston

[23] Doherty, "Voices of Protest from the New South," *Mississippi Valley Historical Review,* XLII, 53–55.

[24] "National Aid to Southern Schools," *The Negro Question,* p. 63. The first version was published as "The Nation and the Illiteracy of the South" in the *Independent* for August 29, 1889. Entitled "A National Debt," it appeared in the Minneapolis *Northwestern Congregationalist* on September 6, 1889.

[25] *The Negro Question,* p. 65.

[26] In a letter to Adelene Moffat, May 11, 1888, he remarked with pride that one group just organized in Mississippi had passed a resolution of thanks to "R. J." The telegram he had sent her on May 7 was signed "R. Jones."

and appeared as an article in the August, 1888, *Forum.* Cable stressed the responsibilities of the Negro and condemned segregation for tending to relieve him of the duties of the citizen.

But the Negro's [27] grievance is, that the discriminations against him are more and more unbearable the better public citizen he is or tries to be; that they are impediments not to the grovelings of his lower nature, but to the aspirations of his higher; that as long as he is content to travel and lodge as a ragamuffin, frequent the vilest places of amusement, laze about the streets, shun the public library and the best churches and colleges and neglect every duty of his citizenship, no white man could be much freer than he finds himself; but that the farther he rises above such life as this the more he is galled and tormented with ignominious discriminations made against him as a public citizen, both by custom and by law; and finally, that as to his mother, his wife, his sister, his daughter, these encouragements to ignoble, and discouragements to nobler, life are only crueler in their case than in his own.[28]

In "What Makes the Color Line?" Cable denounces segregation as a political device. He says that "To deny, abridge or jeopardize a negro's right to vote, to hold office, to sit on jury, or to enjoy any of the public advantages around him on the same terms as others, without any consideration of his own individual values—good, bad or indifferent—except that he is an individual of a certain *race,*" violates the principles and best interests of the nation.[29]

[27] In accordance with the practice of his time, Cable was not consistent about capitalizing this word. On a galley proof of this article in the Cable Collection at Columbia University, he noted that "colored people . . . affect the initial capital." The proof was received too late for correction to be made.

[28] *The Negro Question,* pp. 67–68.

[29] *Ibid.,* pp. 111–12. This essay first appeared in the Chicago *America,* June 13, 1889.

The essay concedes virtues to the freedman's political activity during Reconstruction and scoffs at those who fear that given the right to vote he would do so along purely racial lines.

Probably Cable's most effective plea for the education of the Negro and the poor white is the final essay of this book, "The Southern Struggle for Pure Government." A compilation of speeches Cable had delivered in several Northern cities, this address before the Massachusetts Club, Boston, February 22, 1890, was widely distributed in the South in pamphlet form.[30]

Chesnutt wrote, on March 28, to thank Cable for the copy he had received and to praise the address. "I do not comprehend how a fair-minded opponent, however radically he might differ from you, could find anything harsh to say in reply to so fair and courteous an argument; if any one can lift the race question out of the mire of prejudice and partisanship into the clear light of reason and patriotism, I think you are the man." [31] The speech was also endorsed by an intense young Harvard graduate student who, when he attained prominence later as a scholar, author, and race leader, came to know both Cable and Chesnutt. W. E. B. DuBois sent a short letter praising Cable's clarity and heroism.[32] Almost half a century later the militant Dr. DuBois recalled his meeting with Cable at Northampton, and expressed high regard for the author's interest in furthering the progress of America and the Negro.

[30] Turner, *George W. Cable,* p. 255. It was published in abridgments under various titles in the New York *Tribune,* the *American,* and *Our Day.*

[31] Chesnutt, *Charles Waddell Chesnutt: Pioneer of the Color Line,* p. 53.

[32] DuBois to Cable, February 23, 1890.

"The Southern Struggle for Pure Government" attacks the one-party system of the New South and reveals the absurdity of the racial stereotypes which had become fixed in the national mind. Cable assails the common disparaging generalizations about the intelligence of the exploited race. "The great majority of the Negroes are illiterate, improvident, reckless and degraded. But so is the Irish peasant. So is the Russian serf." [33] He says that black laborers are no more happy and contented when ill used than were the slaves who built the pyramids in Egypt. The same arguments advanced against granting colored men the vote, he says, had also been used against the ignorant, poor, and unintelligent of every race. He denies that Southern whites have had special interest in the Negro because of their daily contact with him. In fact, he says, "every great step thus far taken towards the Negro's real betterment has been first proposed by those remote from him while it has been condemned as idle or dangerous by those nearest him." [34]

To prove that Negroes are not mentally incapable, Cable points to their educational achievements. "Over 1,000,000 of their children, half of their total school population, are enrolled in the public schools, where their average daily attendance is more than 600,000." [35] He asserts that most of the Negro teachers and preachers and ninety-nine hundredths of the lawyers, editors, dentists, and doctors had to get their training in the North or in institutions built, maintained, and staffed by Northerners. And educated Negroes, he says, are not granted in the South the privileges to which their attainments entitle them, not even admittance to public libraries.

[33] *The Negro Question*, p. 125. [34] *Ibid.*, p. 129. [35] *Ibid.*, p. 125.

For twelve years it [the New South] has persuaded an apparent majority of the nation to leave to it the fitting of the Negro for citizenship, even refusing national aid to lift the burden of public education it counts insupportable; yet to this day it has made not the slightest provision for admitting any Negro to the full measure of any civil or political right by virtue of acquired fitness.[36]

Cable refuses to accept the traditional excuses for the inadequacy of Southern schools. He notes that "the Southern States to-day have only schools enough for half their school population, and believe they are bearing as heavy a burden of school tax as any people of equal means can, while the States and territories of the West, under the ideas of free government first and of two parties of equal rights, are taxing themselves far heavier, even where they have less wealth."[37]

It has been much reiterated in the South and re-echoed in the North that the task of public education in the Southern States suffers a unique and unparalleled drawback in the fact that while the Negroes enjoy nearly half the outlay of the school funds, almost the entire amount of those funds is paid by white taxpayers. But assuming this to be quite true in every other regard, there are two points in which it is not so. First, the very alphabet of economics teaches us that all taxes do not rest entirely on those from whom they are collected, but that hundreds of thousands of men who are too poor to be found enumerated on the tax-rolls are for all that reached by taxation through the medium of rents and similar indirections. And, second, that the fact quoted is far from being unique and unparalleled. The only thing peculiar about it is that this lower and unmoneyed mass, which, as a matter of good investment in the whole public interest, is in every State in the Union freely accorded an enjoyment of the school funds out of all proportion to its money

[36] *Ibid.*, p. 145.

[37] *Ibid.*, p. 137.

contributions, happens in the South to be a distinct race which has been working for the last one hundred and fifty years, but has been drawing wages only for the last twenty-five.[38]

By this time Cable had ceased to feel obliged to deliver his criticisms of the South in person before Southern audiences; the platform there was no longer open to him. His final speech of major importance was "What the Negro Must Learn," an address before a meeting of the American Missionary Association in Northampton, October 22, 1890. He gave his New England listeners a spirited attack on the South's colleges, institutions with curricula "antiquated and almost completely innocent of civics and economics," [39] and on laws that "so one-sidedly protect the landlord, creditor and mortgagee that they work intensely toward the perpetuation of the landlessness, penury, unthrift, supineness and vice of the laboring masses," on whom, Cable said, the prosperity of all society rests.[40]

Although the essays Cable published after *The Negro*

[38] *Ibid.*, pp. 138–39.

[39] McIlwaine, *The Southern Poor-White from Lubberland to Tobacco Road,* p. 172, states that as late as 1900 no Southern college or university had established a department of sociology and very few even offered courses in that subject.

[40] *What the Negro Must Learn,* a pamphlet published by the American Missionary Association, p. 6. The address was printed in *American Missionary,* January, 1891. Cable indicates that Negroes very properly regarded education as a means to the attainment of civil and political rights, not as an end in itself.

The laws to which Cable refers here were probably the crop-lien laws of Alabama and Mississippi, by which share-cropping was instituted after the Civil War. Correspondence in the Cable collection at Tulane indicates that he got information about the laws from President Henry S. DeForest, of Talladega College, and Booker T. Washington. Charles H. Otken, a native of New Orleans but a resident of Mississippi, published *The Ills of The South* (1894), in which he spoke out against concentrated wealth, land monopoly, and the crop-

Question continue to emphasize the rights of the freedmen, they pay increasing attention to the rights of the Southern poor white. "Does the Negro Pay for His Education?" which appeared in the July, 1892, *Forum*, analyzes the expenditures for public education in the South. Cable declares, "Out of the South there is no State whose non-property-holder pays so large a share of the whole school tax as the 'poor white' and the Negro pay in the South or in which, for other men's children, the payer of school taxes on property pays so little." [41] He says that "the Negro, so far from being the educational pauper he is commonly reputed to be, comes, in those States, nearer to paying entirely for his children's schooling, such as it is, than any similarly poor man in any part of the enlightened world." [42] Cable laments the disparity in the allotment of funds to white and Negro and urban and rural schools and in the salaries of white and colored teachers. Reasoning that black illiteracy fosters white illiteracy, he demands a pro-rata distribution of state educational funds. "For lack of it, hundreds of thousands of poor children, white and black, are now out of school, and other hundreds of thousands get wretched schooling instead of good." [43]

"Education for the Common People of the South," published in *Cosmopolitan*, November, 1892, praises the achievement of the Reconstruction governments, which, "when they died so widely unmourned, left a public-school system in

---

lien system. See Doherty, "Voices of Protest from the New South," *Mississippi Valley Historical Review*, XLII, 56–58. Cable had attacked the crop-lien laws earlier in "The Southern Struggle for Pure Government."

[41] *Forum*, XIII, 643. [42] *Ibid.*, p. 645. [43] *Ibid.*, p. 648.

complete working order in every southern state, and thousands of schools in operation."[44] Fittingly, it sums up the broad democratic liberalism which the author professed so consistently in his political writing, and it demonstrates that he laid stress upon the hardships of the freedman "not because he is a negro, but because, in such vast numbers, he is the South's poor man and underling; one of the *other men* under a gentlemen's government," and one forbidden to become a gentleman even if he could.[45] "As for the South's white commoner—the sand-hiller, the covite, the cracker, the tar-heel, the 'Cajun—he may become a gentleman if he can," but he must expect no aid from a gentlemen's government.[46]

As if this were still the eighteenth century, it conserves the landed squire as its unit of gentility, and maintains a grotesquely pitiful disproportion between its public outlays for the education of two or three thousand young gentlemen and those teaching the three R's to millions of illiterate children. Nor does there seem to be any ground to hope for an effective change until a real democracy rises up in the South and forever puts away the ancient, idle notion of founding either prosperity, security or political purity on the exclusive and imperial supremacy of the gentleman, or of any race, class or political party which does not concede equal public rights to every other that in any degree shares with it the burdens of a common weal.[47]

[44] *Cosmopolitan,* XIV, 65. [45] *Ibid.,* p. 68.

[46] *Ibid.* Cable did not suppose that these were the only exploited minority groups. In *What the Negro Must Learn* and "The Southern Struggle for Pure Government," he says that the nation had defrauded and oppressed the Indian. And see note 30, p. 64, above.

[47] "Education for the Common People of the South," *Cosmopolitan,* XIV, 68. In this essay and elsewhere, Cable regards the South's failure to attract foreign immigrants as the result of its mistreatment of its native laboring class.

This essay was Cable's last direct effort to persuade his countrymen to accept and act upon the facts, logic, and political principles which he believed to be the foundation for a resolution of the American dilemma. He seemed to have failed, dissipated his creative talents, wasted himself on a lost cause. Now, much as he had done a decade earlier when he made *Dr. Sevier* the vehicle for his interest in prison and asylum reform, he turned to fiction to express his convictions about what seemed to him the most important issue of American life.

VII: "The Facts in the Fiction"

Like Walter Hines Page, the Southern liberal with whom he is sometimes compared, Cable believed in public education for all. His support of education for the Negro, the poor white, the immigrant, and the underprivileged adult was not merely vocal or casual. An incidental interest would not have led him to make the unpopular, even hazardous, endorsement of unsegregated schools he made while still a resident of New Orleans, to expend valuable time and energy on the adult education provided in Northampton by his Home Culture Clubs, or to give money, direction, and moral assistance to certain institutions which he regarded as particularly deserving.

One of these was Berea College in Berea, Kentucky. Founded by Kentucky abolitionists, Berea was a white school which admitted Negro students and for a while even had a bi-racial board of trustees.[1] Most of its financial support came from the American Missionary Association, with which body Cable was thoroughly in accord.[2] With his

[1] Brownlee, "Moving In and Out," *Phylon*, IX, 147. The school vainly contested before the U.S. Supreme Court a state law which, in 1904, prohibited coeducation of the races.

[2] See the draft of his letter to Dr. Dunning, September 12, 1889, in the Cable Collection at Columbia University.

friend Roswell Smith, who gave the college more than $50,000, Cable visited Berea in June, 1885, and spoke at the commencement exercises.[3] He made repeated visits to Berea in later years and urged friends and acquaintances to assist its program.[4] He wrote Edward Atkinson, a New England capitalist who had been a member of the Open Letter Club, that Berea was entitled to national support because it "has always grasped, and is grasping to-day, the whole Southern question with an inoffensive but faithful effectiveness unequaled in our entire country." [5]

Unlike Walter Hines Page, Cable disagreed with the idea that education for Negroes should stress the skills of the farmer, domestic, and laborer.[6] This may account for his failure to appear on the platform in 1897 to help Booker T. Washington raise money for Tuskagee Institute.[7] It is

[3] His address, "Christianity as a Business," was published as "Professional Christianity" in *Advance* (Chicago), July 30, and distributed as a pamphlet.

[4] Cable, *A Memory of Roswell Smith,* pp. 58–59.

[5] Letter, December 26, 1899, in the collection of the Massachusetts Historical Society. See also Cable's correspondence with Roswell Smith and Berea's President Frost in the Cable Collection at Tulane University.

In 1955, again an interracial institution, Berea presented Paul Green's *Wilderness Road* as part of its centennial celebration. This challenging historical drama urged the South to solve its educational problems in accordance with its own best democratic traditions. New York *Times,* June 30, 1955.

[6] Yet instruction in the domestic arts, designed in part to train Northampton girls for domestic service, was a feature of the adult education program of Cable's Home Culture Clubs.

[7] Other explanations are perhaps equally plausible, among them the pressure of Cable's own work, previous lecture commitments, and his withdrawal from public discussion of the race problem. Butcher, "George W. Cable and Booker T. Washington," *Journal of Negro Education,* XVII, 467–68.

significant that *What the Negro Must Learn,* in which Cable specifically repudiated the theory that Negroes should waive civil and political rights in return for schools where they might be taught to be better laborers and servants, was based on "The South's First Needs," a speech he made on May 16, 1890, under the auspices of Howard University, which stressed an academic and professional curriculum. Yet Cable gave financial assistance and active support to Okolona Industrial College of Okolona, Mississippi.[8] Wallace A. Battle, a Negro graduate of both Talladega College, Alabama, and Berea, founded the institution, later called Okolona Normal and Industrial School, in 1902. Cable sent money to the school in 1903 and became a member of the board of trustees in 1905. The next year he arranged for Battle to appear on the platform in Northampton, where he was visiting Cable, and in 1907 Cable himself spoke for Okolona in Springfield, Massachusetts.[9] Mild mannered and ultraconservative, Battle was grateful for Cable's help and praised him as one of the "most sympathetic and lovable" of the board members [10] and "one of the great souls of America." [11]

Another institution in which Cable was actively interested,

[8] See the Cable-Battle correspondence in the Cable Collection at Tulane University.

[9] Turner, *George W. Cable,* p. 340.

[10] "Wallace Battle, the Episcopal Church and Mississippi," *Crisis,* XXXIV, 282. Battle was president of Okolona until 1925, when the commencement-day murder of one of his teachers by resentful local whites led him to resign and move to the North. Neither his board of trustees nor the Episcopal Church, which sponsored the institution, took effective action to punish the murderers or to protect the school and its personnel. (Cable had died on January 31, 1925.) *Ibid.,* pp. 261–62, 282–83.

[11] Turner, *George W. Cable,* p. 357.

this one only about five miles from his home, was Williston Seminary in Easthampton, Massachusetts. He was a member of the board of trustees from June 20, 1887, to November 4, 1922, when, because of his failing health, his resignation was accepted. He sometimes addressed the students, as he did in October, 1899, and he made the Founder's Day speech on June 17, 1907.[12] In 1905, and for several years thereafter, he supervised extensive landscape gardening on the campus.[13] In contrast to many New England preparatory schools, Williston had a liberal admissions policy, and Cable must have been pleased to know that sometimes Asians, Africans, and colored Americans were included in the student body.[14]

Inevitably, Cable's preoccupation with the problems of the New South must find expression in his fiction. He had expounded advanced and positive opinions for several years in the full knowledge that they would lead to outraged criticism from many quarters. Although close study of his

[12] *Willistonian,* June 18, 1907. Northampton's *Daily Hampshire Gazette* reported commencement week events at Williston in its issues of June 17, 18, 19, and 20, but made no reference to Cable's appearance. This was after Cable's break with Adelene Moffat and may be evidence that the paper was out of sympathy with him.

[13] Sawyer, *A History of Williston Seminary,* p. 275; Cable, "Where to Plant What," *Century,* LXXII, 97–98; and the records of the meetings of the board of trustees in the archives of Williston Academy.

[14] One Negro who attained prominence while he was a Williston student was Charles Fred. White, a Spanish War veteran whose *Plea of the Negro Soldier and a Hundred Other Poems* appeared in 1908. He cut the paper, set the type, ran the press at Easthampton's Enterprise Printing Company, and did all the work of publishing the volume except binding it. See the brochure, prepared as an advertisement for the book, in the Moorland Collection at Howard University.

Now Williston Academy, the institution continues its liberal policy. Two Liberian boys, descendants of the founders of that country, were students there in 1957–58. See the Springfield *Union,* March 22, 1958.

career and his writing reveals a gradual withdrawal from the role of Southern critic and champion of minority rights, one would expect to find Cable's liberal convictions clearly and vigorously stated in his Reconstruction novel, *John March, Southerner.* One would also expect to find him relying heavily on fact in his treatment of scene, plot, and characters. The novel meets only the second of these expectations.

No doubt the earliest draft of the book, two chapters of which Cable submitted to *Century* in 1890, was a forthright expression of his views on Reconstruction and the problems resulting from it. In rejecting the manuscript, Richard Watson Gilder, who was now strongly pro-Southern, called it "a tract, not a story" and lamented that the author had crowded into it the same "serious thought on public, political and humanitarian questions" which he was stating in his essays and addresses.[15] Cable submitted three revised chapters the next May. Again the work was unacceptable, an embarrassment to Cable, because he had obtained heavy advances from the company and now owed four thousand dollars.[16] In June, 1893, Gilder turned down the completed manuscript, arguing that it had "less charm" than any of Cable's earlier work.[17] Finally *Scribner's Magazine* accepted it with minor changes. It ran as a serial in 1894 and was then published as a book.

When Cable's hero, young John March, inherits more than a hundred thousand acres of land, he decides to colonize it in order to exploit its industrial potential. Cornelius Leggett, a scheming Negro politician, finally convinces

[15] Biklé, *George W. Cable: His Life and Letters,* pp. 212–13.
[16] Turner, *George W. Cable,* p. 292.
[17] Biklé, *George W. Cable: His Life and Letters,* p. 213.

him that this can be done only by forming a corporation and selling stock to local people until Northern capital can be lured into the enterprise. While March is away—he actually goes to Europe and persuades peasants to migrate to his tract, Widewood—Jeff-Jack Ravenal, newspaper editor, and Major Garnet, president of Rosemont College, contrive to fleece him of his interests. March's fortune is restored with the discovery that, through a mistake in the deeds, he really owns Rosemont.

Cable followed his usual creative method in founding his work on fact. The story of John Moffat's loss of his property through a mistake in the deeds and the machinations of an unscrupulous lawyer Cable probably first heard when he visited Monteagle in August, 1887, after his commencement address at Vanderbilt. His informant might have been his new friend, Adelene Moffat, who was proud of her father and always liked to talk about him. Lilian Moffat Gilfillan and her husband might have mentioned it when Cable visited them in St. Louis.[18] Or he could have learned about it from Mrs. Jennie Weir, Adelene Moffat's older sister, with whom he left a list of questions when he visited Monteagle in 1889 to make notes for the book.[19] There were several reasons why Cable should choose to set his novel in the Monteagle area: the appeal of a convenient true story, the availability of friends who could provide useful details, his approval of Moffat's ideas about immigration, and the fact that the history of the section was particularly appropriate to the story he wished to tell. In 1890 he visited Cartersville, Georgia, a county seat in a piedmont mining area, and took notes there,[20] but the basic scene of the book

[18] See her letter to Cable, December 5, 1889.
[19] Turner, *George W. Cable*, p. 291.
[20] *Ibid.*

appears to be Tennessee rather than Georgia. The main model for Cable's "State of Dixie, County of Clearwater" is Franklin County, Tennessee. "Sandstone County" is his version of Grundy County, and "Blackland County" is actually Lincoln. "Suez" is Sewanee and "Pulaski City" resembles Nashville. Probably Colonel John Moffat served as the prototype for Judge Powhattan March, whose dream of developing his vast tract of land he passes along to his son John. Mrs. Moffat or Mrs. Jennie Weir may have given Cable ideas for the sanctimonious Mrs. March. The Widewood tract, of course, is really Moffat's Monteagle, and young March's immigration scheme has its origin in the similar enterprises Moffat once promoted. Immigrants did settle in Franklin County, so March brings them to "Clearwater." "Rosemont College" is the University of the South, and neighboring "Montrose Academy," operated by the fictional Misses Kensington, is the Fairmount of Mrs. Kells and Mrs. Yerger. Cable was familiar enough with Negro schools to need no model for "Suez University." The unnamed college in the North which the heroine, Barbara Garnet, attends is, naturally, Smith College in Northampton.

The technique which Cable adopted in his efforts to make the book a balanced and unobjectionable picture of those chaotic years of American history following the Civil War and Reconstruction, and to accord with his new belief that the chief function of literature is to entertain, is disconcerting to the reader who expects the facts in this fiction to constitute a significant statement of the author's social and political philosophy. The facts are there, but they are obscured by the inclination toward romance which was growing on Cable during the nineties and which makes his later fiction generally a pale reflection of the work of his early years. The attempt to appease the South by carefully apportioning virtues and vices among the Northern and Southern characters in the book weakened the force of its social criticism and did not win Southern approval.[21]

On the eve of the novel's serial publication, Cable said it was "written for all readers, to all, and at none," and hoped it was a "pleasing story" which would keep readers interested and leave them profited.[22] Looking back now on *The Grandissimes,* he described the plot of that novel as "little more than the very old and familiar one of a feud between two families, the course of true love fretting its way through, and the titles of hero and heroine open to competition between a man and his friend for the one and a mother and daughter for the other." [23] Not only is this a contradiction of his own earlier acknowledgement of the social criticism which motivates that book; it is also evidence of a shift in his character and of his willingness to say what he judged to be expedient. It was a misguided effort to eliminate from the public memory the one quality of *The Grandissimes* which brought it "very close to greatness." [24]

In *The Grandissimes* and *Dr. Sevier* Cable is very much the intrusive author, and there is never any doubt as to which characters have his sympathy and express his opinions on controversial issues. In *John March, Southerner,* Cable

[21] Baskervill, who had helped Cable accumulate notes for the book during his brief stay in Nashville in November of 1889 (*Ibid.,* p. 290), called it "one of the most dismal failures ever made by a man of genius." "George W. Cable," *Chautauquan,* XXV, 184. Chesnutt wrote Cable, on April 11, 1895, that he found it less appealing, for obvious reasons, than the earlier books.

[22] Biklé, *George W. Cable: His Life and Letters,* pp. 213–14.

[23] "After-Thoughts of a Story-Teller," *North American Review,* CLVIII, 17.

[24] Chase, "Cable and His *Grandissimes,*" *Kenyon Review,* XVIII, 383.

intrudes clumsily in the love scenes, but on the issues of Reconstruction and the problems faced by the New South he rarely offers his characteristic and illuminating asides. The figures in the novel speak for themselves, not for the author; there is no *raissonneur* to state the theme Cable expressed so well in private correspondence: "The New South of Coal, Iron and Spindles which our commercial American mind is so tickled with must be kept well to the fore, but with the constant implication that ideas and fundamental principles of justice & order are just as paying & necessary investments as mines & mills." [25] There is no hero—March is too slow-witted, vacillating, and confused to qualify—and the inept characterization makes it difficult to identify the villains and thus to discredit their cause.

It is possible for a casual reader to conclude that Cable endorses much that was done to restore white supremacy in the South. Major Garnet, who champions that movement, seems at first to be cast in the role of hero and author's spokesman; it is not until late in the story that he stands revealed as the villain, and even then there is no repudiation of his racial or his political point of view. Leggett is made so ridiculous a figure that his virtues pass unnoticed, and they are never sufficient to challenge the racial dogmas most of the white characters advance. The Negro characters seldom rise above the level of stereotypes, a level to which the author had not previously descended, and for the first time he introduces the element of minstrelsy into his work.[26] In its presentation of the Negro, this novel is not to be

[25] Cable to Adelene Moffat, May 11, 1888.

[26] Sometimes Cable came "perilously near to caricaturing" Creole life. *The Louisiana Book: Selections from the Literature of the State*, ed. by M'Caleb, p. 43.

grouped with the works of Thomas Nelson Page and Thomas Dixon, but it is a departure from the realistic approach which characterizes Cable's other work.

The principal Negro character is Cornelius Leggett, a lazy, scheming, dissolute mulatto who contrives to gain considerable power during Reconstruction. As a state legislator he devotes himself to filling his pockets in every way he can. He is held up to ridicule as a symbol of presumption, ignorance, and villainy; yet he is clever and industrious in his own way, and there is some nobility in his determined support of public education for all and his concern for the best interests of the poor whites. Having discovered that Major Garnet has unwittingly built Rosemont on property which belongs to March, Leggett blackmails Garnet, but he uses his power over him to get free schools as well as hush money. Often Leggett shows a political acumen beyond that of his white contemporaries. Even when he is drunk, he realizes, as March does not, that Widewood cannot be made to produce its potential wealth until it is a good place for poor men, which it cannot be without schools. And despite his outlandish dialect and minstrel escapades, he knows that the New South cannot lift itself up by holding the Negro and the poor white down.

Several times married and never divorced, Leggett energetically pursues the virtuous Johanna, Barbara Garnet's maid. When he turns his attention to Daphne Jane he is more successful. She had spent two or three terms at Suez University, "where she had learned to read, write, and add —she had been born with a proficiency in subtraction." [27] Her parents place her in service with March's mother to get her away from Leggett, but he contrives to court the

[27] *John March, Southerner,* p. 276.

girl as he drives her to the March home. In this episode Cable abandons all pretense of realism.

"I arrove fum Pussy on the six o'clock train. One o' the fus news I get win' of is that you in town. Well! y'ought to see me!"

But his hearer refused to be flattered. "Wha'd you do—jump in de riveh?"

"Jump in—I reckon not! I flew. Y'ought to see me fly to'a'ds you, sweet lady!"

The maiden laughed. "Law! Mr. Leggett, what a shoo-fly that mus' 'a' been! Was de conducto' ayfteh you?"

Mr. Leggett smiled undaunted. "My mos' num'ous thanks to yo' serenity, but I enjoys fum my frien' Presi*dent* Gamble the propriety of a free paass ove' his road."

"Oh? does you indeed! *Is* dat so! Why you makes me proud o' myse'ff. You hole a free paass on de raailroad, an' yit you countercend to fly to me!" The manner changed to one of sweet curiosity. "Does you fly jess with yo' two feet, aw does you comp'ise de assistance o' yo' ears?"

"Why, eh—why, I declah 'pon my soul, you—you es peart es popcawn! You trebbles me to respond to you with sufficient talk-up-titude." [28]

Another minority group fares no better at the author's hands than does the freedman. Cable's picture of the white mountaineers on the outskirts of Suez is superficial and unsympathetic.[29] They oppose March's plan to colonize Widewood, warning "ef you bring niggehs we'll kill 'em, an' ef you bring white folks we'll make 'em wish they was dead." [30] March supposes they mean what they say, these men who, Cable says, "believed the world was flat and

[28] *Ibid.*, p. 279.

[29] Cable must have read Adelene Moffat's "Mountaineers of Middle Tennessee," *Journal of American Folklore*, V, 314–20, but apparently made little use of it. This article, which praises the work of Charles Egbert Craddock, is far more penetrating and sympathetic in its treatment of the mountaineers than is *John March, Southerner.*

[30] *John March, Southerner,* p. 214.

would trust no man who didn't; who, in their own forests, would shoot on sight any stranger in store clothes; who ate with their boots off and died with them on." [31] Cable makes much of their intent to kill March if he settles European peasants on his land, but when the colonists do arrive the author drops the whole theme and says nothing of the mountaineers' reaction to them.

As is often the case in Cable's fiction, the scene of *John March, Southerner* is its most realistic feature. The major characters are incompletely motivated and poorly realized, but Cable is more successful in handling his setting. It is new for him; there are no Creoles, no quadroons, no decadent aristocrats. He does not deal directly with the Reconstruction government, but he gives a sense of the character of the period. His biting satire reveals the bigotry and selfishness of the politicians, the helplessness of the freed Negro masses, and the unaspiring ignorance and political backwardness of many of the poor whites.

There is a vivid account of the violence which accompanies the imposition of white supremacy. Threatened for daring to vote, thirty Negroes arm to defend themselves. Captain Shotwell explains to Judge March the outcome of this double effrontery.

"Well, of co'se, you know, seh, what was jes' boun' to happm. Some of ow ve'y best young men mounted an' moved to dislodge an' scatteh them befo' they could gatheh numbehs enough to take the offensive an' begin they fiendish work. Well, seh, about daay-break, while sawt o' reconnoiterin' in fo'ce, they come suddenly upon the niggehs' position, an' the niggehs, without the slightes' p'ovocation, up an' fi-ud! P'ovidentially, they shot too high, an' only one man was inju'ed—by fallin' from his hawss. Well, seh, ow boys fi-ud an' cha'ged, an' the

[31] *Ibid.*

niggehs, of co'se, run, leavin' three dead an' fo' wounded; aw, accawdin' to latest accounts, seven dead an' no wounded. The niggehs taken shelter in the church, ow boys fallen back fo' rein-fo'cements, an' about a' hour by sun comes word that the niggehs, frenzied with raage an' liquo', a-comin' this way to the numbeh o' three hund'ed, an' increasin' as they come.—No, seh, I don't know that it *is* unfawtunate. It's just as well faw this thing to happm, an' to happm now. It'll teach both sides, as Garnet said awhile ago addressin' the crowd, that the gov'ment o' Dixie's simply got to paass, this time, away f'om a raace that can't p'eserve awdeh, an' be undividedly transfehed oveh to the raace God-A'mighty appointed to gov'n!" [32]

Cable cannot resist lampooning Southern dogmas. While Garnet is explaining to one Northern guest "why negroes had to be treated not as individuals but as a class," John March is telling another visitor "why it was wise to treat chickens not as a class but as individuals." [33] March is often the agent for Cable's irony. When Suez whites explain to an Englishman how they have circumvented the efforts of Leggett, "the most dangerous demagogue in Dixie," to secure for the colored college a just share of the state's aid to education, the Englishman protests against the rascally trick by which the Negro citizens are cheated. March angrily retorts that he can make such a statement only because he is visiting a free country, and he slaps the visitor for replying, "There's hardly a corner in Europe but's freer." [34]

Few readers found *John March, Southerner* the "pleasing story" Cable had said he hoped it would be. The book lacks the clarity and unity of effect essential even to a romance. March's plans for exploiting his land are never clear; the

[32] *Ibid.*, pp. 69–70. For an account of some of the violent disturbances which Cable may have used as models for this episode, see Taylor, *The Negro in Tennessee, 1865–1880,* p. 60.

[33] *John March, Southerner,* p. 83.

[34] *Ibid.*, pp. 155–56.

complicated arrangements by which he hopes to achieve his vague aims and the schemes by which he nearly loses his property are neither comprehensible nor convincing. The major characters are not static but neither do they really develop; they simply fluctuate, showing first one quality and then another. The dialogue abounds in theatrical heroics and simpering sentimentality. Plot structure is particularly weak; the episodes seem contrived to complicate the conflicts and to postpone the resolution of the long narrative. An inexcusably strained plot device is Barbara Garnet's dream of a trivial incident of her early childhood, a dream which leads to the climactic discovery that Rosemont belongs to March and not to her dissembling father.

Critics who would justify the book and others who would condemn it are sometimes disposed to equate it with the works of John W. De Forest and Albion Tourgée and to regard it, as Gilder did, as a tract for the times. This it is not. Like some sermons on sin, it merely deplores evil and endorses justice and morality. It presents the issues of the time and it depicts, but does not attack, injustice. It does not express directly the convictions of the author, and it proposes no specific solutions to the problems. Often it distorts social reality or obscures it with irrelevant minstrelsy and genteel sentiment. The basic failure of the novel is not to be attributed to what touches of realism it has; these are its strength. Because there is so little effective realism and so much inept romance, *John March, Southerner* is a serious disappointment. It does not do justice to Cable's political insight, his knowledge of American history, or his dedication to principle during the eighties.

However, its satirical thrusts at the errors and hypocrisies of the New South contribute to the author's total achievement as a social critic. Boyesen's review in *Cosmopolitan* labeled it a sociological novel and gave it unstinted praise. Years later, looking back on the whole of Cable's career, Randolph Bourne called it one of his best novels: "Into that book he got pretty nearly the entire life of a turbulent and proud Southern community in its welter of personal and political feuds and aspirations to develop its suddenly discovered resources." [35] The book does include significant foreshadowing of the findings of historians such as C. Vann Woodward, and it anticipates the realistic probing of novelists like Stribling and Faulkner.

For the weaknesses of *John March, Southerner,* the first novel Cable had published since *Dr. Sevier* (1884), several explanations may be advanced. The most obvious but the least likely is his change of residence, his removal from the Southern scene which supplied his material. Others, which have more validity, are the interference of a squeamish publisher, the taste of a public dominated by magazine readers who preferred romance to realism, and Cable's adoption at about this time of the popular and hence convenient belief that the primary function of literature is to entertain. Perhaps there was a waning of his creative powers, dating from the time of his withdrawal from the unrewarding role of civic reformer.[36] The best explanation, however, may be simply that there were changes in the character of the man and in his circumstances.

Cable was fifty when the novel finished its serial run.

[35] "From an Older Time," *Dial,* LXV, 364. *John March, Southerner* foreshadows Booker T. Washington's efforts to attract Northern capital to a Negro community in Mississippi. See Meier, "Booker T. Washington and the Town of Mound Bayou," *Phylon,* XV, 396–401.

[36] In his review of the Biklé biography, E. K. Mitchell remarks that Cable's abilities dwindled after *Dr. Sevier* and suggests "age, security, and possibly diffusion of energies," rather than New England residence, as causes. *American Literature,* I, 219.

Two years earlier, although he had not yet paid the mortgage on Red House, he had moved his wife and children to 23 Dryads' Green, at the corner of Harrison Avenue. The house, which he remodeled extensively, he called Tarryawhile. As the first resident, it was his privilege to name the street; he called it after a street he had known in New Orleans and always insisted that the apostrophe follow the "s," for there was more than one dryad. Like its Southern namesake, it was planted with beds of perennials in the middle of the road. There were spacious grounds around this home at the edge of Paradise Woods, so called because of an admiring description attributed to Jenny Lind, and these were Cable's delight. He transplanted the elm Henry Ward Beecher had planted when he visited Red House, and in later years more souvenir trees were planted by Felix Adler, L. Clark Seelye, Henry van Dyke, Hamilton Wright Mabie, James M. Barrie, W. Robertson Nicoll, Arthur Conan Doyle, Mary E. Burt, Minnie Maddern Fiske, Anna Hempstead Branch, and others.[37] Cable made these trees a part of the garden he loved, and beneath their shelter he built a study around 1904. Mary E. Burt, a friend of the family, shared with him the cost of the red-tiled, red-roofed structure with its gray stone chimney, and she sometimes occupied one floor of the building in the summer.[38]

Some of the visiting notables who stopped at Tarryawhile Cable took to the Smith College campus, where he occasionally spoke to classes or special gatherings—always on literary subjects, never on social or political matters.[39] His

[37] Biklé, *George W. Cable: His Life and Letters*, pp. 280–81.

[38] *Ibid.*, p. xii, and Turner, *George W. Cable*, p. 322.

[39] On at least one occasion, on February 13, 1886, he gave a reading from his works at Smith.

acquaintances included the most renowned writers and editors and wealthy philanthropists of the day; these he undertook to make his friends. The Bible classes were ended, the Open Letter Club was dead, the controversial causes were abandoned. Cable's ambitions now were personal ones. His philosophy was in accord with the conservatism and respectability of the class to which he aspired and the gentility of the age. His platform appearances continued unabated, but they were readings from the early books that had made him famous, and the selections were calculated to give no offense. He had come to handle most of his own bookings and, conscious of his diminutive stature and high voice and anxious to avoid anything that might contribute to a comic or undignified effect, he sent ahead detailed instructions about the setting and properties for the stage, specifying in particular that there must be no heavy furniture or large-patterned draperies. He was a veteran of the reading circuits now and his performance was as polished and dramatic as that of an experienced actor. The routine of constant travel was physically wearing but psychologically rewarding. It was a pleasure to revisit old friends, to meet new distinguished people, and to have frequent reminders that he, too, was an accepted public figure. The applause and the newspaper accounts and the letters of praise contributed to his new image of himself. He appeared on the platform as a literary celebrity, a man with an entertaining story, not as a reformer with an unwelcome message. And whenever he appeared as president of the Home Culture Clubs at the clubhouse, 41 Center Street, Northampton, he did so in the deserved and satisfying role of civic benefactor.

VIII: "The Dear Good Work"

The new headquarters of the Home Culture Clubs was the old Methodist Church, a block from Northampton's Main Street. The steeple had been removed and the building thoroughly remodeled to suit its new functions. Cable insisted upon this, although Adelene Moffat argued that some of the expenditures were unwise and might create resentment on the part of other community enterprises which had found it necessary to retrench.[1] A contemporary description speaks of the building's simple Greek front and its "various elevations unspoiled by eccentricities." [2] A hundred feet long and more than forty feet wide, the structure seemed adequate to its new role. The basement provided possibilities for a large play area for boys and a smoking room for men. The rooms above could serve as reading rooms and meeting places for the various clubs and could accommodate fifty sessions of classes each week. The second floor, in which Cable took particular interest, was refitted as a small theater. At one end was a completely equipped stage, at the other a gallery which would seat a

[1] Letters from Adelene Moffat to Cable, October 3 and 29, 1893. Her judgment may have been affected by the fact that her salary was not being paid regularly.

[2] "The Northampton Home Culture Clubhouse," the *Letter,* IV, 37.

hundred people. The assemblies, lectures, concerts by Smith College girls, and other special programs which had been held at Grand Army Hall could now be presented at the clubhouse. So could the weekly dances which became so important to the young club members.

The building was acquired through the generosity of Edward H. R. Lyman, who had earlier given the town its civic auditorium, the Academy of Music. Born in Northampton in 1819, he went to Boston at fourteen and began the mercantile career that soon made him wealthy.[3] Cable, who was once connected with business himself and was now prone to admire material success, saw romance in "Mr. Lyman's commercial experiences" and his part in "the owning and sending forth in a perpetual round of voyages, of a fleet of the old-fashioned swift-going clipper ships, carrying outward bound around the Horn and across the Pacific the products and wares of America and returning with the teas and silks of China." [4] Lyman spent six months of each year at his Fort Hill estate in Northampton, and he knew that the Home Culture Clubs had gradually assumed the status of a community social service agency. He respected the integrity of Cable and Adelene Moffat [5] and saw the merits of the enterprise to which they were devoted. By 1892 there were more than three hundred members and forty clubs scattered about the country, but most of them

[3] He and his brother-in-law became partners in the firm of A. A. Low & Brothers which, in 1895, was in the hands of younger members of the families. One of these, once a member of the Open Letter Club, was Seth Low, formerly mayor of Brooklyn and then president of Columbia University.

[4] Cable, "Edward H. R. Lyman," the *Letter*, IV, 42.

[5] Cable wrote Adelene Moffat, on March 8, 1907, that Lyman had once said his gifts to the Home Culture Clubs resulted as much from his confidence in the two chief sponsors as in the project itself.

were in Northampton. In that year Smith College girls became important agents in what was soon the main feature of the local program—adult education. The obvious virtues of this work, and the equally obvious limitations which resulted from a lack of facilities, attracted Edward Lyman's benevolence.[6]

At first the classes were limited to about six students each, though they were sometimes held for single individuals. The subjects treated at the clubhouse were related to the needs and interests of the assorted members. Some courses were vaguely cultural: travel, astronomy, literature, music, public questions, etc. Many, such as bookkeeping and mechanics, were practical. A few were academic: geology, German, French, biology, etc. Others, such as gymnastics and dramatics, were evidently recreational. Students included high-school pupils who wanted extra tutoring, people of leisure anxious to pursue a rewarding hobby, and immigrants in need of basic instruction in the language and lore of their new country. Northampton people were "singularly free from destitution,"[7] but the rapid industrial development of the old town and the surrounding area had brought dramatic changes and some problems. In 1845 there were only three voters in Northampton who were not of Yankee stock, but in the years immediately following there was a heavy influx of Irish, Canadian French, Poles, Jews, and others.[8] The principal job of the clubs—

[6] Lyman's widow left the Home Culture Clubs $1,000 when she died. The first bequest the enterprise received was that of J. C. Martin, of Florence, Massachusetts. See Cable's speech at the dedication of Carnegie House, printed in the Northampton *Daily Herald,* April 13, 1905.

[7] Powell, "The Home-Culture Clubs," *Booklovers Magazine,* V, 385.

[8] *The Northampton Book: Chapters from 300 Years in the Life of A New England Town, 1654–1954,* p. 396.

and the principal achievement—was not the spread of culture, in the sense of sweetness and light, but Americanization.

The Smith girls who taught classes were generally juniors; they were required to obtain their parents' consent to volunteer for the work. They served in pairs and employed a complexity of printed forms—record books, attendance slips, report sheets, etc.—hardly matched today by a public school system. The idea of using the college girls as instructors has been attributed to both Cable and Adelene Moffat. It was a natural development, whichever one originated it. Both lived near the college and both must have seen the value of relating the college buildings at one end of the town to the factories at the other. Cable had daughters at Smith and was an active member of the college community. Adelene Moffat, who was directly in charge of the classes and of all other work of the clubs, supervised instruction and at her home held social gatherings and orientation sessions for the club leaders. Several of them became her personal friends. She said that she persuaded teacher agencies in Boston and New York to credit the volunteer instruction as experience, and thus managed to provide some compensation for those of the girls who later sought teaching positions. She preferred, however, to have the classes taught by townspeople, whose tenure need not be limited to one year, whose services were available in the summer, and whose experiences and daily affairs gave them a better understanding of the underprivileged students who were their neighbors and fellow citizens.[9]

Adelene Moffat showed a special talent, and one that Cable lacked, for that part of her job as general secretary

[9] Moffat, "Northampton Clubhouse Work," the *Letter*, IV, 65. See her letters to Cable, January 21, 1892, and March 30, 1893.

which involved direct dealings with the lower classes of Northampton.[10] This is plainly indicated in the newspaper reports over the years and is verified by Northampton residents who remember her work. Cable's correspondence also acknowledges it. She had been taught never to waste the time of a working person, whose time is his only capital. "I knew," she said, "when I entered the house of a working man and found the housewife washing sheets, to grasp one end of her burden and help wring it while I talked with her." Cable was often away on reading engagements; [11] it was Adelene Moffat who personified the Home Culture Clubs, both for the people who frequented the clubhouse and for many of the solid citizens whose contributions enabled the work to go on.

Through her detailed reports in correspondence, Cable was kept informed of the progress and problems of the work and was able to direct its administration. His letters were full of his enthusiasm for its possibilities and accomplishments, full of suggestions for extending its scope and increasing its value, efficiency, and appeal. His was an executive role. He did come to the clubhouse and often presided at the more important special programs. But when he approached, or was approached by, the immigrants and laborers he wanted most to aid, he could find nothing to say to them or said something which his irritation or confusion or patronizing manner made offensive.

[10] For an interesting account of the procedure followed and the difficulties encountered in organizing the reading groups, see her article, "The Story of a Club," *Cosmopolitan,* XVII, 435–39. "Miss Jenny" represents Adelene Moffat. There is an introductory note by Cable.

[11] He still gave some lectures, too, though not on controversial issues. See Turner, *George W. Cable,* pp. 300–1.

One of Adelene Moffat's special interests was a group of urchins, the juvenile delinquents of their day, who were attracted to the clubhouse when they saw recreational possibilities in its large basement. There was no furniture except a water bucket and a dipper, but the furnace cold-air box, which passed along the floor against the inner wall, substituted for chairs. At her first meeting with the thirty-odd boys of the group, Adelene Moffat scattered copies of the *Police Gazette* around the room and won their confidence by feigning an interest in prize fighting and the career of John L. Sullivan, but when the meeting ended she found that they had put tobacco juice in the fingers of her gloves. The boys' energy was directed into more acceptable behavior when a crude monkey-ladder converted the area into a makeshift gymnasium and a half hour of military drill, directed by Lieutenant Moynihan on Saturday nights, was added to the curriculum.[12] In later years several of these boys attained prominence in politics and became respected members of the community which had once regarded them as hopeless ruffians.

Another function which Cable's civic project undertook to perform once the necessary facilities were available was that, he said, of "furnishing social amusements to large assemblages of young people, in competition with concerns doing the same thing purely for commercial gain and totally without social responsibility."[13] The weekly dances proved to be the most popular social amusement and a means of disciplining intractable youngsters, for admission to them was a reward for good behavior. Behavior was a

[12] Moffat, "Northampton Clubhouse Work," the *Letter,* IV, 66. See also the *Letter,* II, 1, and IV, 38 and 50.

[13] Biklé, *George W. Cable: His Life and Letters,* p. 190.

problem on some occasions; once all activity at the clubhouse was suspended for several weeks as punishment for rowdyism. In order to help pay for the improvements to the building, the second floor was leased for private social affairs and theatrical performances, and periodically the members staged plays themselves. They gave Dion Boucicault's *The Octoroon* one spring, and Howells's *The Unexpected Guest* was presented on Wednesday, February 26, 1896.[14] One benefit featured "Queen Stella of the Gonzales of Spain" on "Gypsy Life and Tradition": admission one quarter. Cable was intrigued by the idea of a society circus, but failed to interest enough society participants. When some professional circus performers—including a contortionist and his wife, a boxer—were stranded in Northampton, Cable wanted Adelene Moffat to find jobs for them and have them entertain at the clubhouse.

Cable had not forsaken his original idea, and such modifications as were made either were the result of his other interests, such as his enthusiasm for the theater and for gardening, or were fortuitous and were forced upon him. He described the project to Edward Atkinson as primarily "fireside reading clubs where neighbors by virtue of neighborhoodship and without reference to the diversities of social rank or intellectual accomplishments meet weekly" in the homes of members "for the pursuit of any purpose not too laborious to be amusing nor too idle to be profitable." In this letter of April 27, 1894, in which Cable asked Atkinson to address the annual meeting of the clubs, he remarked that the members came from various social

[14] One of Howells's plays may have been presented in the spring of 1893. See Ekström, "The Cable-Howells Correspondence," *Studia Neophilologica*, XXII, 57–58.

groups, ranging from college girls and professors to Tennessee Negroes and mountain whites.[15] (*John March, Southerner* was appearing at this time, and Cable may have been preoccupied with these latter groups.) Club No. 11 was located at Monteagle, and the club report said the eleven members, who were studying "General Culture," were drawn from "the various social elements in the town —the sojourners there in search of health, some of the mountain families, and representatives of the various business interests"; [16] it seems unlikely that Negroes were included. The possible inaccuracy of Cable's claim is not important, for it is true that a broad cross section of American society did participate in the club work, particularly in Northampton. There, in later years at least, some Negroes attended classes, and others, students at Smith College, served as teachers.[17]

Cable's efforts to propagate the clubs outside Northampton met with some success. By 1897 there were eighty-six clubs in Massachusetts, New York, New Jersey, Pennsylvania, Connecticut, Ohio, South Carolina, Tennessee, Illinois, Michigan, Wisconsin, Colorado, and Nebraska. Most of them were in Massachusetts and about fifty were in Northampton, where the activity had moved outside the home and into the clubhouse. Still the general secretary

[15] The letter is in the collection of the Massachusetts Historical Society. For Atkinson's speech at the meeting, and one by President Cable, see the special supplement to the *Letter,* May 29, 1894; see also the *Letter,* IV, 3 and 7. The speaker in 1895 was Felix Adler. See the *Letter,* IV, [18].

[16] The *Letter,* IV, 7. See also IV, 49.

[17] Adelene Moffat mentioned in her diary on December 7, 1899, that two colored girls from Northampton were enrolled in classes. Helen M. Chesnutt, Charles W. Chesnutt's daughter, taught English to a small class of French Canadians around 1900.

found her time taken up with correspondence and weekly reports tabulating the number of pages read, and she spent many hours in helping to organize new club units in new locations. She came to believe that this part of what Cable called "the dear good work" [18] must be abandoned, or at least curtailed, because the service the work could perform for the motley population of Northampton was more important. That the work had a broad base in Northampton is apparent from the range of occupations of the club members: weaver, buffer, clerk, laundry-hand, spinner, reeler, college student, cook, shingler, farmer, forger, driller, blacksmith, casket-coverer, saloon-keeper, etc.[19] Locally the project had developed into a useful social service agency; elsewhere it retained the vague, pseudo-cultural character of Cable's original concept.

This is supported by the tabulated figures on members and reading. The clubs had a membership of 142 in 1888, and the total reading, according to Cable's system of multiplying the number of pages read at meetings by the number of members present, amounted to 415,000 pages. By 1897 membership had jumped to five hundred, but the number of pages read, 460,000, showed no comparable increase. The explanation is that the reading was being continued largely by the clubs outside Northampton; the main local activity consisted of the clubhouse classes in arithmetic, banjo, dancing, dressmaking, elocution, embroidery, geometry, guitar, psychology, physical culture, spelling, etc. The fact that the work in Northampton was largely class instruction rather than reading clubs is somewhat obscured by the device of referring to the classes as clubs and calling the volunteer teachers club leaders. Some

[18] Letter to Adelene Moffat, January 21, 1897.

[19] Biklé, *George W. Cable: His Life and Letters,* pp. 190–91*n*.

of the groups that met in the clubhouse paid rent and evidently were not Home Culture Clubs at all. One of these was The Rainbow Club, a branch of the Massachusetts Association of Working Girls.

In order to guide and encourage the reading groups, publication of a small newsletter was begun in 1892, under Adelene Moffat's direction. It was composed of letters and reports from the different clubs and suggested courses of study. Gradually the journal expanded, partly because of the financial support of Edward Lyman. The issue dated July 1, 1895, featured a new floral cover designed by Louise Chard, Cable's oldest daughter, and listed Cable, Mabel Loomis Todd, and Adelene Moffat as editors. The first advertisements appeared in the November issue, the last one to bear on its cover reference to the Home Culture Clubs. The content now included brief biographies of living authors and historical sketches of the towns where the clubs were located. These, occasional stories and poems, and a few illustrations made the *Letter* an attractive little monthly. Cable was at home in the editor's chair, a rocker in his study at Tarryawhile, and in his scrupulous attention to detail he dispelled for his staff the idea that writing and editing are easy occupations. He would keep the printer waiting until the right word was found and correctly placed. Once he called attention to the importance of discriminating diction by comparing two titles. "See how much better Howells names his story than Frank Stockton does," he said. "Stockton says, 'What Might Have Been Expected' and Howells, 'A Foregone Conclusion'; both mean exactly the same." [20]

[20] Anna Gertrude Brewster, "George W. Cable: Our Fellow Citizen," an unpublished paper prepared, about 1929, for a meeting of the Northampton Historical Society.

When Cable was away on the platform his editorial tasks fell to his assistants and the work was done at Miss Moffat's home. Some issues were prepared almost entirely by the staff. Planning the reading courses, proofreading, and other details became the responsibility of Anna Gertrude Brewster, who succeeded her sister Mary in these editorial capacities. Direct descendants of Pilgrim William Brewster, the girls had long been friends of the Cable family, and their brother later married Cable's daughter Margaret. One issue of the *Letter* included a contribution by Lucy, who was the only one of Cable's daughters to be graduated from Smith. Walter B. Cox, Nettie's oldest son, sent illustrations from New York, where he was employed by the *Tribune*. Others whose work appeared in the slender magazine were Anna Hempstead Branch, Mabel Loomis Todd, Viola Roseboro', Professor Mary E. Byrd of the Smith College Observatory, Ruth McEnery Stuart, James Whitcomb Riley, Paul Laurence Dunbar,[21] Mary E. Burt, Albert Bigelow Paine, and Eugene Field, with whom Cable had made a reading tour in the winter of 1892–1893. Generally Cable directed the editing or did it himself, and he wrote letters and articles for the later issues. The last one, that for May, 1896, featured an article by Hamlin Garland.

[21] Cable was introduced to the Negro poet in Dayton, Ohio, in 1895 and met him again in New York in the summer of 1896, after Howells's review of Dunbar's poetry had brought him national recognition. (Howells's article on Chesnutt in the *Atlantic Monthly*, May, 1890, performed a similar service for that author.) Dunbar's "Theology" appeared in the *Letter* for August, 1896; this differs slightly from "Theology by Intuition," the version in *Lyrics of the Hearthside* (1899). See my article, "Mutual Appreciation: Dunbar and Cable," *Free Lance: A Magazine of Poetry and Prose,* IV, 2–3; Conover, *Some Dayton Saints and Prophets,* pp. 182–83; and Cunningham, *Paul Dunbar and His Song,* pp. 121–22.

It was obvious that Cable's larger editorial ambitions were about to be realized. The editorial staff moved to quarters in the clubhouse and three more workers were added. When the new magazine, the *Symposium,* appeared in October, almost the only feature of its predecessor that it carried was a section devoted to books and reading. Anna Gertrude Brewster conducted that department, and Adelene Moffat did a "Home and Neighbor" column which stated the theories of social responsibility and community uplift on which the Home Culture Clubs were based. Helen M. Cox, Cable's niece, was one of the illustrators.[22] From the beginning, none of the staff except Cable had much hope, much less confidence, that the journal would succeed. Its name alone, one of the editors said, was enough to kill it. One of its established competitors greeted the first issue with withering contempt: "If there is anything this poor old world needs it is another ten-cent magazine." Contributions from hopeful authors arrived in almost greater numbers than subscriptions. Some established writers were listed in the table of contents, for Cable solicited contributions from his friends. Each of the three issues carried a long piece by Cable: a story, "The Brown Ghost," in October; an essay, "To See Our Life as Romance Sees It," in November; and in December an account of James M. Barrie's memorable visit to Tarryawhile that fall.

All the mechanical work except the printing was done by the staff, headed and driven by Cable. His name appeared on the cover as publisher. He and Edwin Oviatt were the editors; Adelene Moffat and Anna Gertrude Brewster were assistant editors. When the issues were ready for distribution, the staff addressed by hand about three thousand

[22] Turner, *George W. Cable,* p. 298.

wrappers, and Cable did his share. His friends, unimpressed by the journal and its prospects, opposed the waste of his time and money. When the third issue came off the press in December, he was persuaded to abandon the venture. One bleak day he called each of the staff into his office and told them, one by one, of the decision that had been forced upon him. Dejected, he cried as openly as a child.

The *Book Buyer*, a Scribner publication, took over the affairs of the *Symposium*, and Cable found considerable consolation in an invitation to become the editor of *Current Literature*, though the salary was low and his contract short. As soon as his reading commitments were discharged, he went to New York in February, 1897. The issue for that month carried a photograph of Paul Laurence Dunbar, whose talent and blackness seemed to Cable comforting evidence that the Negro could not be inherently inferior; it reprinted poems from Dunbar's *Lyrics of Lowly Life* and Howells's generous introduction for that volume. When Cable took up his editorial duties in March, he looked to Northampton for assistance. Ever since the days of the Open Letter Club he had praised Adelene Moffat's literary ability and had encouraged her to write. She had published some articles and was anxious to do more with her pen than compose letters and reports and handbills on how to organize reading clubs. He promised to use her services but admonished her to "say no word to anyone about writing. There are strong reasons for this." [23] Both her article, "Howard Pyle's Quality as an Illustrator," in the July issue, and her review of James Lane Allen's *The Choir Invisible*, in August, appeared under a pseudonym, Landon Mc-

[23] Cable to Adelene Moffat, March 31, 1897.

Vicar.[24] She may have done other reviews for Cable, who reminded her that *Current Literature* critics must be anonymous.[25]

Cable thought *Current Literature* might possibly provide the financial security which literature itself had not brought him. Affection for his previous publishing venture led him to call his editorial column "Editor's Symposium" when he took over the magazine with the April issue. The column's subtitle is reminiscent, but only faintly, of earlier and more vigorous phases of his career: "An open tabletalk round the literary board, whereat any may speak whose art is not too awkward to unite truth and brevity with courtesy and wit." Also related to his previous work were the magazine's guide to educational reading and the series on "Great Editors"; included among these were five of the men who had published Cable's own writing. His editorial columns, neither profound nor distinguished, treated significant contemporary writers, morality in art, the function of dialect, and other literary matters. Cable was encouraged to believe that his work in New York would revive his creative energies. On June 6, 1897, he wrote to Adelene Moffat about his years of "retirement" at the edge of Paradise Woods, "I was going to pieces. Now I am pulling myself into shape again and believe the coming year (the coming twelve months) will prove the most fruitful term of its length I shall have enjoyed for a great while." He did com-

[24] In several interviews she mentioned to me that she had published poetry and other writing under various pseudonyms and had ghost written articles on public issues for prominent persons. She would give no details, on the ground that it would be unethical to do so, and I have been unable to locate anything except the articles signed Landon McVicar.

[25] Cable to Adelene Moffat, July 19, 1897.

plete "The Entomologist," a novella set in New Orleans, but otherwise the prediction was unfulfilled.

Yet his editorial experience in New York was helpful. It was fortunate for him that the crisis which threatened the Home Culture Clubs when Adelene Moffat announced that she must resign as general secretary occurred at a moment when he believed there was a future for him in the editorial world in the metropolis and when he supposed that his civic activities had, for years, interfered with his more legitimate literary work. In March of 1897 he was able to face with equanimity her possible withdrawal and the end of their joint enterprise. At almost any other time during these years such a prospect would have left him disheartened and appalled.

Adelene Moffat's absorption in Cable's various projects over the past years had been costly for her. She had not intended her stay in the college town to be permanent or her social service and secretarial work there to be other than a means toward the achievement of her aim, a career as a professional artist. Gradually she had turned, or been turned, from the path she had planned to follow, and now she found herself at a dead end. She had come to Northampton in the summer of 1888 as a step toward studying art in New York that winter. Her return to the town the next summer resulted from her failure to get a job as a teacher, as well as from her initial enthusiasm for the Open Letter Club and her sense of obligation to the man who had established himself as both friend and benefactor. Despite the satisfaction she took in her work with the Home Culture Clubs, she held to her artistic ambitions. That fall she started a sketch class. Cable's older daughters were among her pupils, and for a while the eldest, Louise, who studied art at Smith, shared a Northampton studio with her. In 1891 she opened an art studio in nearby Holyoke, and for two years, when the studio was first at 272 High Street and then at 326 Maple,[26] her partner was Helen M. Cox, Cable's niece. For the next two years Adelene Moffat operated the Holyoke studio, now at 14 Essex Street, by herself. When she moved out of Mary Louise Cable's house in Northampton and built her own home at 63 Dryads' Green, the third floor attic was her studio.

A house of her own was a necessity, not only because she wanted space for her art work and a place to entertain, but also because she needed to accommodate the relatives from Tennessee who came to stay in Northampton. The first of these was her nephew Robert B. Weir, who worked at Sidney Bridgman's book shop, which later became Bridgman and Lyman. Harvey Weir, Robert's brother, worked there, too, when he came a few years later. Their sister Mary studied at the Fairmount school in Tennessee for a while, but the family felt she could learn little there and sent her to join her brothers. Julian and Lydia, several years younger than Mary, came later. At times these relatives lived with Adelene Moffat (and, some of them, with Mary Louise Cable), and Mrs. Jennie Weir, now a widow, and Mrs. Moffat visited with her. Apparently Robert Weir, who became steward at Clarke School for the Deaf, helped his aunt to finance the house. She made it pay for itself by the standard Northampton practice of boarding Smith College girls and others. For several years, however, Adelene Moffat and Robert Weir found the house a burden and once they were on the verge of selling it. Weir had bor-

[26] She once reported the address in correspondence as 327 Maple Street; the Holyoke city directory listed it as 326.

rowed money from Cable and wrote him, on August 17, 1897, that he could not meet the note because his aunt had been unable to fill her house, and he had been called on to pay most of her interest and taxes. Although Adelene Moffat's relatives added to her problems, they gave her a home life she must have missed when maturity, marriage, or death took them from her house as the years passed and left her to her own concerns.

In a sense, the Cables were her family too, especially during her early years in Northampton. She was at the deathbed of Cable's mother in 1890. Adelene Moffat admired Cable's wife, as everyone did, and acted upon her advice. She was fond of Willie, whom she took to Portland, Maine, on her vacation in 1893, and of Louise, with whom she maintained friendly relations even after Louise left for art study in New York and, in 1894, marriage. Cable's family, like Adelene Moffat's, gradually dispersed. His nephew, Walter B. Cox, moved to New York in 1893; soon the other Coxes joined him there. With all her relatives gone, Mary Louise Cable abandoned Whitcomb House. She rented a home at 50 Elm Street, next door to St. John's Episcopal Church, and operated it as a "college house," as Northampton called these substitutes for dormitories.

The correspondence of Cable and Adelene Moffat during these years reveals their admiration for one another and their satisfaction in the nobility of the work on which they collaborated. The letters deal with the problems that arose continually in maintaining and administering the project, enlarging the program, and managing the staff. Regardless of the weariness the burdens sometimes brought, every advance, every new hope and prospect, roused them to renewed enthusiasm.

On February 25, 1892, Cable wrote to her, "You are a paying investment." It is clear that she was, and it seems that she did not resent it. She told him on August 11, 1893, "It is only at these rare times when I write to you that I remember how seldom I express what I feel always, a deep gratitude to the providence which has [set] my feet, if only for a little while, in the parallels you have marked out for your own. If I follow with lagging steps, still I follow, with my eyes in the right direction." She added praise that Cable was to apply later to Andrew Carnegie: "I wonder if you can ever know how much better the world is for your being in it."

His letters—addressed to "Adelene" when he wrote them himself, to "Miss Moffat" when they were dictated—are the other side of the same coin. They recount details of his business and personal affairs, record his every triumph, convey instructions, and discuss plans and hopes for their personal careers and mutual interests. In a letter written on April 1, 1892, he acknowledged that the club work had become much more hers than his and said, "Thank you again and again for all you have done for me & for those I love." At the close of the year, on December 13, he wrote, "I shall never cease to be grateful to you, & to the providence that brought you to me, for the many and great services you have rendered and are still rendering to me. Thank you for your faithfulness and loyalty in every hour and your goodness and wisdom and gentleness and truth."

When Adelene Moffat told Cable that she was thinking of resigning, he evidently asked her to prepare a formal statement, for it is significant that the details of his financial arrangements with her, which he would not have wished to make public, are not mentioned in her letter.

Northampton, Mass., Apr. 5th, 1897

My dear Mr. Cable:

In pursuance with your request for a more explicit statement of the question which I intimated in our last interview it would be necessary to discuss very soon, I find this my first opportunity to give my own affairs precedence over the immediate club business which has been so absorbing of late as to leave little time for anything else. In the meantime I have been thinking over affairs very carefully and perhaps it is best that I should have come to my decision without consulting you or anyone else.

To be brief, I do not see how I can continue in the Home-Culture work any longer. I have come to the end of my resources even physically. This year we have enrolled eighty-six clubs with a membership of nearly five hundred. The clerical work alone to be done properly is too much for one person. Each of these five hundred feels that he has a personal claim upon me and cannot be put off with class treatment. But it is not so much the strain of the work that forces me to relinquish it as the realization that I must depend upon my art work for a livelihood and that in the last nine years I have done nothing in that direction. I must take it up where I laid it down for the club work before it is too late. I have made no plans feeling that my first definite action must be to inform you. I need not tell you, at least, how much it costs me to come to this decision. There is much that I wish to talk to you about but since you will be home soon perhaps we had better defer consultation until then. As to the clubs, my great comfort in leaving them is that I leave them in a fully developed and prosperous condition, as the following table will show. The slight falling off in the figures this year is due to the fact that we have not had our usual equipment. There is no reason why the work should not continue to grow indefinitely. Hoping and believing that we may be able to provide for its uninterrupted continuance, I am,

Very sincerely yours,

Adelene Moffat [27]

[27] This letter is in the Cable Collection at Columbia University.

She attached a tabulated report showing the growth of the clubs over the previous ten years. For Cable, who frequently boasted that he had been known as the best bookkeeper in New Orleans, there was a magic in numbers, but she noted: "It is in one sense an injustice to the work to attempt to estimate it in figures for its best, often its largest values cannot be so estimated." She also prepared a detailed financial statement. He replied, on April 17, "The larger sum of your claim for back salary takes me quite by surprise, but I have your statement at home & dare say I shall find the amount as you say."

Cable had been president of the Home Culture Clubs ever since their inception and, although he referred to them as "our" clubs or "the" clubs in his letters to Adelene Moffat, he called them "my" clubs when he wrote to other people. As the organization grew and as its solicitations of public support increased, it seemed wise to incorporate as a means of establishing public confidence. The original members of the Home Culture Clubs Company were Cable, Edward H. R. Lyman, John C. Hammond, Edward R. Nims, William Gaylord, Benjamin C. Blodgett, A. Lyman Williston, a descendant of the founder of Williston Seminary and president of its board of trustees, and L. Clark Seelye, president of Smith College. At the first meeting, on November 2, 1896, Adelene Moffat was appointed secretary, but she was never a member of the corporation, and the minutes of this meeting and of many others over the years that followed are in Cable's hand.[28] Massachusetts granted the corporation a charter as a benevolent and edu-

[28] The minutes are preserved in a bound volume, *Records of the Home-Culture Clubs Company,* in the archives of The People's Institute, Northampton, Massachusetts.

cational institution on the tenth of December. The change was mainly a legal one. The enterprise operated as before, with the management and direction in the hands of President Cable, subject to the nominal approval of a board of directors which met only once a year.

On April 17, 1897, Cable sent the following letter to his board:

Gentlemen:

Herewith I enclose a letter from Miss Moffat resigning her office as General Secretary of the Home-Culture Clubs. After two personal conferences with her I find myself wholly unable to protest. I have for years seen Miss Moffat setting aside (at times partly, at times wholly) her very best ambitions for an artist's life and sacrificing her best strength on the generous work whose burdens have been so much more hers than any other person's.

Nor can I find it in my judgment to recommend that her place be filled by a new appointment and the work so continued. For when Miss Moffat takes from the place her own personality I do not see how it can be filled. Both she and I have always watched diligently for some one—any one—to whom her work might be transferred whenever necessary, but I have never found such a person. To appoint two or three persons to supply her absence would hardly be more practicable, quite aside from the question of expense; for even should Miss Moffat still be persuaded to continue in the secretaryship, it would be an imperative necessity to provide her with a salaried assistant. Moreover, though this difficulty comes at a time when the work is more flourishing than ever before,[29] it comes also at a moment when my professional work [*Current Literature*] is keeping me away from Northampton so much of the time that I do not see how I can myself continue to give the work the attention it has had from me in the past.

[29] Compare this statement with Adelene Moffat's report, in her letter of resignation, that there had been "a slight falling off in the work of the clubs this year."

I believe that you are confident that every part of the money given to this work since it began has been as effectively spent for the general good as that in any region has gone to the support of colleges, asylums, or "social settlements." If there has been any serious mistake it has been in trying for so many years to carry on the work upon too moderate an appeal to the financial support of its many good friends. As one result the general secretary's salary has been borne at my own private expense during a greater part of the whole time.[30] This burden I bore willingly while I could, without other allusion to it than *the omission of this item of expense from the financial reports*[31] from time to time submitted to you; but I can no longer offer to carry it, nor can I propose to ask you or the general public for the necessary increase of donations. Nevertheless, even now when no plan for the work's continuance can be offered based on an outlay of less than twelve hundred dollars a year, the expense is much less than half what any equal amount of benevolent work of which I have knowledge is done for.

Laying these facts and convictions before you, I submit the

[30] This letter exists in several versions. It appears that the typed manuscript in the Cable Collection at Columbia University, which Cable signed, is the original. There is a copy in the archives of The People's Institute which bears his typed signature and some corrections and insertions in longhand.

The manuscript at Columbia has a penciled asterisk in the left margin and a line in the right margin opposite the sentence ending "whole time." At the bottom of the page the following is written in pencil: "A considerable portion of what was paid I earned in my studio at Holyoke." This sentence was written by Adelene Moffat, not by Cable.

When Adelene Moffat was assembling her records so that John C. Hammond could make a formal presentation of her claim for salary arrears, copies were made of the letter. One of these is in my possession. The typist inadvertently inserted Adelene Moffat's sentence in the body of Cable's letter. On my copy the sentence is lined out (though it can still be read) and this statement is written in longhand after "Holyoke": "This erasure was a pencilled note copied by mistake. A.M."

[31] Italics mine.—P.B.

matter to your judgment and pleasure. Should there appear no better course than to discontinue the work, there is nothing in its financial condition that need in consequence be a source of embarrassment. Its floating liabilities are confined to two or three accounts (for coal, gas, insurance and periodicals) aggregating about two hundred and fifty dollars. The clubhouse and janitor's residence are of a commercial value more than ample to extinguish the mortgages on them and these small liabilities.

To this statement, however, I must add the following:

Miss Moffat has been ten years in this work performing her offices always in a spirit the farthest removed from a mercenary attitude. Her salary has never been as large as it should have been; but from time to time I have not been able entirely to cover it. The amounts thus left owing her have in the ten years of the work reached an aggregate of something more than a year and a half's pay, or about fifteen hundred dollars. While this was agreed to between Miss Moffat and myself at the various times of its occurrence, and she preferred, for the good work's sake, to continue it, this was in the hope that, when we should have finished the hard labor of getting the clubhouse and its extensive repairs and alterations paid for, all arrears might eventually be covered, and that meanwhile the establishment itself might stand as, in a sense, a security. I believe that the value of the assets beyond all their liabilities, including the mortgages of $4000 on the clubhouse and $2000 on the janitor's house, is sufficient to do this. But this also is submitted to your judgment.

I have communicated these things by letter instead of through a called meeting because of my unavoidable and almost constant absence, at this time, from Northampton. At any time, however, that it may seem to any member of the board essential to call a meeting I will endeavor as promptly as possible to respond to an expression of that belief.

Very respectfully,

Geo. W. Cable

On an attached sheet Cable tabulated the company's assets and liabilities, including the following arrears in salary to the general secretary:

1892	$486.40
1893	505.47
1894	233.83
1895	327.95
Total	$1,553.65[32]

Cable's figures were based on the statement he had asked Adelene Moffat to prepare for him. Her document, "Account between G. W. Cable and Adelene Moffat,"[33] includes details which he discretely refrained from mentioning to his board and which are not stated in any other records. His letter to the board remarked that he had not always been able to pay her the $840.00 she was due annually; he did not reveal that in 1891 her first salary payment ($10.00) had been made on January 3 and the second not until May 18. More important, he said nothing about the fact that the net income from Adelene Moffat's studio in Holyoke was credited as payment on her salary as general secretary of the Home Culture Clubs! Her statement of the account may be summarized briefly:

	1891	
Paid by Cable	$305.00	
Balance due Cable from A.M.	48.60	
Total credited to salary	$353.60	Arrears—$486.40
	1892	
Paid by Cable	$240.00	
Income from the Holyoke studio	94.53	
Total credited to salary	$334.53	Arrears—$505.47
	1893	
Paid by Cable	$251.00	
Income from the Holyoke studio	355.17	
Total credited to salary	$606.17	Arrears—$233.83

[32] It appears that the figure for 1895 should be $317.95 and the total, therefore, $1,543.65.

[33] Typed manuscript in the Cable Collection at Columbia University.

1894			
Paid by Cable	$325.00		
Income from the Holyoke studio	197.05		
Total credited to salary	$522.05	Arrears—	$317.95
		Total	$1,543.65

While Adelene Moffat's resignation was still pending, Cable wrote for her the letter of reference she had requested.

Mrs. Young Fulton,—
Dear Madam:

Miss Adelene Moffat has been intimately associated with me for ten years, in the work of the Home Culture Clubs, acting as General Secretary of the movement. The office has required, and to it she has brought, untiring diligence, initiative energy and inventiveness, rare tact, broad, sympathetic, tolerant and unselfish kindness, skill in correspondence, social attractiveness, great courage, buoyant spirits and a rare quick demonstrative knowledge of men, women and children in both unrefined and refined society, the qualities, in short, of one fitted to lead and govern without the support of arbitrary authority. I consider that no occupation whatever its honors can do her justice which does not give scope to these combined administrative and executive powers.

I have the honor to remain, dear madam,

Yours truly,

G. W. Cable [34]

Any employer would wish to retain the services of so exceptional an employee. Cable needed Adelene Moffat for the "dear good work" and he managed to persuade her to remain, even at a reduced salary. He was able to provide a guarantee that at least half of her salary would be paid promptly in the future and to give her less work and more

[34] This letter, undated, is in the Cable Collection at Columbia University.

time for her art by reducing the scope of the Home Culture Clubs. He sent the following letter to the board on May 4, 1897.

Gentlemen:

On reading the General Secretary's letter of resignation and my letter to the Board presenting it Mr. E. H. R. Lyman authorized me to make for him, the following proposition:

That if the General Secretary will withdraw her resignation; and if the work of the clubs can be so planned as not to curtail its operations in Northampton Clubhouse; and if the Board can and will find sources of revenue sufficient to cover all other running expenses of the work for one year from the first of May 1897 in addition to the two hundred dollars which he annually contributes by waiver of interest on mortgages, he will guarantee the payment of one half (say three hundred and sixty dollars) of the General Secretary's salary for that period.

I find no way in which the Home-Culture club work can be continued another season except by dropping the work wherever it lies beyond Northampton and its immediate vicinity. This part comprises about one-fourth the whole number of clubs. For although this branch of the work is the least expensive and is besides more distinctly the Home-Culture Club work as originally conceived and as I would therefore still prefer to carry it on, the large and almost spontaneous growth of the opposite branch of the work in the club-house has given it rightly a superior claim upon the interest and financial support of the town. The work beyond our own borders does not need to be continued in order to preserve the value of what has been done. Its results are secured and the outlay made for it has had its full return.[35]

Cable remarked that this change in the work would reduce printing and other costs and lighten the burdens of the general secretary. He gave a detailed report of anticipated income and present liabilities—this time excluding

[35] This letter is in the Cable Collection at Columbia University.

all reference to Adelene Moffat's back salary—and expressed confidence that the work at the clubhouse could be continued to the great advantage of the public.[36]

At the meeting of May 10, 1897, the Board of Managers considered Adelene Moffat's resignation and Cable's proposals to change the program of the Home Culture Clubs in order to retain her. The minutes of the meeting, at which she served as secretary, make no reference to arrears of salary. The board agreed to discontinue the activities outside Northampton and accepted Edward Lyman's offer to guarantee half the amount of the general secretary's reduced salary. Evidently she worried about the other half. Cable wrote her on June 26: "You ask if money collected now can be applied on your salary. It can be applied on one-half of it. The other half, you know, is Mr. Lyman's obligation. You have got ahead of me; I wanted to tell you this little pleasant word before you should ask." This arrangement antedated her letter of resignation. One of her functions as general manager was soliciting contributions, and Cable had written her on March 13: "If you will try to get a check from Dimcock and one from the Beldings you shall have whatever you get on a/c your salary. Yet I don't mean by that that you may not expect anything else from me; I shall do my utmost & earliest for you besides." The problem of Cable's indebtedness to her for her work of previous years was partly resolved by his letter offering as security for the arrears a corner lot he owned on Dryads' Green, adjacent to one belonging to Mary Louise Cable. Board members must have convinced her that the debt

[36] Under "Annual Subscriptions," Cable's report lists $50 pledged by himself. It also lists $50 paid by Mr. Hammond as "Advanced to Mr. Cable and pledged to be raised by him."

would be discharged; on the eighteenth of the following April they voted unanimously that it should be accepted as an obligation of the company, though perhaps not a legal one, and should be paid as soon as practicable.

Adelene Moffat could not know that it would not seem practicable to the management of the corporation to make any payments to her for five years.[37] In 1903 and 1904 she received a total of $675.00, reducing the indebtedness to $868.65. On the strength of this evidence that the account would be paid, Adelene Moffat was prevailed on to give President Cable a written release on the Dryads' Green property he had assigned to her as security for the arrears; no payments were made after that.[38] But now, in 1897, the

[37] The minutes of the meetings of the board are not in agreement with Adelene Moffat's record of payments. The minutes for the meeting of May 30, 1902, report that, on Hammond's motion, it was voted to turn over to Adelene Moffat the piano which had been bought for $240 in the previous year. Adelene Moffat had paid $180 of this amount. The $60.00 paid by the Home Culture Clubs was to be credited against arrears of salary, and, on Frank Lyman's motion, it was voted to pay her $200 in cash. A pencil note in the margin of the minutes for the meeting of September 12, 1903, suggests that she might have been paid an additional $200, reducing the arrears to "$1,082.62." But Adelene Moffat's statement, "The Home Culture Clubs, In account with Adelene Moffat" (in the Cable Collection at Columbia University) lists no payments until August 28, 1903, when she received $100. Another payment of the same amount was made on September 21. Evidently Adelene Moffat's record is correct, for it was prepared as the basis for legal action and there is no evidence that her figures were disputed.

The minutes of the meetings are not full accounts of the transactions. Evidently some of them were added to the official record book later, since they are not always in proper chronological order. They are laconic after May 8, 1905, when Calvin Coolidge was elected secretary.

[38] A copy of the release, dated September 26, 1905, is in the Cable Collection at Columbia University. See also the Hammond & Ham-

reduction in the program of the Home Culture Clubs and, hence, in the burdens of the general secretary, and the improved salary arrangements were sufficient inducements to persuade her to withdraw her resignation. She and Cable continued, on as amicable terms as before, their labors for the welfare of the community. The danger to Cable's benefaction, his bid to be remembered when he died, was past.

---

mond papers in the Cable Collection at Tulane University. Adelene Moffat may at first have supposed that the lot was given to her in payment of the arrears. She wrote a letter, undated, to ask Cable's advice about selling "the corner lot of mine." No doubt this precipitated the payments on the arrears by the Home Culture Clubs which ultimately resulted in Cable's recovery of the property.

IX: The Fruitful Life

Cable's connection with *Current Literature* came to an end with the publication of the September issue, and that winter he went to the Midwest on a reading tour. From Bloomington, Illinois, he wrote to Adelene Moffat on February 2, 1898, "You must not mind my being a little jealous of you, that you should be in the very forefront of the work where (very justly) you visibly stand for it in the eyes of all who come in touch with it." In the same letter he said: "But let me also say how I thank you for taking off my hands the collection of our subscribers' checks. Yet this is only one item in the work which I love to feel is my work, and am proud to have credited (in whatever degree) to me, but which you are the real performer in, and, in which you rightly earn the gratitude of the hundreds who are being made better & happier by it."

Near the end of that month he went to New Orleans in search of literary material. He once told Anna Gertrude Brewster that the Crescent City was "a dreadful place to live if it ever turns against you," but he wrote Adelene Moffat, on February 28, that his visit was "successful, delightful and profitable beyond all expectation." It was, however, only a minor pleasure compared to his triumphant trip to England in the spring of 1898.

On his visit to America in the fall of 1896, James M. Barrie had spent three days with Cable in Northampton, and the admiration of the two men for each other's writing developed into personal affection. Cable's local prestige was much enhanced by his role as host and by the praise the celebrated visitor gave his work. At Smith College, where Barrie spoke on condition that he might keep his hands in his pockets, the author of *The Little Minister* said that "no American novelist merits a higher rank than Mr. George W. Cable." [1] Cable's reception for Barrie, his wife, and Dr. W. Robertson Nicoll was an event neither the Cables nor their many guests from the town and college ever forgot. The visitors were also entertained at an informal affair at Adelene Moffat's studio, where the two small authors—Barrie was heavier than Cable but about equally short—sat with their arms about each other while Nicoll, editor of the London *British Weekly*, led the conversation. Before Barrie left America he urged Cable to come to England and promised to arrange for a series of drawing-room readings from the Creole stories which would defray his expenses. The proposal was an attractive one but could not be acted upon because Cable was in the midst of his magazine venture. His brief stay in New York as editor of *Current Literature* gave him a taste of a different life from that he had been following in Northampton and made him long to extend his acquaintance with the wide world of literature and affairs. He came to think of residence in Northampton as a kind of retirement which had led him, by way of rebound, "to bible-class teaching, Home-Culture Clubs and all that. With these I am done," he told his wife in August of 1897, when he knew his work

[1] Turner, *George W. Cable,* p. 305.

in New York was ending, "and I am going to use my wisest judgment to allot my hours and activities henceforth so as to make my life—our life—still as fruitful as it possibly may be."[2] Barrie's suggestion accorded perfectly with Cable's present idea of the fruitful life. He sailed for England, alone, on April 20, 1898.

The trip was a great success. English audiences were charmed by Cable's dramatic recitations from *Dr. Sevier*, "Grande Pointe," and "Posson Jone'"—written over twenty years earlier—and the sales of English editions of his work mounted. He reveled in the company of the literati and other notables and took deep satisfaction in their acceptance of him as one of themselves. The detailed diary he kept—and revised before sending it home to his family—shows his delight in dressing for dinner with the lords and ladies, in visiting the tourist spots hallowed by memories of Shakespeare and Chaucer and Burns, in sipping Burgundy in Scott's valley of the Tweed.

One of the men whom Cable met and who is mentioned frequently in his account of the trip was Henry James, a "clean, true man" whose stammer and foibles Cable described in the reports he mailed to Northampton.[3] But the most impressive experience of his holiday abroad, and ultimately the most fruitful, was his stay with Andrew Carnegie, whom he had met in 1883 through Richard Watson Gilder and with whom he dined in London. He wrote Carnegie from Liverpool, June 7, 1898, and asked if he might visit him at Skibo Castle; he added that if he came he must stay three or four days and said he had already

[2] *Ibid.*, p. 300.

[3] *Ibid.*, p. 309, and Biklé, *George W. Cable: His Life and Letters*, p. 231.

taken the liberty of having his mail sent there.[4] Three days later he wrote from Edinburgh to tell the Carnegies exactly when to expect him.[5] At Carnegie's twenty-thousand-acre estate six hundred miles from London, Cable's appetite for romance was fed by the Scottish pageantry and his materialism by the display of wealth. Cable's songs and readings, his clever occasional verse, his enthusiastic approval of the things in which his hosts took pleasure, and his effusive expressions of appreciation for their hospitality won their friendship and support. On their way to the loch to fish one day, Cable and Carnegie discussed plans for a garden competition, modeled on one Carnegie sponsored in Dunfermline, to be held under the auspices of the Home Culture Clubs.[6] When he left Skibo, Cable had Carnegie's promise to provide money for the prizes.

Adelene Moffat was happy to learn from Cable's letters the details of his triumphs abroad. On April 16, 1898, she wrote: "So many years have I coveted this experience for you,—my oldest and best friend, I think there is no sacrifice I would not have made to buy it for you. I knew what it would mean to you—you who keep for yourself so little of what you earn." She was despondent because her work seemed weary and monotonous, and she asked what had become of the old Adelene Moffat, the creature of passionate protest who burned to reform the world. From her letter of April 24 it may be inferred that financial problems were one cause of her feeling of depression; she had evidently had to borrow money from the Lymans. On the last

[4] The letter is in the New York Public Library.

[5] The letter is in the Library of Congress.

[6] See Cable's letter to Mrs. Carnegie, November 9, 1898, in the New York Public Library.

day of the previous January she had written Cable that the income from her house had paid the month's expenses, enabling her to apply her salary on back debts. But her pleasure over her momentary prosperity that month was tempered by the illness of her mother and of Edward Lyman. She was surprised to find, she wrote Cable on January 28, that her affection for them was very similar and differed only in degree. Her regard for the old man was based on his disinterested kindness, which had given her an insight into the problems of philanthropy from the viewpoint of the philanthropist. The problems of the social worker she knew from her own experience and study. She spoke to the Smith College Current Events Club on "Special Mental Attitudes in Philanthropic Work" in February, 1896. On June 22, 1898, there was enough of the "old Adelene Moffat" left for her to write Cable of her disappointment when a fall from her wheel put her knee in a plaster cast and prevented her from going to New York "to join a class of philanthropic workers and to live in a college settlement." She had hoped to see "the most approved methods of applied philanthropy" and to benefit from the "contact with trained workers devoted to their profession." Instead she spent her enforced idleness with a stack of books on sociology.

Cable's letters to Adelene Moffat from abroad praised her management of their social service project but repeatedly reminded them both of his own part in it. From London, enclosing sheets of the pencil draft of his diary, he wrote on May 6, 1898, "It is that ability to pick the kernel of worth out of the burr and shell of toughness & hardness that makes you so valuable for the work you do so well." On July 8, when his visit to England was nearing its close, he remarked, "When I look at the year's work [of the Home Culture Clubs] and think that in a certain sense I can claim it as my own I am very grateful to you."

Cable returned to Northampton in July and remained there, busy with his writing, through the summer and fall. Refreshed by the holiday abroad, he also resumed his functions as president of the Home Culture Clubs. On January 10, 1899, he presided at a program at which veterans of the war with Spain gave accounts of their experiences, and he addressed an assembly on January 14. Adelene Moffat noted in her diary that half the net profit of the war program was paid to the speakers, leaving the sponsors with a gain of only $18.50. "The entertainments that bring in the most money are such things as the Italian fiesta in which many of the townspeople take part. They come then for the social interest." She might have added that "the social interest" sometimes kept patrons and members away from the clubhouse. The Northampton *Gazette* of June 2, 1899, remarked that, because of the excellent reputation the clubhouse enjoyed, evening meetings there made "an excellent excuse for the young misses to be away from home in company with boy friends until a late hour." And when the girls did attend the affairs to which they told their parents they were going, sometimes they went, said the *Gazette*, because "the entertainments, dances and the meetings make a harboring place for meeting associates that they would not dare invite to their homes." The paper acknowledged that only a few youngsters took advantage of the "grand work" done at the clubhouse.

Edward H. R. Lyman, who had long been the Home Culture Clubs' chief financial support, died in January, 1899, while Cable was away on a reading tour. Cable wrote

Adelene Moffat from Des Moines on January 20 that he was determined to continue the work somehow. She replied on the twenty-sixth that she had draped the portrait of Mr. Lyman that hung in the clubhouse and said, "Yes the work must go on—as long as we can carry it." She admonished: "Keep well and strong and help me to be of more help to you." On February 13 she was able to write Cable that Frank Lyman had indicated his intent to continue his father's gifts to the agency. This was a relief to Cable in Chicago and contributed to his elation in telling her, on the nineteenth, that he had been "the only literary notable" at a banquet where he learned of a man "who leaves two millions to education in the South moved to do so by my essays on Southern conditions."

The Home Culture Clubs deserved the aid of Frank Lyman, who was elected to the board in May to replace his father, and largely because of it the program went on without interruption. On March 7 Cable presided at a meeting at Adelene Moffat's house which led to the organization of a Women's Council.[7] This became a useful device for enlisting the services of local clubwomen in support of the enterprise. Adelene Moffat and other women members of the Home Culture Clubs staff were active in the work of this unofficial auxiliary group, which in later years gave particular attention to the program in the household arts.

When the new term began the next fall, classes were offered in reading, writing, arithmetic, French, German, Latin, elocution, algebra, geometry, nature study, piano, dressmaking, sewing, embroidery, and plain cooking. Except for some of the courses in household arts, which re-

[7] The minutes of the meetings of the Women's Council are in the archives of The People's Institute.

quired payment of a special fee, classes were open to all on payment of a dollar initiation fee and another dollar for annual membership. The emphasis, said the *Daily Herald* of September 29, 1899, would be on practical rather than academic training.

> The dressmaking and cooking will be under the direction of a thoroughly trained professional teacher, who has had practical experience. A feature of the latter class will be bills of fare made out with a view to economical living. There will be, for instance, bills of fare arranged for families of four able to spend but $6. a week or even less, for food; also bills of fare for families spending $12 a week, with the receipts for each. The dressmaking classes will be taught the use of patterns, as this seems more practical than chart systems. These classes are practical. They are designed to help people live within their income comfortably and daintily.

Instruction on how to live "comfortably and daintily" on a small income was of great value for club members. In her diary, on December 21, 1899, Adelene Moffat listed the income of a sample family, four members of which were working, as $28.50 per week. Most of the students who enrolled for this adult education, a program far removed from the founder's original idea, came from the laboring classes. The *Daily Herald* reported in its issue of November 27: "There are teachers and business men, women in domestic service and day laborers, trainmen, printers, dress makers, tailors and clerks, bookkeepers and cigar-makers, but a large majority are employed in the silk mills, cutleries and other shops in Northampton, Florence, Heydenville, Leeds and Easthampton." The students were as varied in race and nationality as in occupation. There were whites and Negroes, Americans, Canadians, English, French, Germans, Italians, Irish, Jews, Poles, Portuguese, Russians, and

Swiss. All the Poles came through the efforts of one man, who had been advised by a French-Canadian neighbor to learn English at the clubhouse. Many of the immigrants knew no English at all when they began their study in the evening classes.

The various racial and national groups established and maintained amicable relations with one another because of the firm guidance of the management. Each new set of arrivals met with what Adelene Moffat called the "unintelligent tendency to race prejudice" and a wish to deny to them the benefits of membership.

> The first to appear on the scene were the Irish, the next were the French-Canadians; upon the approach of the latter the Irish rose in a body and demanded that the French-Canadians be excluded, saying that they did not want them coming there, that they would break up the club if they came, and that many of the best members would leave. The reply of the authorities was: "This institution is open to all nationalities and all creeds. The only basis of admission is good character and good behavior. The French-Canadian members fulfil those requirements. The house is here for those who come to it; if you do not come, then you have nothing to say about how it shall be run." The Irish and French-Canadians soon found that they liked each other very well indeed. The Jews were the next to approach. Both Irish and French-Canadians united against them. Again the management stood firm and the results were the same.
>
> This experience was repeated with more than fifteen nationalities. Finally all combined against the Negro. The management again withstood the combined pressure, saying cheerfully, "If you all leave, the place can still be run for colored people, and if you remain and make it uncomfortable for them or any other nationality you most certainly will be requested to leave." Again the result was the same as on previous occasions. Almost immediately the whole incident was forgotten.[8]

[8] Moffat, *Views of a Southern Woman,* p. [4].

Thus by precept and example, the Home Culture Clubs gave instruction in democracy, a subject of more critical importance to club members and the community as a whole than any listed among the courses of the agency's expanding curriculum.

The September, 1899, enrollment seemed an auspicious start for the year's work. Even more encouraging to Cable was the response to *Strong Hearts*, his first book of fiction since *John March, Southerner*. He wrote Adelene Moffat on the twentieth that the whole issue of five thousand copies was disposed of and his other books were selling better than they had for years. Like *Bonaventure*, *Strong Hearts* was a collection of two short stories and a novella; they had first appeared in *Scribner's Magazine*. Based upon Cable's memories of events that took place years earlier, the stories use a common scene, New Orleans, and the same narrator, but otherwise are unrelated. Richard Thorndike Smith, the narrator, also appears in *The Cavalier* and in "The Speculations of a Story-Teller," an essay published in the July, 1896, *Atlantic Monthly*. Smith, whose age and condition necessarily vary in his several appearances in Cable's works, is an obvious projection of the history and character of his creator; Smith is Cable's representation of himself as he thought of himself—and wanted other people to think of him—at this time. His choice of a name for his alter ego is revealing. He had written a memorial volume in 1885 for Roswell Smith, the earnest friend and philanthropist who was the mainstay of his early career. Cable's home in Northampton was adjacent to Smith College, with which he had many associations. Northampton was unique among towns of its size for the number and extent of the charitable, educational, and benevolent institutions which were the gifts of philanthropic citizens of the area. The largest—at least the wealthiest—of these were Smith College and the Smith Charities, the gifts of Sophia Smith and Oliver Smith, her uncle, respectively. Cable's choice of a name for his narrator did not stem from the equalitarian doctrines he once espoused. He chose Smith, consciously or otherwise, not because it was a common name but because, especially when joined to Richard Thorndyke, it suggested a reputation and social position (and, perhaps, a national origin) which he liked to apply to himself. Even more obvious in its connotations is Philip Castleton, the name Cable chose for his alter ego in his final novel, *Lovers of Louisiana* (1918).

Several magazine editors rejected *The Cavalier*, but when the book appeared in 1901 its initial sale was greater than that of any of Cable's previous works. A hundred thousand copies were sold before the year was out. *The Cavalier* is a conventional sentimental Civil War romance which ignores the conflicting ideologies and the brutal reality of that struggle: it adheres perfectly to the belief Cable had adopted that the purpose of a novel should be to amuse.[9] The major characters are Confederates, but the author is not partisan; he glorifies the heroism and nobility of both the contending forces. The book is remarkably free of any social criticism and, whatever its virtues, seems hardly the product of the same imagination and energy that created *The Grandissimes*. "The Clock in the Sky," which came out in *Scribner's Magazine* in September, 1901, has more than a touch of Cable's earlier manner and message; it is an effective attack on slavery, and its characters are blacks, not quadroons. The plot is contrived, but the characterization is realistic and the story is generally convincing. Not

[9] See his letter to Whitman Barbe, April 7, 1900, in Biklé, *George W. Cable: His Life and Letters,* pp. 247–49.

so its sequel, "The Angel of the Lord," which was published in 1901 in *A House Party*, a collection of a dozen unsigned stories by famous American authors. For a thousand-dollar prize, readers tried to identify the writers. Naturally Cable went to some trouble to obscure his views on slavery and the Negro in order to avoid revealing his authorship. The resulting story was an appropriate item for the contest, and Cable made later use of it and "The Clock in the Sky" in *The Flower of the Chapdelaines* (1918), but it adds nothing to his literary reputation. The same might be said for "Père Raphaël," a sequel to "Posson Jone'," which *Century* printed in August, 1901, and for *Bylow Hill*, the novel Cable developed from a plot given to him by S. Weir Mitchell.[10]

Bylow Hill, Cable's only novel with a Northern setting, completed its serial run in the *Atlantic Monthly* for May, 1902. On the thirtieth of the month the board of the Home Culture Clubs, acting with Cable's approval, granted Adelene Moffat a year's leave of absence. She had worked faithfully—Cable wrote her on November 14, 1901, of "your noble work—yours and mine, but in performance so nearly wholly yours"—and deserved this chance to take advantage of a promising opportunity, one which would let her devote herself completely to art. The plan was that she was to draw her full year's pay, $1,000, and out of that was to arrange for a substitute who would be acceptable to President Cable. Frank Lyman and his sister, Mrs. Alfred T. White, advanced the $1,000, and Adelene Moffat left enough of this amount in Northampton to cover the salary of the substitute, $50.00 per month. The substitute did not serve out the year, and other complications developed. The

[10] *Ibid.*, pp. 249–51.

final result, according to Adelene Moffat, was some loss to herself and a saving of $146.81 for the Home Culture Clubs.[11]

She left Northampton on June 25 to accompany an American Exploration Society expedition to Crete, where she was to paint whatever artifacts were discovered. Soon after she arrived in Paris in July, a telegram announced that the expedition was postponed until the following spring. Cable and his wife, to whom Adelene Moffat asked that her revised plans be submitted, approved her decision to remain in Paris and fulfill one of the dreams of her life by studying at the Beaux Arts and in noted ateliers. Cable held her power of attorney, conducted her personal business in Northampton, and kept her posted on the affairs of the Home Culture Clubs. She offered several times to return home if her absence placed too many burdens on him. She was grateful for his interest in her art and for the sundry loans from Frank Lyman which made her stay abroad possible. On October 2, 1903, she wrote that she was as happy as she could expect to be "in a world where my mother is not." She sent "love to Mrs. Cable and the family" and affectionate gratitude to the author himself, "my truest and best friend always."

In the spring of 1903 she went to Athens and then to Crete, where she wrote, while doing a set of drawings in color for the Museum of Philadelphia, "I do not find my work for the expedition either arduous or interesting so the Home-Culture Clubs need fear no rival—my own dear blessed old Home-Culture clubs." [12] She said her head was

[11] Undated note, probably written in 1907, in the Cable Collection at Columbia University.

[12] Letter to Cable, dated merely "Easter Sunday."

full of hopes and dreams for their social work. Naturally she was elated by the news Cable sent in his letter of April 3, 1903. "Two years ago," he said, "I asked Mr. Carnegie for money for the Home-Culture Clubs, and at last I have got it. I can see you shrink with pain as I tell you that I let myself take the attitude of a solicitor for a bequest from our dear Skibo friends; but you will never shrink with as much pain as I did when I did so, nor one tenth as many times as I have since." Aided by a loan from Cable, Adelene Moffat hurried home as soon as her work with the expedition—and an attack of the flu and oleander poisoning—would permit. "How glad I shall be to see you all again," she wrote on June 3, "how glad, how glad!"

Cable's formal request for the Carnegie grant should have come as no surprise to the philanthropist. Cable had written Mrs. Carnegie, whom he evidently found more approachable than her husband, to report, on November 9, 1898, that he had presented the idea for a Carnegie Garden Competition in Northampton and had received an enthusiastic response. He asked her to arrange for him to meet Mr. Carnegie, then in New York, to discuss details. The long letter, which included many ingratiating reminders of his visit to Skibo Castle, mentioned that Mrs. Cable was in a New York hospital awaiting a minor operation. On December 20, Cable wrote the Carnegies that the proposed rules for the garden contest had been adopted by a Northampton committee, and hence he forwarded them for approval. He sent Carnegie a brief letter of thanks on January 13, 1899. The Cables were luncheon guests of the Carnegies in April. On June 16, when the Carnegies were back in Scotland, Cable sent them the following remarkable letter.

Dear Mr. & Mrs. Carnegie:

A number of impulses move me today to bring myself to your minds in dearly-remembered Skibo.

A year ago today I first saw the lovely domain. I wish with all my heart I were with you this very hour; but my mistress is Duty—a dear old girl more just than merciful—and she stands over my desk like a schoolmarm and every now and then drops innuendoes concerning the slowness of my literary pen and the fixity of my obligations.

But I write also to say that

> Our Northampton Amateur Prize Flower G———
> Flower Garden, that is,—Competition
> Still promises all that in reason could be
> The hope of my fullest ambition.

Now I propose to draw upon Mr. R. A. Franks, Carnegie Building, Pittsburgh, for the $66 prize fund, as kindly directed by Mr. Carnegie in his letter of the last day of last year. I do this for the purpose of turning the fund into gold-pieces and putting them into a bank window on exhibition to salivate the public, as it were.

Last Monday evening we held in our city hall the twelvth [sic] anniversary of our Home-Culture Clubs—only thing in this big world that I am, or ever was, president of—and heard a notable address on the Public Duty of the Private Citizen. The title was suggested to the speaker's mind by our own motto, "The Private Home is the Public Hope."

Well, me! I was so stirred, so stimulated in my sense of public duty that I went off Tuesday to a Commencement in Springfield and preached, myself, a lay-sermon on the text (or somewheres round about the text) "A man's life consisteth not in the abundance of the *things* which he possesseth." Think of me enlarging upon that to a lot of rich-girl graduates a majority, probably, of whose fathers' lives consist of almost nothing else! But I did it in hope; and hope never shone brighter on the earth than it shines today.

Yes, we had our anniversary, and I rejoiced to be able to tell our town that we had raised more money, spent more, and have more left over in the treasury than ever before; [13] that we have done more work and done it better, and have more in sight that we can do and that we could do if we weren't so slim-pursed, than ever before. I shouldn't venture to tell you even thus much about this pet work of mine had I not been lately to see your workingmen's clubs in Braddock & Homestead [near Pittsburgh, Pennsylvania]. My Home-Culture Clubs seem related to that sort of work very much as a wife is to a husband. I wish you might have heard me say "Over fifteen thousand visits to our clubhouse this year which in every probability were more profitable to those who made them [than] would have [been] the same time if spent anywhere else where they would have gone; over twenty-eight hundred meetings of small classes or clubs under the evening lamp in pursuit of every simple matter that can be taught unlaboriously to those whose bodies are weary with daily manual labor, or whose aspirations have yet to be lifted up to good stature." I wasn't eloquent, but to me the facts were eloquent. The work is carried on by young men and young women of high social life and education, the young women being largely students of Smith College, and the ultimate aim of it is not so much to educate from books as to communicate the tastes, refinement, and spiritual ambitions of the cultivated to the uncultivated, and to establish the sentiments and practical offices of friendship between houses which fortune and social tendencies naturally separate and estrange.

Now the benefits of this work—within these limitations—naturally fall almost wholly to young people, and as they pass on into married [This incomplete sentence lightly crossed out.]

You observe I score out two lines. That means that my paternal solicitude for the work I am only less in love with than with my literary calling, was leading me to mix up things in this letter that will not really and gracefully mix. So let me back off those sands and begin again.

As I was saying, I want lately to see your workingmen's clubs at Braddock and Homestead. I was on my way south to view

[13] If this is true, it is interesting that none of the surplus was used to begin payment on the debt to Adelene Moffat.

the field of the story I am still writing, as I was last summer at Skibo, (The Cavalier), and at Pittsburgh I dropped in at the Carnegie Building. Thence they ever so kindly sent me, under escort, to see the clubhouse. I was greatly pleased with all I saw. I have some features in my Home-Culture Clubs that I wish you had, but you have a larger number that I wish I could have. Some are too costly for me to attempt to mimic on any scale, but some I must copy, in miniature, somehow. Nay, I have already begun. Haven't we just got one pool-table and one (not too new) billiard-table, in our clubhouse basement, and the men just waiting for us to paint up the room and open the door? Well, then! True, our opportunity is fifty times our ability, and if Margaret Carnegie—who I hear, has birthdays—were old enough to go into the saloon-business with me in a way to furnish everything but liquor (say newspapers, light, warmth, cheer, games, coffee and the right to smoke & talk)—

No, but, really, I am determined to make the experiment this coming season anyhow, just as a small initial item in the cautious evolution of a Workingmen's Club. You will not mind my appropriating your idea, will you? "It's no lost what a freen gets," and I'm so sure you're my friends that I'm sure you'll let me call myself yours.

This is not the kind of writing I did at Skibo last year. Do you remember my scribbling jingles? I have scarcely done one since last summer until yesterday. The head gardener of Smith College, a man highly accomplished in his craft did me lately some delightful services, and asked me for a copy of "Strong Hearts." This is how I inscribed it:

"To one whose calling none fairer
Has been since fair living began;
A reader, a writer, a bearer,
Of nature's love letters to man."

Do you like the tinkle? I wish I could hear you say so.

Daughter Mary's wedding is over and she is in Nova Scotia, Mrs. Alfred Dennis now, and we rejoice in a second most lovable son-in-law. I believe Mrs. Carnegie knows Alfred's aunt Mrs. Sam Dennis. She and I have been having a pleasant talk about you that makes us better acquainted with each other. I like her for liking you so well.

Mrs. Cable bears you ever most gratefully in remembrance and sends her warmest regards. I have not written so long a letter as this since last summer, when I was writing to her across the same Atlantic, but hitherward, from your side.

Please give my most cordial wishes to Miss Whitfield and to Mr. Lauder [a cousin of Carnegie] and his daughters.

Ever Yours truly

G. W. Cable [14]

Five months later the Carnegies were again in America. Cable wrote a long letter of welcome on November 15, announcing the success of the garden competition of the previous summer and inviting assurances that Carnegie would underwrite the activity the next season. In December he lunched with the Carnegies in New York, and he wrote Mrs. Carnegie a short letter in January about a triumphant reading in Philadelphia before what he described proudly as a huge and appreciative audience. Other letters to Mrs. Carnegie indicate that Cable was anxious to have a talk with her husband. He had not achieved this when he wrote her on November 27, 1900, to introduce Adelene Moffat, who had just gone down to New York. "I want you to know her because in Northampton, where her charm and worth are universally known and valued, she is an especially attractive sign of your own and Mr. Carnegie's generous hand in our Flower Garden Competition." He asked, however, that she not be told about the project he had mentioned to Mrs. Carnegie but had not yet been able to broach to her husband. Cable sent Carnegie a

[14] This letter and the other letters from Cable to the Carnegies which are mentioned are in the New York Public Library, unless some other location is stated in footnotes.

formal resolution of thanks for the garden prizes, accompanied by his personal statement of appreciation, on November 7, 1901. He reached the philanthropist at some later time with a direct appeal for money for the Home Culture Clubs. There was no immediate response, and when Adelene Moffat visited Skibo Castle in the summer of 1902 she learned nothing of Cable's solicitations.

In January, 1903, the Home Culture Clubs owned the clubhouse, a housekeeper's cottage, and the quarter acre of ground on which these buildings stood, a plant worth altogether about ten thousand dollars. The principal benefactors were the Lymans. Mrs. Lyman donated a thousand dollars in her will in 1898; Edward H. R. Lyman's gifts had allowed the agency to acquire the clubhouse and repair it; Frank Lyman and his sister gave the building outright in 1899. February, 1903, began auspiciously when Arthur Curtis James of New York and his wife, formerly Harriet Parsons of Northampton, gave five hundred dollars to be used to establish a school of household arts for extending the program, begun two or three years earlier, designed to raise the standard of domestic service by offering instruction to cooks, waitresses, maids, and laundresses. A few days later, Andrew Carnegie sent an unexpected and favorable response to Cable's appeal. He offered to give fifty thousand dollars to be invested in buildings and grounds, provided only that for five years the annual income be raised to five thousand dollars, double the usual amount. Cable wrote on February 7 asking to meet with him for discussion of this proviso and requesting permission to bring Frank Lyman along. On the eleventh the Home Culture Clubs board met and formally accepted Carnegie's proposal. Two day later Cable wrote to report this vote and the board's gratitude for Carnegie's generosity and to ask that the news be withheld from the public for a while so that real estate values in Northampton would not be affected. It was probably this practical consideration that led Cable to refrain from telling Adelene Moffat about the gift until his letter of April 3.

Frank Lyman, Mrs. White, Mr. and Mrs. James, and other faithful supporters of the agency pledged about one fourth of the guarantee required to secure Carnegie's gift, and other subscriptions were obtained to meet the balance. The Whitcomb property, a tract of land on Gothic Street adjoining the rear of the original property of the Home Culture Clubs, was purchased. This included the Boise home, an attractive frame mansion, built around 1850, the front of which featured the white columns and pediment of a Greek temple. Remodeled and refitted, this became James House, the household arts building. The clubhouse was refurbished and christened Lyman House, and the housekeeper's cottage, moved to a new location on the three-acre site, was converted into a model Northampton workingman's home. A New York architect, Edward L. Tilton, was commissioned to draw plans for a new main building to be called Carnegie House. When Adelene Moffat returned to Northampton on August 17, 1903, she and Cable busied themselves, not always in agreement, in planning the expanded activities the new facilities would make possible. The expenditures for land, remodeling the two old buildings, and additions to the paid staff cost about sixteen thousand dollars and would have been an embarrassment to the management had not Carnegie made a second gift to cover this expense. Cable sent to Carnegie on December 23 his Christmas wishes and effusive praise for his benevolence: "Oh, my friend, what happiness and what a crown you have given yourself—to have beautified the history of the world." [15] In a sentimental postscript he described his announcement of Carnegie's second gift at the Christmas party at the clubhouse, as the members gathered around a tree decorated with the humble presents they exchanged with one another.

Cable's labors for the agency, his platform readings, and his work on a second Civil War romance, *Kincaid's Battery* (1908), were interrupted that winter by the severe illness of his wife. Mrs. Cable, too, had enjoyed a taste of the fruitful life Cable had resolved upon for them both after the failure of his venture with *Current Literature*. In 1901 she and Mary E. Burt went to England, and in March, 1903, she visited New Orleans. Early in January, 1904, she went to New York for an operation and Cable accompanied her. The Carnegies, with whom Cable dined on February 11, were there, too. Mrs. Cable died in the hospital on the twenty-seventh.

Mrs. Cable had been in poor health during much of her married life. It is difficult now to know this frail woman,[16] apparently held in affection by everyone who knew her, who bore Cable's children and shared with him the finest years of his life, for it was her husband who pulled himself —and the family—up by his boot-straps, and it is he, the great man, about whom available public records center. She was often ill or indisposed or exhausted, and this may help to explain some of her husband's less attractive per-

[15] This letter is in the Library of Congress.

[16] On November 1, 1873, Cable wrote to his mother: "My poor wife's feeble frame stands like a sunken wreck right in the channel of all my plans for our mutual comfort and happiness." Turner, *George W. Cable*, p. 71.

sonal characteristics, but her beneficial influence on him, especially in his public relations, must have been important to his reputation. Very few people, if any, knew George W. Cable during his lifetime. If more were known about Louise Bartlett Cable it might be possible to understand more fully the man—not merely the author and public figure—who was her husband.

Early in March, Cable wrote a characteristic letter to thank Henry van Dyke for his expressions of sympathy. "My beloved rejoiced for me in your affection for me, and now I bless you for your sweet words of her. I want to speak for a moment of her to you," he said, but he spoke really of himself in explaining why his wife's death "grows on me from hour to hour." One reason, he said, was her beauty and another was "her worship of me. It was glorious to see—it is glorious to remember. . . . And a third of these reasons is her dependence on me. She never breathed of happiness, of any gladness, while believing that I was unhappy."[17] On April 17, Cable sent the Carnegies a Home Culture Clubs report, which he urged them to read, and thanked them for their condolences to him and his "little flock." But the flock was soon scattered. Lucy, the eldest of Cable's single daughters, became a reader for *Collier's* in New York; Margaret, Isabel, William, and Dorothea were often away from Northampton after their mother's death. The children who had sat upon Cable's lap as he wrote his first books were now grown. He was no longer driven by the necessity to provide for their needs, and he could not get from them the help and guidance their mother had supplied in her lifetime of service and devotion.

[17] *Ibid.*, p. 328.

x: "Personal Differences"

The Home Culture Clubs were seldom out of Cable's mind at this time. Even at his wife's bedside in February, 1904, he continued to plan and direct the growth and transition that followed on Andrew Carneigie's gift of money for buildings and grounds. There were frequent meetings of the board, to which Calvin Coolidge, a rising Northampton lawyer was unanimously elected on May 16, 1904. Cable was impressed by the taciturn young man. Anna Gertrude Brewster said that he told Harry B. Taplin, who joined the agency staff at about this time, not to be misled because Coolidge was so quiet. Cable admitted that Coolidge "never says anything," but he remarked that "he thinks a lot. You watch that young man; you will hear of him later." [1] Some months after he joined the board, Coolidge spoke on "The Use of Money in Political Campaigns" at a meeting of the Men's Branch of the Old Members' Association, a group Adelene Moffat had organized in January, 1904.

Cable, too, spoke to a group of club members, competitors in the annual flower garden competition, on "Amateur Flower Gardening." The Carnegie Prize Flower Garden

[1] Anna Gertrude Brewster, "George W. Cable: Our Fellow Citizen," unpublished paper prepared, about 1929, for a meeting of the Northampton Historical Society.

Competition was the feature of the agency's program in which Cable took full delight. For him "the noble work" became "the beautiful work." Much of this was just drudgery to Adelene Moffat, who had to visit hundreds of gardens, encourage and advise the competitors, and eliminate the poorer entries. Cable personally supervised the program when he was in Northampton. He went from garden to garden on his bicycle, the most convenient form of transportation for the purpose; he was a skillful rider and some of the townspeople regarded him as a "scorcher." Reared in the garden district of New Orleans, Cable had loved flowers all his life. He invited the competitors to come to Tarryawhile, where he had made his "Joyous Gard" [2] a beautiful blending of lawns, walks, flowers, woods, and ponds. The garden competition became an elaborate affair and a spectacular success which was imitated in other communities. It transformed Northampton during the summer months, when Cable could speak of having a whole town for his garden.

The names of both Cable and Coolidge were among the hundreds attached to a petition presented to the mayor on April 30, 1903, requesting that a fitting program be held the next year to celebrate the 250th anniversary of the settlement of Northampton. The celebration took place on June 5, 6, and 7, 1904. Northampton stores and public buildings were decorated with flags, and streamers spanned Main Street. There were special church services, family and other reunions, concerts, fireworks, and many speeches by dis-

[2] The name is a reminder of Cable's long affection for Malory. Cable called Mark Twain's attention to the *Morte d'Arthur* and he said, after Twain's death, that the author of *A Connecticut Yankee in King Arthur's Court* had once referred to him as the book's godfather. Turner, *George W. Cable,* pp. 43, 173.

tinguished residents and visitors, including Joseph H. Sawyer, principal of Williston Seminary, Mayor Henry C. Hallett, Governor John L. Bates, and Samuel S. Campion, who delivered greetings from Northampton, England. The Betty Allen Chapter of the Daughters of the American Revolution, which Mrs. Cable had founded in 1896 with the assistance of Mabel Loomis Todd, gave a colonial reception at City Hall. Cable and Coolidge were among the dignitaries who sat on the stage at the Academy of Music and heard the address of President Seelye of Smith College and the oration of ex-Governor John D. Long; Cable was a member of the committee which planned the Academy program.

Probably the biggest attraction of the three-day program was the parade on June 7, with its pageantry, marching groups, decorated automobiles, and many floats. The one sponsored by the Home Culture Clubs was a three-tiered platform drawn along by white horses in green and rose trappings. At the topmost level, four men of different nationalities sat around a study table, at work on their books under the guidance of a student in academic costume. Four particularly stalwart men represented the physical culture courses. There were members of the cooking classes making bread, waitresses polishing silver, and dressmaking students draping a figure. On the lowest part of the platform little girls in flower costumes made of crepe paper symbolized the garden competition. The motto—"The Private Home Is the Public Hope"—was prominently displayed.

Evidence justifying the celebration was supplied by a large collection of antiques and historic relics put on display in James House. A number of articles in the collection were loaned by Adelene Moffat: a pewter lamp made to burn whale oil, a pair of buckskin breeches, china, costumes, embroideries, and tapestries. The institutional furniture and equipment of James House were removed, and the borrowed items were arranged in such a way as to create a facsimile of a home of an earlier period. More than 2,500 people from twenty-nine states and several foreign countries visited James House to see the collection, which had been arranged in the buliding by Adelene Moffat and Mrs. William H. Clapp.

Lyman House was put to more prosaic use as a public comfort house and restaurant.

The main reading-room on the ground floor was converted into a general reception room. Easy-chairs, magazines and papers, fans, writing materials, the telephone and many other little conveniences, were at the service of the visitors. Opening out from this room were the quarters used ordinarily for classrooms, which were converted, respectively, into a thoroughly equipped hospital room, with a trained nurse from the Dickinson Hospital in attendance, toilet-room and lavatory for men, a comfort much appreciated by some visitors quite old and infirm, for whom the effort to come had been a trial of strength. A similar room for women, with a darkened room for "sick headaches," or persons requiring absolute quiet, were arranged in the more retired quarters at the rear of the building. These rooms were equipped with cots, an abundance of clean towels and every conceivable necessity, and the committee might well have a justifiable pride in the fact that not a single article asked for by any of the hundreds who patronized the rooms had been forgotten or misplaced. These requests varied, from a needle and thread, a hot fire or a clean handkerchief, to a baby carriage and a temporary foster mother. Over a thousand people used this building on the Tuesday of the Celebration. The large art room became a kindergarten and day nursery, in which very young children might be left while their mothers went to the parade or elsewhere.

On the floor above, the gymnasium and amusement hall was transformed into a banquet hall, and mid-day and evening meals were served by a committee from the women's council, assisted by committees from the churches of the center and Florence. The unqualified co-operation of all the denominations, under the auspices of a purely sociological organization, was in itself, as one of the visitors said, worth coming to Northampton to see. The co-operation of the churches was not confined to the older and richer churches, but an almost equal service was rendered by such small societies as the Hebrew congregation of B'nai Israel and the newly-formed Polish congregation, St. John of Cantius.[3]

Andrew Carnegie's gifts to the Home Culture Clubs brought Adelene Moffat some personal reward for her long service. Payments were made on her salary arrears and, before they stopped in 1904, she received $675 of the money which had been due her since 1895. But she also received a demotion and found herself no longer general secretary, but secretary for women's work. Harry B. Taplin, a 1902 Amherst graduate, was brought from Hale House in Boston and hired as secretary for men's work. His appointment and the others that followed resulted from the need to increase the staff in order to conduct the enlarged program made possible by the acquisition of James House and to anticipate the expansion that would occur when Carnegie House was built. The agency now had more land than many small colleges could boast and it soon would have really fine

[3] *The Meadow City's Quarter-Millennial Book*, pp. 430–31. Among the illustrations in this handsome volume, published by the town as a record of the occasion, are several fine interior views of James House and small photographs of Cable and Adelene Moffat.

The article on the Home Culture Clubs does not mention Cable's name. In one of his speeches, Seelye listed the agency, "the generous enterprise of Mr. George W. Cable," as one of Northampton's many charitable, benevolent, and educational institutions. Scattered throughout the book are a number of quotations from prose and poetry about Northampton and the vicinity, but none of these is from Cable's books and articles. Nowhere is he mentioned as an author.

facilities for a full program of adult education and associated functions. Its activities were not readily divisible into men's work and women's work. It must have seemed to Adelene Moffat that the position of general secretary was not being abolished, but that Taplin's appointment and her own demotion were merely steps in supplanting her, now that the chief administrative position offered a new dignity and security.

Whether Taplin's appointment resulted from a change in the attitudes of Adelene Moffat and Cable toward one another or whether it merely contributed to the change is difficult to determine. Certainly there is a new note in the Moffat-Cable correspondence after her return from Crete, and particularly after Mrs. Cable's death. Often their letters to one another were critical or unsympathetic. Adelene Moffat wrote on August 2, 1904, "I know you will admire my self restraint when I tell you that it was Saturday at noon that I finished the last garden call and behold it is Tuesday and I have not written to tell you so." The next day she reported on various details of club business and discussed her niece, Mary Weir, who had lived at her home and whose illness had taken Adelene Moffat to her bedside in a Philadelphia hospital in March. On August 4, she wrote an abrupt note informing Cable that salaries for the staff were due and that there was no money on hand to pay them. Later that month, when a vacation in the Adirondacks was reviving her energies and restoring her disposition, she sent Cable a friendly letter, but the earnest, worshipful phrases of her earlier letters were missing.

Cable wrote Carnegie a note on November 4, 1904, which set a pattern for the birthday and Christmas messages he sent the philanthropist regularly from then on. He greeted him as one "given to the world to bless it." The architect's plans for Carnegie House had been accepted the previous spring, and the building was under construction. Responsibility for the dedicatory exercises was assigned by the board to Calvin Coolidge, though, as usual, Cable was empowered to act for the committee. Cable wrote to Mrs. Carnegie on March 27, 1905, to announce his pleasure at the prospect that the Carnegies would be present for the exercises on April 12, and asked to meet with them to discuss plans for the ceremony.

The Carnegies' visit, their first to Northampton, was a proud occasion for Cable and for the little town of 20,000 people, many of whom labored to produce silks, cutlery, baskets, brushes, and stockings in local mills and factories. Few would have disagreed with the *Gazette* of April 12, which said that Carnegie was "in some respects the most distinguished man who has ever visited Northampton." Once a bobbin boy in a mill at a salary of $1.20 a week, he had an income of $23,000,000 from steel alone in 1900, when there was no income tax and when one could hire a couple as cook and houseman and pay them a combined salary of $50.00 a month. Carnegie was world-renowned, and the town exerted itself to show appreciation to its benefactor.

On the morning of the dedication, April 12, Cable and the Carnegies attended an assembly at Smith College, where both men spoke briefly and the Smith girls sang "The Blue Bells of Scotland" and "Auld Lang Syne" in honor of the visitors. Adelene Moffat was among the guests at the luncheon held for them at the Lyman estate. That afternoon there was a public program at the Home Culture Clubs, in which Mayor Connor, former mayors, and various other officials participated. The architect handed President Cable an oak chest containing a silver key, products of Northampton artisans, which Cable presented to Mrs. Carnegie. Then followed an inspection of Carnegie House and the other facilities.

The offices of the agency were located in three rooms in the new brick building, just opposite the main entrance. Adjacent to these were two lounges. There were twenty rooms of assorted sizes for classes and committee uses. In the basement, where Smith girls conducted many auction sales, there was space for bowling alleys. One room on the ground floor which had its own street entrance was a lounge where men in working clothes could read or rest or smoke and where those seeking work could register, at no cost, for employment through a labor exchange; the room had a telephone for the convenience of employers. For only two cents a cue, the public could use the six tables available in the large billiard room. On the second floor was an auditorium which came to be known as Carnegie Hall and which, like other facilities of the agency, was often rented or leased for special purposes. Here were held the adult dancing classes and the regular Saturday night dances. The auditorium would seat five hundred people for concerts. It was an ideal place for the display of a collection of illustrations, in color and black and white, which were made for various editions of Cable's works and had been borrowed for the occasion from Scribner's and the Century Company.

The whole plant of the Home Culture Clubs now consisted of three large buildings and two small ones—the housekeeper's cottage and a house rented for a laundry. Altogether there were two assembly halls and more than fifty rooms for club and class use. The old billiard room in Lyman House became a club room for street urchins. The

Lyman House assembly hall continued to function in many capacities but served principally as a gymnasium, the scene of spirited basketball games between the Home Culture Clubs and the St. John's Church Ushers, the St. Jerome Juniors, and the Commercial College.

Cable had a dinner party for the Carnegies before the main event of the dedication services, an evening program at the Academy of Music. Admission was by invitation only and all the 1,300 seats were reserved. The stage was crowded with dignitaries from Smith, Amherst, and Williston, the Home Culture Clubs chorus of forty, and delegations from Springfield—Carnegie had recently given that city $150,000 for a library—and neighboring communities. Many members of the Home Culture Clubs sat in groups in the audience. One of these was the Old Members' Association. Another was the staff, which Adelene Moffat, who sat with them, had coached in protocol for the ceremonies.

After an invocation by the Reverend Father P. H. Gallen, pastor of the Chuch of the Annunciation in Florence, and a selection by the chorus, Mayor Connor extended official greetings and praised the Home Culture Clubs as truly "a people's college." In his long "Report of the President," Cable traced the sponsorship of the enterprise, naming the persons and businesses which had contributed over the years and stressing the munificence of Edward H. R. Lyman, an appropriate reference, since Lyman had given the town the theater in which Cable was speaking. He told the story of Carnegie's gifts and described the new building and the plant as a whole. He lauded the board members and the volunteer teachers, announced the work of the various committees, and commented on the wide range of activities planned and in progress. To the five hundred club members he said: "Young ladies and gentlemen, your People's College is proud of you." He said the agency was a municipal institution and that he spoke for Northampton as a whole in praising Andrew Carnegie. He ended, without once mentioning the name of Adelene Moffat, by reciting "Abou Ben Adhem." Carnegie, who called Cable a "valued friend and model worker for the good of others," gave an address which was shorter than Cable's introduction. There was another selection by the chorus, and the program closed with a benediction by the Reverend Dr. Henry T. Rose of the First Congregational Church, of which Jonathan Edwards had once been pastor.[4]

A month later, Cable and the oldest of his unmarried daughters, Lucy, sailed for England. He wrote Andrew Carnegie on May 19 to announce their vacation plans and to ask when it would be convenient for them to visit Skibo. Traveling as a tourist rather than as a celebrity, Cable planned no readings. He and Lucy saw the sights of London, Oxford, and Edinburgh, and this time Cable got to Dunfermline, Carnegie's birthplace and Scotland's ancient capital, where Carnegie's money supported the park and the garden competition which was the model for Cable's pet project in Northampton. They spent a week at Skibo; Cable wrote Adelene Moffat from there on June 14 and spoke of Mrs. Carnegie's high regard for her. He sent Carnegie a note on the twentieth, offering a benediction on "those who forgive our faults and strive to fulfil our hopes."[5]

Back in Northampton in July, he resumed work on *Kin-*

[4] See the Springfield *Daily Republican,* April 13, 1905; Northampton *Daily Herald,* April 13, 1905; Northampton *Daily Hampshire Gazette,* April 12, 1905; and invitations and program in the archives of The People's Institute.

[5] The letter is in the New York Public Library.

caid's Battery. Adelade Moffat left in August for a vacation at North Perry, Maine, where she was the guest of the Lymans.

Cable also returned to work on his civic enterprises. Though he sometimes blamed them for keeping him from his writing, it is doubtful that they constituted any real interference. He found that he could do literary work for only a few hours each day; the pattern had been established when he was writing *Old Creole Days* and *The Grandissimes* and he could not break it. Now his community activities must have helped him to combat the loneliness that faced him at Tarryawhile.

On July 6, Cable suggested to Joseph Henry Sawyer that Harry Taplin might be asked to give a course of lectures at Williston Seminary. Principal Sawyer replied on August 30 that the school had no money for the purpose. He also suggested, diplomatically, that because of lack of funds and other problems, it would be helpful if Cable would refrain from further landscaping of the Williston grounds for a while. This work resulted from action taken by the board of trustees in the fall of 1904. Friends had given the school $250 and the board had voted an equal amount, the entire sum to be used for landscaping. Cable headed the Committee on Improvement of the Seminary Grounds; the other members were Sawyer and Robert L. Williston, the school treasurer. For many years the landscaping was in Cable's hands, as he was the trustee most competent and most interested in this project. Often Sawyer wrote him for advice and assistance; sometimes he asked that Cable postpone some projected planting or improvement because of lack of money or interference with other phases of the school program.

Once Williston authorities hoped that Cable's influence with Carnegie, made evident by the gifts to the Home Culture Clubs, might be turned to account. Sawyer suggested to Cable that Carnegie might be approached about contributing a library to the school. A letter to Cable from Sawyer, written on November 9, 1903, indicates that the two men had discussed the idea and that Cable had suggested a request for $50,000, a larger sum than Sawyer had contemplated. A. Lyman Williston, who was on the board of the Home Culture Clubs and was president of the Williston trustees, wrote to Cable on December 28, asking advice about the application and supporting papers he was assembling. The request was held in abeyance for several months. On November 25, 1904, Sawyer wrote to Cable about it again, asking Carnegie's address and Cable's support of the application. But Carnegie gave Williston no money.

The expanded program of his Home Culture Clubs demanded a great deal of Cable's attention when he returned from his trip to England in 1905. Classes began in September, with the usual emphasis on practical training which would benefit both the student and the community. Adelene Moffat's circulars announcing the courses in cooking expressed the philosophy of the agency much better than the official motto did: she said, "The more good cooks there are in the world the fewer bad saloons!"

Cable was seriously ill late in the fall and had a minor operation, but he was well enough in December to attend the banquet in New York honoring Mark Twain.[6] He gave Adelene Moffat a Christmas present, for which she sent him a short note of thanks on the second of January. Calvin Coolidge wrote him four days later, from his law office in

[6] Turner, *George W. Cable,* p. 335.

Northampton's Masonic Building, to remind him that it was his turn to lead the discussion of the Economic Club at the meeting of February 13. Coolidge, evidently serving as secretary for the club, wanted to know Cable's subject so that notices could be mailed to the members. There was a public lecture on city planning at Lyman House on February 15th, and President Cable was on hand to introduce the speaker of the evening.

Cable was making little progress with his writing and was beset by personal problems. In March, when Gilder rejected one of his manuscrpts, Cable acknowledged its shortcomings, but felt obliged to try to get it in print without putting his name on it. The scattering of Cable's "little flock" continued; Margaret was now Mrs. Harold Brewster, and Isabel married in May. On the twenty-second, John C. Hammond, one of the original members of the board of managers of the Home Culture Clubs, politely resigned. Cable paid a visit to his eldest daughter, Louise, in June, but returned to Northampton in time for the board meeting on the twenty-fifth. Though the treasurer was absent, the board accepted a financial report, audited by Calvin Coolidge, and voted to continue to employ Adelene Moffat, Harry Taplin, and other staff members; there were now nine full-time employees and five part-time. Dorothea, who had kept house for her father since her mother's death, went to Wisconsin to stay with the Dennises. Tarryawhile was rented for the third straight summer. Cable and his son lived in the study at the rear of the property and boarded with Mary Louise Cable. The family in Northampton was much reduced since the days, twenty years earlier, when it had filled two houses.

In September, just when the Home Culture Clubs

normally began the main work of the year, Harry Taplin resigned as secretary for men's work. Probably acting upon Cable's recommendation, the board authorized him to employ Herbert D. Hemenway in Taplin's place. Hemenway was not trained in social service work. After graduation from college he was in charge of the grounds on an estate in Providence and then worked for a Boston market gardener and florist. For a while he had charge of the greenhouses and grounds at the Massachusetts Agricultural College. In 1900 he was in Hartford as director of the School of Horticulture.[7] One of his first tasks on his new job in Northampton was to try to dissuade the town from its sudden interest in taxing the Home Culture Clubs for the caretaker's house in which Joseph Ashwanden and his wife, employed as general housekeeper, lived, and for which they paid no rent. Hemenway's main function, however, seems to have been to lecture to the clubs on gardening in preparation for the summer prize competition and to conduct nature study walks and field trips in good weather. At the same time that the board authorized Cable to hire him, it voted to purchase the Loomis property and to establish there the Northampton Nurseries, largely for the convenience of garden club competitors.

On October 31, Cable wrote to tell the Carnegies that he was to be married late in the next month to Eva C. Stevenson, of Lexington, Kentucky, "a woman of forty-eight, of charming social accomplishments, a beautiful musician, large in mind and heart, of a mirthful temper and ardent affections." He denied newspaper stories that she was "a woman of large fortune," and said, "She has merely enough income to assure her that our marriage adds nothing to my

[7] Northampton *Daily Herald,* January 8, 1907.

burdens."[8] Cable wrote on November 15 to invite the Carnegies to attend the wedding, to be held in Philadelphia at the Church of the Incarnation; three days later he sent word that it would take place in Christ's Church instead.[9]

George W. Cable was sixty-two when he brought his second wife home to Northampton. His build was as slight as ever, his movements as agile and nervous. The keen, quizzical eyes set in the broad oval of his face had a youthful twinkle. At forty-four he had written his mother that he had not a single gray hair except in his beard and mustache;[10] now the neatly trimmed beard was white. In the grip of an absent-mindedness that was so notorious that it sometimes gave him concern, he would rout around in his beard with his fingers until he located some particular hair that bothered him. With him, absent-mindedness was not a sign of age. On November 17, 1886, he had written to Mrs. Annie T. Fields: "Please don't laugh at a poor witless fellow: when I reached home from your house Mrs. Cable walked straight into my valise and drew forth the missing teaspoon! She sends her love and will cause the spoon to follow ere long."[11] Cable's memory was frequently inaccurate,[12] but his mind was as alert as ever.

Mrs. Eva Cable became active in her husband's affairs

[8] The letter, which is in the Library of Congress, is printed in part in Turner, *George W. Cable,* p. 336.

[9] The letters are in the New York Public Library.

[10] Biklé, *George W. Cable: His Life and Letters,* p. vii.

[11] The letter is in the Henry E. Huntington Library. Cable had written Mrs. Fields on August 2, 1884, that he hoped she would soon meet his family—"the mother bird and nestlings."

[12] Furthermore, some of his recollections may have been feigned rather than real. See Turner, "George W. Cable's Recollections of General Forrest," *Journal of Southern History,* XXI, 225–26, and the same writer's *George W. Cable,* p. 348.

in Northampton. She and Adelene Moffat must have been on amicable terms, since it was at Miss Moffat's home that she met Anna Gertrude Brewster. For two months that winter Mrs. Cable was bothered by facial neuralgia, and in March she went to Atlantic City to recover. On March 4, the Northampton *Daily Herald* announced Andrew Carnegie's gift of $8,500 to the Home Culture Clubs for the garden program and revealed that the money had been used to buy the Loomis greenhouse, nursery ground, dwelling, and barn on three lots on Jewett Street between Forbes Avenue and Vernon Place. What money was left from the grant was to be used to stock the greenhouse.

When Cable was at work on his fiction he sat in a rocker, a writing pad on his lap and a pencil in his hand. He wrote first drafts with his left hand—he was naturally left-handed—but shifted to his right for the final copy.[13] He used a desk for his correspondence, and important or difficult letters, like his writing for publication, were often done in more than one version. He must have labored for some time to compose this letter on March 8, 1907.

Dear Miss Moffat:

Last April I had to report an excess of the year's running expenses over our income, of more than $1,000, and was plainly and rightly told by our board that in one way or another this discrepancy must be removed.

I dismissed Miss Parsons [14] and undertook to fill the place of bookkeeper and cashier myself, and you know with what vigilance I have studied every economy and worked daily and nightly with my own accountant's pen. We have reduced expenses and increased our income, but the reduction is barely half enough (as I must presently show our finance committee from our books) and in simple duty to the concern's interests I

[13] Biklé, *George W. Cable: His Life and Letters*, pp. xii–xiii.

[14] Helen Parsons was registrar from 1900 to 1906.

must relieve the president's office of the clerk-work I have temporarily assumed.

The only chance for a full reduction lies in our payroll, which I plainly perceive our board considers too large. Yet we are in constant need of more clerical work rather than less, and the fact is forced upon me by its own weight, that our administrative work must be done by one secretary and that he must be a man. Its nature has been changing for years in a direction to demand this, and the wonder of our friends is that, even as it was, you handled so much of it so well.

In plain words, then, the work we have so long pursued together offers you that release which I have longed to see it offer me these ten years and which I would joyfully accept in your place if I could.

Allowing the strong probability that you will promptly be sought by other managements and will have large choice of appointments suited to your talents, it yet has taken all my moral courage to present the matter to you as you see it now stands. You have shared with me the public trust on which all our work has been builded, and one of Mr. E. H. R. Lyman's latest words to me was that he gave his gifts with confidence because they were given "to G. W. Cable and Miss Moffat.["] But this situation has come about totally contrary to my purpose and to all my expectations, by the natural growth of an enterprise which must be allowed its natural growth or presently end in a failure we have no right to risk.

I write this to you in strictest confidence and shall not submit it to our board, or mention it to anyone, until I hear from you.

With every wish for your welfare, I am—

Yours truly

G. W. Cable [15]

Adelene Moffat replied on the tenth in one sentence: "Your letter of March 9th [sic] comes to me as so great a

[15] I quote the draft of the letter which is in the Cable Collection at Tulane University. The original Adelene Moffat turned over to her attorney. It is clear that the final version of the letter did not differ appreciably, if at all, from this corrected draft.

surprise that I must ask for a little time before replying to it formally." Her surprise was natural. The Women's Council had met at her home on the sixth, and she had reported on the agency's activities with no thought that she was about to be dismissed. She consulted with her friends when she recovered somewhat from her shock, and Frank Lyman wrote for her to the management to say that she felt her only course was to retire from her work with the Home Culture Clubs, effective whenever the board should wish.[16] Her resignation was presented at a special board meeting on March 18. In Coolidge's absence, Dr. John A. Houston acted as secretary, with the result that the record of the meeting is more detailed than usual. On Seelye's motion, the resignation was accepted and the following resolution was adopted.

In accepting with regret the resignation of Miss Moffat to take effect April 30, the end of the present fiscal year, the Directors of the Home-Culture Clubs desire to place on record their cordial commendation of the intelligence, tact and self-sacrificing spirit she has manifested in fulfilling the duties of her position, and their high appreciation of the many invaluable services she has rendered to the clubs in their development during the past eighteen years.

Frank Lyman had submitted his own resignation, but it was voted to ask him to reconsider and to continue on the board.

Both local newspapers printed on March 20 the news of Adelene Moffat's resignation and the board's commendation of her services. The source of the stories was a news release

[16] The extent of Cable's control of the Home Culture Clubs is indicated by the fact that this letter, like others directed to that agency, is in the Cable Collection at Tulane University, not in the files of The People's Institute.

provided by the agency. The articles said nothing about a need to reduce the agency's payroll, and neither did Cable when he wrote to Andrew Carnegie on the twenty-ninth. He said he planned to attend the dedication ceremonies at Carnegie Institute in Pittsburgh in April but doubted that Mrs. Cable could accompany him.

> We have done finely this year. Unhappily the growth of the work has put it into such shape that it seemed best for Miss Moffat to lay down her long office in favor of a successor who could stand to the work more like the male president of a co-educational college than a woman could. It made an unpleasant moment for both of us. I must tell you more about it when next it is my fortune to see you.[17]

The unpleasantness had just begun. The Women's Council held its regular meeting on April 3 and, after routine business was concluded, Miss Helen Sergeant proposed a resolution praising Adelene Moffat and petitioning the president and the board to induce her to continue with the agency. A copy of this petition was to be sent to each member of the board. Miss Julia E. Peck, librarian of the Home Culture Clubs and secretary of the Women's Council, reported in the minutes of the meeting that Cable, who was present, proposed that only one copy of the petition be prepared and that that be sent to Calvin Coolidge, secretary of the board. According to the minutes, this motion was not carried. In a letter to the local newspapers in which Cable said he had "pointedly commended" the resolution, he stated that the motion was carried and that it was offered by someone other than himself.[18] On April 4, the *Daily Herald* printed the resolution which praised Adelene Mof-

[17] The letter is in the Library of Congress.
[18] *Daily Herald* and *Daily Hampshire Gazette,* April 6, 1907.

fat for her "tact, enthusiasm, adaptability and untiring zeal," observed that her withdrawal might "seriously imperil the future welfare of the clubs," and asked the president and board to persuade her to remain.[19]

Coolidge, now a member of the state legislature, wrote Cable the next day to advise that he receive the petition and convey it to Adelene Moffat but that he state that the trustees regarded her resignation as final; A. Lyman Williston wrote on the sixth that since the resignation had been carefully considered and had been announced to the public, it seemed to him it would be best to let the matter rest. Cable would have been glad to do so, but the newspapers and the public would not let him. The *Daily Herald* of April 5 published a long article on the state of the controversy at that point, suggesting strongly that the general public favored Adelene Moffat and was out of sympathy with Cable and critical of his agency.

> There is no use in anyone's denying the fact that things are seething hot in Home Culture Clubs' circles or that the intensity of the heat is increasing as the days pass. There is, of course, a vast amount of current street and household gossip regarding the matter. . . . In the first place, it should be stated that Miss Adelene Moffat did not resign the secretaryship in a voluntary way, but at request. . . . Very strong was the sentiment that the good of the Clubs demanded the retention of Miss Moffat if possible, as it was felt that her earnestness, energy and genius in execution had been for all these years one of their chief mainstays and causes of success. . . . Soon came the further announcement of the resignation of Miss Edith Baer as head of the Household Arts Department—and, whether or not connected with that of Miss Moffat, it added to the mystery by reason of its quick sequence, and there arose a demand on

[19] The original of the resolution is in the Cable Collection at Tulane University.

all sides for an explanation. This soon came in the revelation of personal differences between President Cable and Miss Moffat. . . . As a culmination came about the meeting reported in yesterday's Herald, with the adoption of a strong resolution in favor of using every effort to induce Miss Moffat to withdraw her resignation. The meeting was a very lively one, and the resolution was adopted in opposition to the protests of the president.

Now it is declared by leaders of the Women's Council that they and the other members will resign and withdraw entirely from the Home Culture Clubs, unless Miss Moffat is re-instated with honor. The management of the Clubs they declare to be, in their opinion, altogether too autocratic and the same sentiment is voiced by many others of both sexes.

Furthermore, the treasurer, John J. Raleigh, declares that he is determined to resign unless there is a change. He considers himself, he says, only a "dummy" treasurer. For three or four years past, he states, not a penny of the Clubs' money has passed through his hands, although originally he did handle the funds, and all that he has to do now is to sign checks and notes drawn for the benefit of the organization and the annual treasurer's report—which is made out and brought to him to sign. . . .

It is greatly to be feared that the efficiency of the Home Culture Clubs, for a time at least, may be much diminished, as a result of the present controversy. . . .

It should be stated, further, that Mr. Cable expressed himself to the Herald as very much gratified over its editorial comment on Miss Moffat's resignation, published the day following the announcement.

Years before this, on February 8, 1889, Adelene Moffat said in an admiring letter to Cable: "If ever I should have to write an article . . . 'What I know about George Cable' —one thing I shall be able to say very certainly. He knows how to write letters." The long controversy that resulted from Cable's dismissal of Adelene Moffat called on all his skill as an ambidextrous correspondent. Many of the charges which were made against him or his enterprise he readily refuted, others he parried, some he adroitly ignored. For instance, in his long letter replying to the *Herald*, published on April 6, he made no reference to the statement that members of the Women's Council had threatened to resign.

Editor of the Herald:

The extended remarks in your issue of to-day (Friday) upon the condition of affairs in the Home Culture Clubs give me equal pain and surprise. Had you consulted me, even by telephone, I could have saved you from misleading statements which can only injure a valuable and extremely sensitive public interest.

I was present at the late meeting of our Women's Council and pointedly commended their resolution so complimentary to Miss Moffat. My only protest was against what seemed to me a faulty way of communicating it to the Board, and that form was modified, though by the motion of another, not of mine.

Miss Baer, our instructor in Household Arts, has resigned to accept a position very attractive to her, because in her home city of Philadelphia, and has done so, as far as I know, without the slightest reference to the matter of Miss Moffat.[20]

Any implication that the funds of the company have been handled with the slightest irregularity or informality is absolutely without foundation. Not a dollar can be drawn from [the] bank, and not a dollar ever has been put into [the] bank without the treasurer's signature and the only reason why Mr. Raleigh has not had the clerical work of the Treasureship himself is because it has been done by a cashier [21] with a strictness of form which makes it possible to audit the entire cash movement of a year

[20] The position was that of instructor at Drexel Institute. At the Home Culture Clubs reception for Edith Baer, who had been on the staff for three years, and her replacement, Miss Emily Stevens, Cable spoke briefly and presented certificates of efficiency in cooking to selected club members. See the *Daily Herald* and *Daily Hampshire Gazette,* June 5, 1907.

[21] As Cable stated to Adelene Moffat in his letter of dismissal, and as the ledgers in the archives of The People's Institute show, he was the cashier.

upon its vouchers, within the space of an hour. Mr. Raleigh knows and will inform you that he has not been called to meetings of the directors only because he is not a director. He has just authorized me to state that since conferring with me, he has no present intention to resign.

As to Miss Moffat's resignation I do not know what either she or the board may desire to say or leave unsaid, and shall not speak on my own responsibility until I do know.

I have also to regret, greatly, that an imperative engagement calls me out of town to-morrow for an absence of several days and requires me to be more hurried and brief in this communication than I should wish to be.[22]

Let me add, however, in all good-nature, that your allusion to "autocratic" behavior is amusing. The presidency of the Home Culture Clubs is a laborious, unpaid office which I have been longing to be rid of these ten years, and any one may have the place to-morrow who is willing to fill it and will satisfy the board of directors of his ability and good faith.

George W. Cable
Northampton, Mass., April 5, 1907

Immediately below Cable's letter, the newspaper stated its regret that it could not "withdraw or palliate the statement made yesterday. To enter further into details would only necessitate . . . the telling of some unpleasant facts which neither Mr. Cable, his friends or the Clubs would care to have known." Mr. Raleigh, it said, confirmed the accuracy of the paper's account of his statements but did not "intend the slightest implication against Mr. Cable's integrity." In an editorial the *Herald* politely praised Cable's benevolence in founding the Home Culture Clubs, but insisted that the quasi-public agency must have a treasurer who was more than a figurehead and must inform the public of its financial status and business transactions in

[22] Cable went to Pittsburgh for the dedication of Carnegie Institute.

order to hold local confidence and support. The paper expressed praise and sympathy for Adelene Moffat in its issue of April 9. "Who has done for this city the self-denying work that she has done? and for such a small salary! No man would have thought of accepting it."

On April 23, Pauline A. Shaw (Mrs. Quincy A. Shaw) wrote to Cable, saying she had heard that Adelene Moffat was leaving her post wth the Home Culture Clubs and asking his opinion of her fitness for an executive position in social service work. Mrs. Shaw, daughter of Louis Agassiz and sister of Mrs. Henry L. Higginson, conducted a number of philanthropies in the Boston area. Cable replied immediately. He said it was not easy to answer all Mrs. Shaw's questions; "I can do so at all only on the assurance that you will treat this reply as strictly confidential." Thus protected, he remarked that Adelene Moffat applied herself to her work only fitfully, was intolerant of routine, and was "constitutionally incapable of sustained concerted action with others or of carrying out the instructions of others." He said she had a "keen intelligence and a singular lack of judgment" and that this was particularly apparent in the superintendence or reconstruction of a building.[23]

But the woman whose shortcomings it had taken Cable nearly twenty years to discover and act upon must be replaced. He wrote to Mrs. Annie T. Fields, hoping she might be able to recommend someone who would fill the position for four hundred dollars less than the salary paid to Adelene Moffat, who, he said, "leaves the place vacant on the first of May. We may or may not—that is, we need not,—fill it this summer. It will not be the same place Miss

[23] Mrs. Shaw's letter and a typed copy of Cable's reply are in the Cable Collection at Tulane University.

Moffat is leaving, but more limited to a woman's capacity. Yet it will demand tact, refinement, along with the ability to make oneself attractive at once to the working girl, the college girl and the social woman." [24]

Adelene Moffat's services to the Home Culture Clubs were given appropriate public recognition at Carnegie Hall after the closing session of Harry Lane's dancing class. Lane's Springfield students gave exhibitions of fancy dancing, ice cream was served, and Cable spoke briefly. The surprise event of the evening was the presentation of a silver loving cup, inscribed: "Presented to Adelene Moffat by members and past members of the Home Culture Clubs, April 29, 1907." Hemenway made a "very happy presentation speech." The *Daily Herald* reported that the retiring secretary "was taken completely by surprise and was quite overcome by emotion, but responded feelingly with the following sentiments: that she thought it was about time that she should be retiring, when a thing requiring so much time and trouble as the planning for and purchasing of her present could happen without her knowing anything about it; that the expressions of regard and appreciation coming to her since her resignation would be the things of greatest inspiration in her new work and would never be forgotten." The paper said that, having decided not to reconsider her resignation, she would remain in Northampton until the first of July, "when she will go to Boston for a year of research." [25]

It must have been obvious that Adelene Moffat needed a job, not a year of research, and equally obvious that she

[24] The letter is in the Henry E. Huntington Library.

[25] *Daily Herald*, April 30, 1907. See also Northampton's *Daily Hampshire Gazette* of the same date.

intended to leave Northampton. She visited New York early in May, perhaps to recover from the work and worry of the past few weeks and to look for employment. She was buying from Cable a ten-foot strip of land adjacent to her Dryads' Green property on the southwest, and when she returned to Northampton on the sixth she found that he had delivered the deed. Apparently she understood this as a hint, not a gift, and the next day she sent her check for fifty dollars, completing payment for the land. About the hundreds of dollars in salary arrears the agency owed her, nothing whatever had been said in President Cable's letter of dismissal.

XI: "A Bare Question of Veracity"

The reason George W. Cable discharged Adelene Moffat in March of 1907 was not stated in his letter to her or in the newspapers, though the *Daily Herald* did mention that there was "a vast amount of current street and household gossip regarding the matter" and spoke of "unpleasant facts" which it would not print. Cable's real motive is revealed in an exchange of letters that took place in April. He wrote Harold Brewster, his son-in-law, on the eighteenth, asking confirmation of Mary Louise Cable's statement that Adelene Moffat had made derogatory remarks about the first Mrs. Cable to Harry Taplin. Harold answered the next day that he had not heard any such remarks but thought his sister Gertrude had.[1] In any case, he said, the incident should be disregarded, because people were familiar with Adelene Moffat's inclination to gossip and would discount what she said. Taplin sent Cable an indignant letter on the twentieth, saying that the whole story was false and ridiculous. Taplin pointed out obvious errors in Mary Louise Cable's report,

[1] Anna Gertrude Brewster could not be reached conveniently for confirmation because she was in England during most of 1906–07. From October, 1898, to June, 1906, she had been at home only during school vacations. She has said in several letters to me that she knew nothing of the cause of the break between Cable and Adelene Moffat.

and said he had never heard Adelene Moffat make disparaging remarks about Cable's first wife but, on the contrary, he had often heard his colleague speak highly of her. Although Adelene Moffat's reputed remarks were supposedly made to Taplin and Taplin specifically denied that she had made them, Cable chose to insist that the story was true. The charge that Adelene Moffat had slandered their mother made her *persona non grata* with the family, who rallied to the support of their father and "Aunt Eva." On April 22 Cable wrote that Taplin himself had not escaped Adelene Moffat's tongue, as he would tell him in detail when next they met. "Let me further explain that I should never have found out the thing I enquired of you about, had Miss Moffat not filled the air of this good little town with base slanders of me which I could not contradict without reducing the matter to a bare question of veracity between us."

The Home Culture Clubs board reluctantly accepted Frank Lyman's resignation when it met on May 13, 1907. It rejected the petition of the Women's Council, on the ground that it was inexpedient to reconsider Adelene Moffat's resignation. Coolidge's minutes indicate that the finance committee was authorized to borrow $1,500 and to deal with an "alleged claim" of the former secretary for women's work. At a meeting on the thirtieth the board authorized an audit of the books,[2] and when it met again on the first of June the finance committee was instructed to borrow another $1,500.

These loans, the first of many, are evidence of the financial problems which plagued the agency for several years

[2] Coolidge was absent and Dr. Houston acted as secretary, but his signature has been erased from the minutes. Here, as elsewhere in the record book, the minutes are out of chronological order.

and which were solved only by reducing the plant and operations. It appears to be obvious that the enterprise no longer had the support of the community, or at least of many persons in the community who had contributed to its development. The management changed. John C. Hammond's resignation in May of 1906 was perhaps not unrelated to the rumors circulating in Northampton. Frank Lyman's withdrawal was followed the next year by that of A. Lyman Williston. Raleigh resigned as treasurer in February, 1908. Cable acknowledged that the Women's Council kept up a "lively ferment" for three months after Adelene Moffat's dismissal, and apparently many of the officers and members finally resigned. When it was reorganized in the fall of 1907, Mrs. George W. Cable, first vice-president, and Miss Mary Louise Cable were seemingly dominant in its activities.

A letter, dated June 10, 1907, which Cable must have been expecting, came into his hands shortly after it was delivered to the treasurer. It was Adelene Moffat's formal request that Raleigh submit to the directors her statement of the corporation's indebtedness to her for back salary. Cable did not reply. But he could not ignore the letter Frank Lyman wrote him on June 18. Speaking for himself and his sister, Mrs. White, Lyman said they found it impossible to continue their financial support of the agency, for to do so would seem to express approval of a management with which they were quite out of accord. He enclosed a copy of an agreement, dated February 18, 1903, promising to contribute a sum not to exceed $3,000 a year, payable semiannually, with the proviso that the obligation might be voided at any time after three months' notice had been given. Frank Lyman had given notice for himself on March 13; he now gave it for his sister. He asked what amount was still due under the agreement and requested a written acknowledgment of receipt of the letter. Cable sent it the following day, saying he would answer at length at a later date.

He wrote three drafts before he achieved a long letter of defense that satisfied him. Admitting that Lyman's obligation had been fully discharged, he pleaded for continued support of the agency, at least for one year, so that it could prove it still merited public confidence and assistance. For years, he said, he had devoted to the enterprise time and labor from which he might otherwise have earned far more than the amount of Lyman's annual gift. And he insisted, "I have for years been most unfortunately misled as to the character of our retiring secretary."

Some further information about the "base slanders" that were circulating is provided in the documents and the letter Cable sent to L. Clark Seelye on June 26. Perhaps at Seelye's suggestion, he forwarded statements about Adelene Moffat he had obtained from Mary Louise Cable, Helen Cox, and two employees of the Home Culture Clubs. He said he was surprised by Adelene Moffat's alleged remarks about him, for all the while she had professed to consider him her most valued friend. He told Seelye that at about the time of his second marriage Adelene Moffat had remarked to him that she supposed her own status would continue to be that of a member of the family. She had never been so regarded, he said, and he quoted some of the more sensational passages of the attached documents.

Mary Louise Cable's statement in support of her brother accused Adelene Moffat, whom she said she had never liked, of being untruthful and unfaithful, and she cited instances intended to prove the charge: she said Adelene Moffat denied the obvious when she claimed that her mother, who had died in 1901, had not been a Christian Science practitioner.[3] Helen Cox, Cable's niece and at one time Adelene Moffat's partner in an art studio in Holyoke, was represented by a typed undated extract from her letter quoting a New York woman who said she had known Miss Moffat since childhood and did not think highly of her.

Julia E. Peck, librarian of the Home Culture Clubs for the past three years, testified in her two-page statement that the former secretary for women's work procrastinated and took credit for the work of others (including, it might be inferred, the librarian). Then she went on to more personal and crucial matters. Adelene Moffat, she said, had remarked that Cable wanted her to resign but would not dismiss her for fear of losing his contributors. On one occasion Miss Moffat told the staff that she was thoroughly acquainted with Cable's character before she came to Northampton, but a day or two later she said that for years Cable had been a symbol to her of all that was noble and good and that her awakening to his true nature was a slow process; the contradiction, said Miss Peck, was so evident that the staff disregarded her. More recently, the librarian stated, Adelene Moffat had made direct charges against Cable's moral character, saying that three women had confided their grievances to her since his marriage to Eva C. Stevenson. Miss Peck reported that Adelene Moffat had told her that each woman claimed that he had promised to marry her in

[3] There are two versions of Mary Louise Cable's statement in the Cable Collection at Tulane University. One is her longhand original; the other, a typed manuscript edited by Cable, is the version sent to Seelye.

case his wife Louise should die and that Miss Moffat had asserted more than once that only her influence kept Cable out of the law courts.

Cable could not resist adding a comment to Miss Peck's document and typing insertions on the five pages of misspelled and ungrammatical longhand notes supplied by H. D. Hemenway. The secretary for men's work charged that Adelene Moffat tried harder to get on good terms with the contributors than to do her job and that it was the contributors, for the most part, rather than the club members, who said they were sorry about her departure. She was, he said, inefficient, unreliable, and disloyal, and had told him that Cable had only two passions, one of which was vanity.

In a note contradicting one of Hemenway's statements, Cable said that Adelene Moffat told him in an interview that she was taken completely by surprise when Frank Lyman announced his intention to make no further contributions to the Home Culture Clubs.

The *Daily Gazette* of July 31, 1907, reported that Hemenway had decided not to join the faculty of an agricultural college in Alabama and rejoiced that he was to remain in Northampton. At the board meeting on September 7, his salary was increased to $1,200; Miss Peck's helpfulness brought her no similar reward and she did not remain with the agency long. The *Herald* said on March 11, 1908, that Hemenway, a "whole-souled and genial man," was resigning to take a better, but unspecified, job. Two days later the board authorized the finance committee to borrow not over $500 and to offer Hemenway not over $1,400, if necessary to ensure zeal on his part. This salary, together with a promotion to general secretary, was granted him at the meeting of July 13. Hemenway continued as general secretary until 1919, when he took a job in horticulture at the University of Massachusetts.

This "whole-souled and genial man" was evidently the author of two suprising articles. *The Gentlewoman* for October 15, 1908, published a long illustrated article, signed "H. D. Hemmingway," which traced the history of the Home Culture Clubs but put particular stress on the garden work, the feature Hemenway—and Cable—most relished. The writer did not choose to name Adelene Moffat or Edward H. R. Lyman, though the latter was referred to indirectly as the public-spirited donor of the first building. The account said that Arthur Stone [4] was the first secretary and that Hemenway was made general secretary in 1907. A second article, "The People's Institute of Northampton, Mass.," attributed to Hemenway, published around 1912, did mention Edward H. R. Lyman and Harry Taplin and spoke of Adelene Moffat as Cable's private secretary, but did not give her name. (There is a clipping of this article in the files of The People's Institute, but the name and date of the periodical from which the clipping was taken have not been preserved.) The articles are surprising because they are signed by Hemenway, but they fit a pattern which was already established. Cable had not mentioned Adelene Moffat's name in his *Century* article in 1888, in his 1906 article in the *World's Work,* or in his remarks at the dedication of Carnegie House in 1905. Cable's agency received a great deal of newspaper publicity in the years after Adelene Moffat was discharged, some of it in connection with the audits and general controversies, much of it routine

[4] Arthur Fairbanks Stone wrote Cable to report on some class on December 11, 1885.

promotion or Sunday journalism, but her name virtually disappeared from the public record.

When Adelene Moffat's letter of June 10, 1907, about her salary arrears brought no response from the treasurer of the Home Culture Clubs, she turned the collection of the claim over to her attorney, John C. Hammond. On the twenty-fifth Hammond sent a copy of her account to Cable and to each of the members of the board. Adelene Moffat wrote to Hammond the next day:

My lack of confidence is confined entirely to Mr. Cable. He is very subtle and clever and his misrepresentations since the development of this situation have been so amazing that I agree entirely with Mr. Lyman that it is much safer and more dignified to decline to have any more direct communication with him and I am more grateful to you than I can say for acting for me in this matter. . . . I am pressing this claim because I need the money badly, not as a measure of retaliation. . . . Mr. Cable's constant assurances [were] that I was building up a work here which as I grew older would be in a position to reward my "years of devotion" with an honorable place and an adequate means of support. I do not say that I would not have worked just as hard and as willingly without such assurances but Mr. Cable's lack of business honesty on this point quite changes my point of view as far as he is concerned.[5]

Cable wrote Hammond on June 27, 1907, that the matter would be attended to at the earliest practicable moment, but not until the following March, when Hammond implied that his client might resort to legal action, was anything done. Cable made no reference whatever to the salary arrears in the long letter he wrote Andrew Carnegie, apparently in July of 1907.

[5] A copy of this letter is in the Cable Collection at Columbia University.

Dear Mr. Carnegie:—

There are things with which I have no right to trouble you. But there are things of which I have no right to leave you uninformed. Here is one of them:—

Early last March I had to ask the resignation of our secretary for women's work, Miss Moffat. She had always been fitfully neglectful of her work, but in the last two seasons had become continuously so. She had also grown flagrantly and aggressively disloyal and was constantly laboring to alienate my whole staff of workers from me by the most amazing statements against my personal character and conduct. So glaring had these faults become, that when I asked for her resignation and she had gone round to the members of our board individually and privately pleaded her own case before they heard a word of serious criticism from me or any one, the Board, after a discussion of less than thirty minutes, sustained my action by a unanimous vote, Mr. Lyman only being absent.

This exception of Mr. Lyman, however, is a grave one. The board are all contributory to our yearly revenue, but he and his sister, Mrs. White, as heirs of their father, have for years been our financial mainstay, giving $1,200. annually toward our running expenses. Miss Moffat had made herself their protegée and now appealed to them. So Mr. Lyman, without a moment's conference with me, tendered his resignation with Miss Moffat's and announced the permanent withdrawal of his annual support. The board, while sustaining me, solicited him to reconsider, but in vain. Then the secretary proceeded to rouse to her aid our "Women's Council," who formally met and petitioned the board to reinstate her. The board kindly declined, but the council kept up a lively ferment for three months, yet now have come completely round and make profuse pledges of sympathy and support in the coming season.

Hardly was this phase of the trouble past when Mr. Lyman wrote me, repeating for his sister (till then in Europe) all he had said for himself, and inviting me to say what, if anything, I thought they should do to fulfill conclusively the terms of their five-years pledge of support, which does not expire until next April. I showed my reply to Dr. Seelye and at his suggestion procured from a number of persons their written statements of what they had for years known of Miss Moffat's misconduct to be [sic]. This he found so convincing that he undertook himself to lay it before Mr. Lyman, who is the husband of his niece. But Mr. Lyman refused to see it or consider it, replying to Dr. Seelye only by letter and that letter so objectionably phrased that Dr. Seelye, in a board meeting, withheld one part of it entirely and read only that portion which insisted that in order to restore Mr. Lyman's confidence, it would be essential to have a public accountant examine our books for the last five years and make a public report, while the board should hold my resignation in hand for action in accordance with results. Mr. Lyman did not know that this is what I had already myself proposed to the board and they had declined to do. Nevertheless they now decided to have this examination made, not by a public accountant but by a small committee of private experts acceptable to Mr. Lyman. But at the same time they reelected me, requesting me not to resign and offering me such expressions of confidence and esteem as I shall be grateful for as long as I live. The books and vouchers are all ready and the committee will probably be selected in a few days. Along with this I send a copy of my letter to Mr. Lyman, which I beg you will do me the great favor to read.

Our beautiful work has received a prostrating blow which is likely to cripple it for years. Of course you have the right to expect that I shall say that from this blow it nevertheless must and shall recover, and I say it. I even hope we can gain some advantage, eventually, out of this very disaster. Already it has shown our friends the great risk of being subject to the caprice of individual financial supporters. In the talk I had with you on the evening when you made us your $50,000 grant, you pointed out this weak spot in our condition—our lack of all provision against sudden financial mishaps. Now I shall make this one my plea for the establishment of a such a provision by every possible means however small, or process however gradual.[6] We have right before us a year of shrinkage and privation. But I

[6] At his speech at the dedication of Carnegie House, April 12, 1905, Cable said that the Old Members' Association had begun a campaign

have told our board that, while for the work's own sake no less than mine I must use every effort and opportunity to press it into younger hands, I count myself in honor bound not to insist on any release of myself from duty or hardship contrary to their sense of the work's need, and I now say the same to you.[7]

The board meeting which Cable described was that of July 2, 1907, at which the officers were reelected and an audit of the books authorized. An audit had also been authorized at the meeting of May 30, but this must have been merely a routine review of the treasurer's annual report by the finance committee. The second audit was made by persons not connected with the agency. Joseph Pickett, head of Northampton Commercial College, and G. C. Rowley, accountant for A. McCallum & Company, audited the treasurer's report, which the board had already approved, and this account of the year's transactions appeared in the *Daily Herald,* September 25, 1907. This audit was not enough to silence all the unpleasant rumors about financial irregularities, so Seelye commissioned Walter W. Eaton & Company, Springfield corporation auditors, to conduct a thorough study of the agency's accounts from May 1, 1903, through November 1, 1907. Seelye also appointed a committee of four Northampton residents, John W. Mason, Georgia Laura White, Jean Murray Ganong, and Theobald M. Connor, to inquire into the work of the Home Culture

---

to raise a permanent fund of $2,500, as protection "against days of adversity when public support may falter in the face of hard times." Northampton *Daily Herald,* April 13, 1905.

[7] I quote in its entirety the draft of the letter which is in the Cable Collection at Tulane University. Carnegie contributed to an operation to remove a cataract from Cable's eye in 1913 (see Cable's letter to Carnegie, January 9, 1914, in the Library of Congress), sent him money on other occasions, and, when he died in 1919, left Cable $5,000 a year for life. See Turner, *George W. Cable,* pp. 345, 355.

Clubs and also the public reaction to it. The reports of these two investigations, together with Cable's letter transmitting them to the board of managers, were published in the *Herald* on January 10, 1908.

The Eaton report disclosed no important irregularities but criticized the manner in which the accounts were kept. Judge Mason's committee, quoting Cable as authority, answered objections which had been raised to the leasing of Lyman Hall for theatrical purposes and wrestling matches and to the operation of a greenhouse in competition with established businesses in Northampton. Acknowledging that public confidence was at a low ebb, it devoted most of its attention to the problem of enlisting support from the community. The public, it said, regarded the agency almost as "Mr. Cable's private business enterprise."

We understand from Mr. Cable that he feels the burden very heavy upon him and that there is under consideration a plan for increasing the number of directors and having the Board of Directors as enlarged, appoint responsible working committees to take charge of the several branches of the work. This would seem . . . to be the best way to insure the public interest, systematize the work, and provide for its continuance.

Cable's long letter of transmittal called the audit a "gratifying statement" that all funds had been properly accounted for.

Their chief criticism would, I am confident, have been much modified had I not been unavoidably absent in New York City when they made their report. They certainly would [not] have called the shifting of entries to which they allude "constant," since fully nineteen-twentieths of all our entries are a mere cash account—cash to sundries and sundries to cash. All shifting of entries will count up hardly a dozen instances and occurred mainly during the time of receiving the successive installments of $50,000 and $16,000 grants. . . . Three or four cross-entries are in mere correction of a young clerk's errors and need no special apology.

He was gratified too by the "approving tone" of the report of Judge Mason's committee, but he differed at length with some of its observations. He said the agency's name was perhaps inappropriate, for it failed to "cover all the good things we seek, and have always sought to do." The institution, he said, was "not charitable, but distinctly educational and benevolent, and many of its best benevolences are in the nature of amusements." There was nothing wrong with wrestling matches and motion pictures as such, and since young people would attend such shows somewhere, they might as well do so in the wholesome atmosphere of the Home Culture Clubs.

The renting of one of our halls to theatrical shows and wrestling matches when it would otherwise have been idle is a matter of the moment—of the last few weeks at most—and of so experimentary [sic] a character in a work nearly twenty-one years old, that it seems to me hardly a feature to be singled out in a discussion of that work's permanent management. . . .

As to our nurseries and greenhouses in Jewett street, they are bought wholly with money given by Mr. Carnegie, and no money has ever been raised in Northampton either to equip or maintain them. No part of the special contributions from our Northampton people for our Model Flower-Garden in Gothic street has ever been used for the nurseries, greenhouses or flower-store.

Cable might have spared himself the trouble of defending this particular part of the Home Culture Clubs program, for he knew it was to be discontinued. On June 12, 1907, plans had been announced for making the three acres surrounding the agency's plant a park or model garden,[8]

[8] *Daily Hampshire Gazette,* June 12, 1907.

and some work on the project was done that summer. There was no reason to object to the model garden, but the greenhouse and florist shop did not receive local support, and on October 8 the board instructed the finance committee to rent the Northampton Nurseries and sell the stock. The *Herald* announced on March 31 that Thomas Foulds, gardener for the Home Culture Clubs, had resigned to take a job in Amherst as manager of an estate. On the following day the *Gazette* reported that Foulds would not be replaced and that the greenhouse and flower store, which for about a year had been operating in competition with local florists, would be disposed of. On May 16 the board approved the sale of the business property to Alexander Parks.

The report of Judge Mason's committee and the audits of the corporation's books may have strengthened public confidence, but they did not succeed in persuading Frank Lyman and his sister to resume their financial support. From Brooklyn, New York, a letter was sent to Seelye on January 20, 1908, signed by Alfred T. White for himself and his wife and by Frank Lyman for himself and Mrs. Lyman. It thanked Seelye for the reports from the committee and the auditors, whose bill the Lymans paid. It then specifically disagreed with the committee statement that the success of the agency in the past had been due largely to Cable's work and influence. Acknowledging that Cable had made generous contributions of his time and energy, the Lymans argued that the success of the enterprise could be traced directly to Adelene Moffat's efforts, not to Cable's. It was because of her work that they had felt the agency deserved support. Cable's failure at the dedication of Carnegie House to express appreciation for her services made the Lymans feel that he withheld from her the recognition to which she was entitled and which could have done much to increase the value of the enterprise. The letter said nothing about resuming contributions.

Cable was a charter member of the National Institute of Arts and Letters, formed in 1888, and was honored by election to the American Academy of Arts and Letters in 1908. On February 5 he sent his acceptance of the invitation to become a member; [9] the honor was some consolation for the unhappy state of affairs in Northampton. He wrote Mrs. Andrew Carnegie on the twenty-third: "The Home Culture matter has reduced itself to the problem of financial support, the Lymans still withholding theirs and being more unfair than I can believe they have any notion they are." [10] On the twenty-fifth he sent Seelye his comments on the Lymans' letter, which Seelye had passed along to him. He said in part:

> I note their admission that their sympathy and approval have been with Miss Moffat and apart from me since Carnegie House was built, the date when her failure to bring to the work either a devotion or an ability commensurate with its expansion began to be especially conspicuous; the date also marks the beginning of my practical efforts to procure other workers fit for the work for which she was not adapted; workers not to displace her, but to relieve me and (while retaining her) to allow the work to grow in the direction of a better efficiency and self-care than she showed any capacity or reassuring purpose to give it.
>
> And lastly I protest that when the annual contribution of Mr. Lyman and Mrs. White was raised from $600 to $1200, the increase was solicited and granted specifically to secure Mr. Carnegie's gif [sic] that no reference was ever made to Miss Moffat's salary in that connection, and that Miss Moffat's salary was never raised or lowered on account of it.[11]

[9] This letter, together with other Cable correspondence and memorabilia, is in the archives of the American Academy of Arts and Letters.

[10] The letter is in the New York Public Library.

[11] A copy of this letter is in the Cable Collection at Tulane University.

None of the audits mentioned as a liability the money owed to Adelene Moffat for back salary. John C. Hammond wrote on March 7, 1908, asking that the board give attention to her claim and make some payment on account; he said she needed the money. His hint that legal action might be taken probably had some effect. On March 14 the board decided that her claim should be left up to Coolidge. Hammond submitted to the board on the twenty-fourth a full statement of Adelene Moffat's account. He specified the amount due as one thousand dollars and stated that his earlier requests, which had not included interest charges, were in the nature of a compromise and no longer applied. The amount owed Adelene Moffat on January 1, 1895, was $1,543.65 and payments during 1903 and 1904 had reduced this to $869.65. Hammond's review of the case, with frequent quotations from documents in Adelene Moffat's possession, was not only support of her claim but also an attack upon the injustice of her abrupt dismissal. He argued that the board had officially accepted her old salary claim as a moral obligation, that its assets were adequate to permit payment, and that Cable had acknowledged responsibility by assigning a lot to her as collateral security. He pointed out that Cable could not properly ask that his business letter terminating her services be kept confidential. During much of this time when Adelene Moffat was owed approximately a year's salary, Hammond said, she was in debt to Cable for a substantial amount *and paid him the usual rate of interest.*

A. Lyman Williston's resignation was submitted to the board at the meeting of April 4, at which it was voted that Coolidge should confer with Hammond in an effort to settle Adelene Moffat's claim at its face value. Coolidge did not succeed. Two weeks later the board decided to mortgage Lyman House.

Cable's son, who had suffered from a weak heart all his life, died on June 2, 1908, and evidently the board did not meet during that month. Adelene Moffat's letter of condolence, June 7, 1908, brought to a close the correspondence which had begun more than twenty years earlier. She wrote to Cable from Cambridge, Massachusetts, of her deep affection for Willie and her real sorrow over his death. "Do not feel that you must answer this. It will be hard—and I shall understand."

The Northampton Institute of Savings granted the Home Culture Clubs a thousand-dollar loan on June 18, and on the twentieth Hammond signed a receipt for that amount in full settlement of Adelene Moffat's claims.

L. Clark Seelye submitted his resignation to the Home Culture Clubs board when it met on November 5, 1908; two years later he also retired from the presidency of Smith College, a position he was the first to hold and one he had filled with distinction for thirty-seven years. The name of Cable's agency was changed to The People's Institute of Northampton in August, 1909. Cable continued as president and Coolidge, who was mayor of Northampton in 1910 and 1911, as secretary. Cable's "people's college," which had been a vital and growing enterprise a few years earlier, gradually regained some of the stability and prestige it had lost when Adelene Moffat was discharged, but it never recovered the position it had enjoyed under her management. In February, 1911, Lyman House was sold to James W. O'Brien, and this brought an end to the years of borrowing.[12] The purchase money paid off current obligations, and

[12] The building is now the Elks' Home.

$12,000 was left on deposit as the permanent fund Cable had so long wished for. The personnel of the board and the staff changed frequently, but Cable and Coolidge continued in their familiar roles. They spoke at a union peace meeting in the Methodist Church in 1914.[13] In 1915 and 1916 Coolidge missed the meetings at which the board reelected him as secretary; in the first year he was president of the Senate of Massachusetts, in the second he was lieutenant governor. The next year Harry Norman Gardiner succeeded him as secretary, but Coolidge and his wife, who also served on the board at one time, continued to give The People's Institute their support. Despite their long collaboration on the civic agency, Cable and the Coolidges never became in any sense intimate friends. Mrs. Grace Coolidge, who had come to Northampton in 1901 to teach at Clarke School for the Deaf and who had married Coolidge in 1905, saw Cable once or twice on the street but never met him.[14]

Cable continued as president of the agency he had founded, but his management was far less direct than it had been. After his son died, Cable and his wife spent the winters, the busy months for The People's Institute, in a warmer climate than that of Massachusetts and were in Northampton only in the summer. Because of this, and because of ill health, Cable resigned in 1920 and was succeeded by Chauncey H. Pierce, but he did not sever all connection with the enterprise. In the spring he visited the gardens entered in the annual contest, and two years later, in an emergency, he assumed direction of the whole gar-

[13] *The Northampton Book: Chapters from 300 Years in the Life of A New England Town, 1654–1954,* p. 312.

[14] Personal letter from Mrs. Coolidge, March 18, 1949.

SPONSORS OF THE PEOPLE'S INSTITUTE, 1921

First row, left to right: Dr. John A. Houston, Calvin Coolidge, George W. Cable, Chauncey H. Pierce, William Allan Neilson. *Second row, left to right:* William Cordes, Edwin K. Abbott, Mrs. J. W. Heffernan, H. N. Gardiner, Helen C. Coty, Mrs. L. M. Scoville, W. E. Shannon.

den competition, though illness prevented him from being present when the prizes were awarded.[15]

At the present time, The People's Institute of Northampton occupies Carnegie House and James House on Gothic Street. A member agency of the Community Chest, it still conducts an evening school for adults, taught by Smith College students. The largest enrollment is in the course in English for the foreign-born, and in 1957 the twenty-eight students in this group were of nine different nationalities; but the adult education program is much reduced from what it was years ago, when an immigrant peasant boy like Stephen P. Mizwa could begin at The People's Institute an education that could lead him through Harvard and on to a career as a college professor.[16] The decline in the adult classes is not a reflection on the present agency but a tribute to the achievements of its earlier years. It is evidence of the change in social patterns in Northampton and elsewhere; the Americanization of immigrants is no longer a major problem in Northampton. The Institute operates an after-school play program for small children and a summer day camp. James House is headquarters for the Young Women's City Club, an organization of about fifty young women who sponsor club suppers, parties, picnics, lectures, and discussions. A Golden Age Club, composed of people over sixty, meets in James House for group singing, movies, and various social activities, and the Carnegie Coin Club also gathers there. Other organizations rent office space or meet in the buildings, among them the Boy Scout Council,

[15] For an interesting picture of Cable in Bermuda in 1922, see Chesnutt, *Charles Waddell Chesnutt: Pioneer of the Color Line,* pp. 290–91.

[16] Gray, "From the Steerage to a College Chair in 11 Years," *American,* XCVII, 46–47.

the Girl Scout Council, the Community Chest, the Children's Aid Association, the Bricklayers, Masons, and Plasterers' Union, the Sunday School classes of Congregation B'nai Israel, and the Pioneer Investment Club. There are square dances on Saturday nights and many rummage sales. In general, the program of The People's Institute is comparable to that conducted in cities and towns throughout the nation by various community agencies.[17] It is a useful and respected civic enterprise.

Mrs. Eva Cable died on June 7, 1923. On December 16, at the age of seventy-nine, Cable married Mrs. Hanna Cowing of Northampton. He died in St. Petersburg, Florida, on January 31, 1925, and was buried in Northampton. It was the third Mrs. Cable who sent to The People's Institute in 1934 the only reminder it keeps on display of his role as founder of the agency, a framed photograph which hangs in the foyer opposite a portrait of Abraham Lincoln. Brochures of the Institute make reference to Cable, and Northampton newspaper stories occasionally speak of his distinction as an author and a civic-minded citizen; but popularly the Institute is identified with Andrew Carnegie, for whom the main building is named, rather than with Cable. His name does not appear on the literature circulated by the Chamber of Commerce, though there is much there about Coolidge and Carnegie. The Lyman family connection with the Institute is nowhere acknowledged. Adelene Moffat, of course, is known only to a few people

[17] In 1897, when Cable was editing *Current Literature* and hoping for a career in New York, the Home Culture Clubs board met to consider Adelene Moffat's letter of resignation. It not only decided to abandon activities outside Northampton, but also authorized Seelye to consult with the YMCA with a view toward consolidating the two agencies. After conferring with YMCA officials, he reported at the meeting of December 14, 1897, that the idea was impractical.

with whom she was personally acquainted and to antiquarians.

Despite Cable's ungenerous letter to Mrs. Quincy A. Shaw, Adelene Moffat found employment with the Boston philanthropist, and until Mrs. Shaw died in March, 1917, Miss Moffat worked with her in an executive capacity. She was director of Cambridge Neighborhood House, Cottage Place Day Nursery, Cottage Place Library, Long-Sought-for-Lodge, North Bennet Street Day Nursery, Moore Street Day Nursery, and Ruggles Street Neighborhood House. Her interest in the underprivileged never waned. The clubs and classes of Cambridge Neighborhood House were open to Negroes and whites without distinction and encouraged those who felt that segregation must not prevail in the Boston area.[18] She supported the National Association for the Advancement of Colored People during its early years. On January 21, 1913, she addressed the third annual conference of the NAACP in New York, citing her experience with the Home Culture Clubs and the social settlement in Cambridge as evidence that whites and Negroes could work and play together amicably and with mutual benefit when those in authority refused to give countenance to discrimination. She stressed the responsibility of social agencies to oppose unintelligent racial, religious, and national prejudices of all kinds.[19]

Her article, "Exhibition of Italian Arts and Crafts in

[18] Ovington, *The Walls Came Tumbling Down,* p. 22. Adelene Moffat wrote to Cable on February 2, 1899, that Mary White Ovington praised the work of the Home Culture Clubs at a meeting in New York.

[19] Her address was printed by the NAACP and circulated in pamphlet form. Adelene Moffat told me she objected to the title, *Views of a Southern Woman,* under which it appeared, as she did not consider herself a Southerner.

Boston,"[20] demonstrates that she did not lose interest in the immigrant or in art after she left Northampton. On later trips abroad she studied the paintings of the old masters in the galleries of Great Britain, continental Europe, and Russia. She was an octogenarian in April, 1942, when Argent Galleries, 42 West 57th Street, New York City, held a one-man show of her work, including copies of masterpieces, some of the paintings of Mycenaean pottery she had made in Crete in 1903, still lifes, portraits, and landscapes. In her nineties Adelene Moffat was still active as a professional artist, still writing, and still deeply concerned about equal opportunity and justice for all. Her last years were devoted to investigating the possibility that Princess Anastasia had survived the massacre of the family of Czar Nicholas II by the Bolsheviks in 1918, and she was regarded by some as an authority on the subject.[21] She was a member of several organizations and was particularly interested in the Society of Women Geographers, to which she left the bulk of her estate when she died in New York on February 10, 1956. Some of the objects she brought from Crete were bequeathed to the Museum of Art in Boston; other items and paintings were given to museums in Memphis and Brooklyn. Her body was cremated and the ashes were sent in an urn to Monteagle. In the center of the circular family plot in the cemetery stands a pedestal of Scotch marble bearing a copper sundial and an inscription honoring her father, John Moffat, as founder of the town.

Adelene Moffat had visited Northampton in 1951, and news of her death brought a brief revival of interest in her

[20] *Survey*, XXII, 51–53.

[21] New York *Times*, February 12, 1956. This obituary contains a number of errors.

collaboration with George W. Cable in building the Home Culture Clubs. But there was no general recognition of her part in developing, from an insipid scheme for spreading "culture," an important social service agency that had contributed, and is still contributing, to the welfare of the city and its citizens.

XII: The Record of His Years

The break with Adelene Moffat and the resulting public controversy did not permanently affect Cable's reputation as a philanthropist and public benefactor who, almost alone, conceived and established a notable social service project.[1] It may be thought that his project for assisting Northampton's masses to help themselves was merely a perverted philanthropy which sprang less from Cable's concern for the welfare of the lower classes than from an inner compulsion to establish his own social standing in the community and win the regard of future generations. This interpretation would explain Cable's consistent unwillingness to acknowledge publicly Adelene Moffat's contributions and, in part, his abrupt dismissal of the woman with whom he would otherwise have had to share the regrets of posterity. But whatever psychological motivation induced Cable to sacrifice his limited resources of time and energy and money, and however misguided some of his efforts may

[1] See the obituary in *Nation,* CXX, 133, and William Allan Neilson's address at the funeral service held at Edwards Church on February 8, 1925. This was printed as a pamphlet, *In Memoriam: George W. Cable,* and excerpts appeared in the *Daily Hampshire Gazette,* February 9, 1925. Then president of Smith College, Neilson was also president of the board of The People's Institute from 1933 to 1938.

have been, his action in founding and maintaining the Home Culture Clubs is praiseworthy.

It was not affection for the freedmen and Acadians and poor whites and the inmates of asylums and prisons that impelled Cable to champion their cause, and he evidently had no feeling of affinity with those people in Northampton whom he wanted most to help. With his equals Cable was inclined to take the lead, to be autocratic; with his supposed superiors he adopted a humility and charm that won him quick acceptance; but he was uncomfortable in the company of people whom he could regard as his intellectual or social inferiors, and his only recourse was to patronize them. Mark Twain, whose aspersions on Cable may be partially discounted as characteristic of his moodiness or sensitivity or acerbity, was irritated by what he regarded as Cable's insulting ways with servants, and he said servants hated Cable.[2] In the paper she read at a meeting of the Northampton Historical Society, Anna Gertrude Brewster remarked on Cable's inability to establish rapport with the masses.

There was an ever-present irony in the fact that "the cross-section of society" did not understand or appreciate him. Moved as he was by a sincere wish to benefit his fellow men and make them happy he, in turn, did not understand them. His absent-mindedness, lack of tact, and some decided mannerisms repelled the

[2] Cardwell, "Mark Twain's Row with George Cable," *Modern Language Quarterly,* XIII, 365. Twain complained to his wife about what he considered Cable's religiosity, conceit, avarice, and trivial dishonesty on their reading tour. "This pious ass allows an 'entirely new program' to be announced from the stage & in the papers, & then comes out without a wince or an apology & jerks that same old Night Ride [from *Dr. Sevier*] on the audience again." *Ibid.* But see Turner, "Mark Twain, Cable, and 'A Professional Newspaper Liar,'" *New England Quarterly,* XXVIII, 18–33.

people he was most eager to serve. They comprehended neither his intentions nor his language and club work always went better if he did not appear directly connected with it.

His inability to mix with the lower classes in Northampton perhaps accounts for the fact that the books that followed *John March, Southerner* failed to extend the area or sharpen the impact of his social criticism. He spent some forty years in that industrial community and had an opportunity to observe the immigrants and others who worked in its mills and factories, but he wrote nothing significant about the problems or the people. His increased age, his reading tours, and his changed circumstances may be offered in explanation. The Puritan became the cosmopolite; he wrote Adelene Moffat on February 6, 1898, from Chicago, about the ugliness of the prairie country: "Morality everywhere; no harm in that assuredly; but by whose warrant in heaven or earth has *morality* earned the right to be ugly or dirty?" The family man was so much away from home that he became a man of the world and quietly adapted the rigid standards of his youth to suit the comfortable mores of his society. The reversal of his attitude toward the theater is symbolic. Once he thought it sinful. In the North he not only relaxed this view; he tried to make a play of *Bonaventure* and was overjoyed when a dramatization of *The Cavalier*, with Julia Marlowe as the star, ran on Broadway. He spoke proudly of his "theatre business" and hoped for a dramatization of *Madame Delphine*. He was disappointed in 1921 when a contract for making movies of some of his works was allowed to lapse.[3] As Cable modified his convictions, the very qualities which had led

[3] See Cable's letters to Adelene Moffat, January 15 and 19, 1902, and June 1, 1902; Biklé, *George W. Cable: His Life and Letters*, pp. 251–54; and Turner, *George W. Cable*, pp. 324–26, 354.

to success and for which he is now remembered—his crusading zeal for justice and reform, his broad sympathy for the underprivileged, his piety—gradually but surely diminished. His essays became innocuous discussions of nature and gardening and banal statements of his philosophy, statements so vague that they did not even identify the issues he had once discussed with outstanding foresight and vigor.

The novels he published after Adelene Moffat left Northampton resemble his best fiction in superficial details of scene and style, but they do not have the heart, the compelling purpose of *Old Creole Days* and *The Grandissimes. Kincaid's Battery,* published in November of 1908, can be dismissed, like *The Cavalier,* as a traditional Civil War romance.

The final fiction of his career more nearly approaches his fine books of the eighties, probably because it returns to the scenes best suited to his special talent. *Gideon's Band* (1914) is another romance, hackneyed in subject and plot, but it includes effective social criticism in its presentation of the evils of slavery and caste and the tragedy of the quadroon. Although this story of the Mississippi is theatrical and contrived, there are moving episodes, and Joy, the black nurse, is as realistic a figure as Clemence of *The Grandissimes. The Flower of the Chapdelaines* (1918) treats Creole life in the New Orleans of the First World War, but the characters and themes look to the past, and the bulk of the book is composed of tales the author had published years earlier. In thus presenting again the stories of the white girl unjustly enslaved, the West Indian insurrection, and the escape of a slave family which wins freedom in the North by following "the clock in the sky," Cable reaffirmed the democratic doctrines implicit in those narratives.

Lovers of Louisiana (1918), Cable's final book, seems a direct return to the issues with which he was concerned at the height of his career. The hero, Philip Castleton, is a liberal Southern intellectual, and the glamorous heroine is a Creole of the romantic tradition.[4] Cable gave the book a contemporary flavor by intruding discussions about the position of the South in the modern world, but most of the action seems concurrent with that of *The Grandissimes* or *John March, Southerner.* Ovide Landry, the Negro who is a key figure in both of Cable's last novels, has devoted himself to the welfare of his race as though he were following the advice Frowenfeld gave the colored Honoré Grandissime.[5] When Landry prevails on Philip Castleton to speak to a literary society at a Negro college, one feels that the address is both an echo of some of Cable's own speeches and is what the author would have wanted John March to say if that confused hero had remembered his promise to speak at Suez University.

[4] Jay B. Hubbell sees in Cable's work "a certain susceptibility to the voluptuous." *The South in American Literature: 1607–1900,* p. 817.

It is interesting that Cable's heroines often possess more vigor and strength of character than his heroes.

[5] Apparently Ovide Landry is based on a learned Negro bookseller whom Cable discovered in New Orleans when he was doing research for the book in 1915 and on Oscar J. Dunn, a black lieutenant governor of Louisiana who fought corruption and extravagance in the Reconstruction government. See Biklé, *George W. Cable: His Life and Letters,* pp. 291, 293; Turner, *George W. Cable,* p. 351; and Cable's letter to Carter G. Woodson, editor of the *Journal of Negro History,* November 7, 1916, in the Carter G. Woodson Collection of Negro Papers in the Library of Congress. Cable subscribed to the journal and wrote Woodson, August 20, 1918, that he endorsed its purpose and achievement.

Castleton is like his creator in many ways. He has written an article, "The Southern Answer," which has estranged him from his friends because of its liberal views. In his speech, Castleton's advice to the Negroes is that they must rely on an "inner liberty": "By use of the splendid rights you now enjoy—which millions of white men are still deprived of—make yourselves privately so estimable and publicly so valuable that the few rights yet denied you will come by natural gravitation if not to you to your children's children." [6] The mild address would not have offended Castleton's white associates had he not prefaced it with a request that his colored listeners forget that he is white. This apology is a social blunder as damning as Cable's meal with the Napiers. When his friends reject him in disgust, Castleton remarks to Landry:

"Really, Landry, your old-time abolitionist friends had certain advantages over to-day's."

"Yes," said Ovide, with his touch of pomp, "conditions were more flagrant, sir. Also they had faith in us."

"They were illusioned; we are disillusioned."

"Yes," Ovide further admitted, "to most of the world my people are no longer even interesting."

"Yet the world," said Philip, "has really grown kinder. Trouble is, it's harder than ever for even the kindest to take the colored race in earnest. Pardon me, but it seems a race of children."

"Say, rather, a child race, professor, which every peasantry is, isn't it? But we're not all children and we claim the inalienable, individual child's right to grow up to such modern manhood as we individually can. Sir, our deprivation of that right is the rock our ship of freedom has stuck on these fifty years." [7]

For the most part, the issues of the novel are the old problems of slavery, Reconstruction, and segregation. The

[6] *Lovers of Louisiana,* p. 107.

[7] *Ibid.,* p. 111.

arguments are academic and Cable's solutions are tenuous. But the virtue of the book as social criticism lies in the recognition that the issues of the Civil War have not been resolved in accordance with the principles of democracy and that the status of the Negro results from historic conditions and events which have continued to influence the structure of American society. Randolph Bourne said that Philip Castleton "is always less a lover, less even a reformer, than he is a walking idea of what Mr. Cable would like the effective modern Louisiana young man to be."[8] *Lovers of Louisiana* shows that Cable never lost his conviction that the citizen, whatever his race or class, is entitled to be treated as an individual. This was the very keystone of his philosophy.

One may summarize the tenets on which Cable based his social criticism, as Edmund Wilson did, by labeling him a Jeffersonian democrat who wholeheartedly endorsed the equalitarian theories of the American revolution.[9] Cable saw that men are not equal and he considered that classes are therefore both natural and proper, but he believed that no man's status should be imposed by society without regard for his personal merits and deficiencies. Slavery was categorically wrong, and segregation was an injustice whether or not it involved injury or unequal treatment, for it fixed individual status on the basis of group identification.

The citizen, Cable felt, must discharge his obligations to the state to the best of his ability; the state, however, must fulfill obligations to the citizen in accordance with his

[8] "From an Older Time," *Dial,* LXV, 364. This discerning review of the book sums up Cable's virtues as a social critic. Bourne's praise of Cable's total achievement is sound, but his appraisal of *Lovers of Louisiana* seems unduly generous.

[9] "Citizen of the Union," *New Republic,* LVII, 353.

needs. The criminal, the asylum inmate, must not be expected to reimburse society for the cost of his incarceration or care. A child is entitled to an education at public expense, whatever the amount of taxes paid by his parents, and if his immediate community cannot provide that education the nation as a whole must assist it to do so.[10]

One of the citizen's responsibilities is to vote wisely. That he cannot do if the franchise is denied him or if, as in the New South, a one-party system prevents the voter from making a genuine choice among candidates and policies. Much as he favored industrial progress, Cable could not approve the New South, because it was not an advance toward his principles but a return to the undemocratic practices of the past. It reestablished caste, failed to provide adequate public education, exploited the poor, countenanced violence as a means of controlling a disfranchised peasantry, and violated the right of an accused man to a trial by a jury of his peers and of a convicted man to humane punishment suited to his crime. Reconstruction, "that great war without battlefields,"[11] despite its humiliations, mistakes, and corruption, was not an ignoble failure, for it attempted to improve the lot of the masses and established a system of public education where none had existed before.

Cable professed to love the South and never ceased to regard himself as a Southerner, but he did not believe in regional partisanship or states' rights, and he held that the

[10] In "Does the Negro Pay for His Education?" *Forum,* XIII, 642. Cable urged the adoption of a poll tax by Southern states as a means of providing funds for public education. Massachusetts had a poll tax at that time.

[11] Cable, "Education for the Common People in the South," *Cosmopolitan,* XIV, 64.

citizen's loyalty must be to the nation. The South was wrong in fighting the Civil War, not alone because it was defending slavery but because secession was untenable in theory. The contemporary race problem, rooted in history and in "a moral error as wide as the nation,"[12] was a national responsibility and must be solved in the best interests of the whole people.

Cable's advocacy of civil rights for the Negro was often confused, through ignorance or malice, with a demand for social equality. He consistently distinguished between the two, and called social equality "a fool's dream."[13] Many of those who did not understand his position either did not wish to do so or were emotionally incapable of viewing the race question logically.

Cable was an idealist and an optimist. His was a philosophy of progress. Man can attain perfection; this is the best of all possible worlds, even though there is a pressing need for improvement; right makes might and will ultimately prevail. An informed electorate will choose wise leaders, and those noble statesmen will adopt just measures unmotivated by self-interest. Some of this optimism the author outgrew as time and disillusioning experience corrected his naïveté. He learned, for instance, that a sensitive South welcomed criticism no more from a Southerner speaking in his native section than it did from anyone else. And the Open Letter Club proved that, whatever the values of the public forum, the dissemination of facts and the exercise of logic would not correct injustices which the nation looked upon with apathy.

[12] Cable, "National Aid to Southern Schools," *The Negro Question,* p. 65.

[13] Cable, "The Silent South," *The Silent South,* p. 52.

He insisted, however, that there is a virtue in facts and logic, a special virtue in truth. "Whatever the truth is," he said, "I believe it is best to know the truth, best for all, best that all know it, and that all of it is better than any part of it." [14] Had he been able to apply this reverence for truth as an inflexible guide to conduct, the record of his years would indeed be, as it has been called, a stainless one. But George W. Cable was human, "a more interestingly complex person than has been generally supposed." [15]

To Fred Lewis Pattee Cable wrote on July 21, 1914: "It would give me much pleasure to tell you how I came to drop into the writing of romances; but I cannot; I just dropt. Money, fame, didactic or controversial impulse I scarcely felt a throb of. I just wanted to do it because it seemed a pity for the stuff to go so to waste." [16] Rarely has a writer so directly contradicted himself, denied the obvious, misstated his motives, and misjudged his achievement. Before he wrote his first published story Cable had shown himself to be a reformer by instinct, and his didactic bent is discernible in nearly everything he wrote. Cable was not miserly,[17] as Mark Twain sometimes supposed, but

[14] "Does the Negro Pay for His Education?" *Forum,* XIII, 649.

[15] Cardwell, "The First Public Address of George W. Cable, Southern Liberal," *Studies in Memory of Frank Martindale Webster,* p. 75. The comment is in reference to Cable's letter to Mark Twain, June 29, 1882, which is printed on p. 72. Cable told Twain of his commencement address at the University of Mississippi, "I am said to have scored a decided success," and asserted that he was heard by nearly all of the eight hundred people present. Cardwell feels that the letter glosses over the hostility of Cable's audience and his difficulties in addressing a large group of people. But see Turner, *George W. Cable,* p. 135*n.*

[16] Biklé, *George W. Cable: His Life and Letters,* p. 48.

[17] He was never wealthy or even secure, but he contributed consistently to what he regarded as deserving enterprises. He gave money to his church, to Negro education, and to the Home Culture Clubs. It

neither was he indifferent to money; his responsibilities made such an attitude impossible. As to the wish for fame, that was the core of his ambition, the clue to correspondence and behavior which would otherwise be inexplicable. Cable's letter was written not to Pattee but to posterity.

In conversation Cable was sometimes less careful and calculating. Perhaps the most important conversational indiscretion for which documentation is available was that which led to strained relations with Hjalmar H. Boyesen, the man who assured the publication of *Old Creole Days* by guaranteeing the publishers against loss. Boyesen wrote Cable to praise his magazine stories and encourage his ambitions, and Cable responded with details about his personal affairs and professional plans. In 1882, several years after he had learned of Boyesen's part in getting *Old Creole Days* into print, Cable met a Russian professor, Waldemir Kowaledsky, who arrived in New Orleans with a letter of introduction from Boyesen. Cable entertained him. Later the Russian published an article quoting Cable's remarks about Creoles and attributing to him a statement that Boyesen had less talent than Howells. Much to Cable's discomfiture, the *Critic* printed a condensed version of the article on July 28, 1883. When Cable wrote to the magazine in an attempt to undo the damage, he did not say he had been misquoted and he made no specific reference to the reputed remarks about Creoles; he did say he could not remember making the statements Kowaledsky reported. He praised Boyesen's abilities as an artist, disparaged his own

---

was his custom to donate fifty dollars a year to the Northampton YMCA. He made many loans to friends and relatives, even when he was in debt to others or to the bank or to his publishers. Probably this commendable generosity sprang partly from his need to identify himself with the class of people who could afford such benevolence.

pretensions as a critic, and cleverly evaded any comparison between Boyesen and Howells.[18] Although this incident did not quite end the relationship between Cable and Boyesen, it seems that they were never on intimate terms again.

No doubt Cable sincerely regretted the incident. Having adopted the role of social critic and civic reformer, he could not hope for general popularity, but he did want the approval of his peers. It was not the acclaim of the mob he cared about but the regard of the learned, the upright, the wealthy, the accomplished and successful, the urbane and sophisticated. These were the select who had the sort of status he longed to achieve. On November 23, 1883, he wrote his wife from Boston that he was to be the guest of the St. Botolph Club at a dinner. "The evening is specially Mr. Matthew Arnold's, but it is very pleasant to know that I am his junior partner in the honor." The next night he wrote again. He spoke of his pride as he read the proofs of his *Century* article on the convict lease system, but it was not as a dedicated reformer that he named the celebrities who were present for the dinner and reported his triumphs there. "We don't like the attention, do we? It makes us pout, eh? We're not vain, and so it displeases us. And when we're waltzed out to the long supper-table at the head of the column, of course it's very unpleasant, & all that sort o' thing." [19] For the class of people Cable aspired to join,

[18] See Ekström, "Cable's *Grandissimes* and the Creoles," *Studia Neophilologica,* XXI, 192–93, and Turner, "A Novelist Discovers a Novelist: The Correspondence of H. H. Boyesen and George W. Cable," *Western Humanities Review,* V, 370–72. Cable's associations with some other literary figures, among them Lafcadio Hearn, Joel Chandler Harris, John Greenleaf Whittier, and Mark Twain, were also marred by controversies or incidents. Generally his biographers assign the blame for these, perhaps too readily, to persons other than Cable.

[19] Biklé, *George W. Cable: His Life and Letters,* pp. 109–10.

as for the nation as a whole, reform did not remain in fashion. So it is not strange that although at the outset of his career Cable led the fight against the major abuses of his time, at the close he was content with quiet efforts to revise the nation's orthography.[20]

But the important consideration in an appraisal of Cable's record as a man and an author is his achievement. When his powers were at their height he risked his material security and devoted his intellectual and physical energies to the service of the oppressed and exploited and thus, in a democratic society, to the service of all. His controversial essays, "restrained in tone and earnest with a high-minded persuasiveness," [21] are brilliant arguments for extending democracy to America's second-class citizens, white and black. They were so far ahead of their time that it is only within the past decade that the nation has officially adopted his definition of the nature of civil rights and has begun to take steps to guarantee these rights to all Americans.

Cable was not a professional social scientist, and it was in literature, primarily, that he sought his livelihood and his fame. Fortunately he contrived in his finest writing to combine his chief interests. As Randolph Bourne said, "Cable always blended his romance and sociology." [22] He did this effectively in *Old Creole Days, The Grandissimes,* and, for the most part, *Dr. Sevier;* critics and anthologists damn Cable to an unmerited obscurity when they praise these works as local color and ignore Cable's significance as a social critic. As he grew older he kept the same ingredients, sentiment and sociology, but altered their proportions, and

[20] He became a member of the Simplified Spelling Board in 1913 and was made a vice-president in 1921. *Ibid.*, p. 290*n*.

[21] Bourne, "From an Older Time," *Dial,* LXV, 364.

[22] *Ibid.*

the resulting blend, neither a bitter medicinal stimulant nor a soothing opiate, was less successful. In the early books Cable is an incisive critic of a bygone regime, but his real attack is on the injustices of his own time rather than on those of the past; the Creole is a romantic symbol for the white South. In the later novels Cable seems hardly more than a dispassionate observer, the historian of the dated culture he depicts.[23] When he obscured his beliefs, or said only what was expedient, or, as in *The Cavalier,* wrote to fit a vogue, he added little to his stature, but when his pen was driven by his convictions he produced works of lasting value.

Many literary reputations rest on fewer fine books than George W. Cable produced, and if Howells erred in ranking him with Hardy and James and Turgenev and Tolstoy,[24] an error just as great is made by those who place him with Grace King and Thomas Nelson Page, Ruth McEnery Stuart and F. Hopkinson Smith. Edward Laroque Tinker said that Cable was a pioneer among Southern writers in treating objectively and realistically the life he saw around him.[25] Other perceptive critics have commented upon the intellectuality, the social insight, the "sudden lapses into realism" [26] which characterized his work at a time when Southern fiction "was for the most part mellow and moon-drenched." [27] Hamilton Basso has called Cable the spiritual godfather of Faulkner, Caldwell, Wolfe, and other Southern writers who question the validity of the

[23] Flory, *Economic Criticism in American Fiction: 1792 to 1900,* pp. 56–57.

[24] *Literature and Life,* p. 132.

[25] "Cable and the Creoles," *American Literature,* V, 326.

[26] Cash, *The Mind of the South,* p. 143.

[27] Dabney, *Liberalism in the South,* p. 380.

plantation tradition and probe their culture in order to disclose and treat its afflictions,[28] and Edmund Wilson, likening Cable to Dickens and Charles Reade, said he was less a dealer in lavender and old lace than a sociologist.[29]

Cable made a distinguished contribution to American literature, but he was not satisfied with this achievement. Early in his career he wanted also to be an effective reformer, and as late as May 24, 1897, when he no longer thought of himself as the conscience of the nation and the champion of exploited minorities, he wrote his wife, "I long to be a good man and a man who can look his town in the face and say the only debt between him & it is to him." [30] In his years in Northampton he did more than discharge the normal obligations of the conscientious citizen. When he died, few of the tributes and obituaries failed to mention that George W. Cable had performed a notable service by developing in Northampton an agency which put into practice the democratic principles that are the theme of his finest literary work.

[28] "Letters in the South," *New Republic,* LXXXIII, 162–63.
[29] "Citizen of the Union," *New Republic,* LVII, 352.
[30] Turner, *George W. Cable,* p. 299.

Bibliography

I. WORKS BY CABLE

A. BOOKS

1879. Old Creole Days. New York, Scribner's.
1880. The Grandissimes. New York, Scribner's.
1881. Madame Delphine. New York, Scribner's.
1884. The Creoles of Louisiana. New York, Scribner's.
1884. Dr. Sevier. Boston, J. R. Osgood.
1885. The Silent South. New York, Scribner's.
1888. Bonaventure. New York, Scribner's.
1889. Strange True Stories of Louisiana. New York, Scribner's.
1890. The Negro Question. New York, Scribner's.
1891. The Busy Man's Bible. Meadville, Pa., Flood & Vincent.
1892. A Memory of Roswell Smith. New York, De Vinne Press.
1894. John March, Southerner. New York, Scribner's.
1899. Strong Hearts. New York, Scribner's.
1899. Burt, Mary E., and Lucy Leffingwell Cable, eds. The Cable Story Book. Selections for School Reading. New York, Scribner's.
1901. The Cavalier. New York, Scribner's.
1902. Bylow Hill. New York, Scribners.
1908. Kincaid's Battery. New York, Scribner's.
1909. "Posson Jone' " and Père Raphaël. New York, Scribner's.

1914. Gideon's Band. New York, Scribner's.
1914. The Amateur Garden. New York, Scribner's.
1918. The Flower of the Chapdelaines. New York, Scribner's.
1918. Lovers of Louisiana. New York, Scribner's.
1958. Turner, Arlin, ed. The Negro Question: A Selection of Writings on Civil Rights in the South by George W. Cable. Garden City, N.Y., Doubleday.

B. OTHER PUBLICATIONS

This list includes articles, stories, serial publication of novels, pamphlets, and minor contributions to books.

1873. " 'Sieur George," *Scribner's Monthly,* VI (October), 739–45.
1874. "Belles Demoiselles Plantation," *Scribner's Monthly,* VII (April), 739–47.
1874. " 'Tite Poulette," *Scribner's Monthly,* VIII (October), 674–84.
1875. "Jean-ah Poquelin," *Scribner's Monthly,* X (May), 91–100.
1875. "Madame Délicieuse," *Scribner's Monthly,* X (August), 498–508.
1876. "Don Joaquin," *Harper's Magazine,* LII (January), 281–89.
1876. "Café des Exilés," *Scribner's Monthly,* XI (March), 727–36.
1879–80. The Grandissimes, *Scribner's Monthly,* XIX (November–April), 97–110, 251–65, 369–83, 582–92, 690–703, 841–59; XX (May–October), 24–34, 194–204, 380–91, 527–35, 696–704, 812–24.
1881. "Madame Delphine," *Scribner's Monthly,* XXII (May–July), 22–31, 191–99, 436–43.
1881. "Historical Sketch" of New Orleans, in *History and Present Condition of New Orleans, Louisiana, and Report on the City of Austin, Texas.* Washington, Government Printing Office, 1881. (Reproduced in Tenth Census, *Report on the Social Statistics of Cities,* 1887, compiled by George E. Waring, Jr.)

1883. "Who Are the Creoles?" *Century Magazine,* XXV (January), 384–98.

1883. "The Creoles in the American Revolution," *Century Magazine,* XXV (February), 538–51.

1883. "The End of Foreign Dominion in Louisiana," *Century Magazine,* XXV (March), 643–54.

1883. "Plotters and Pirates of Louisiana," *Century Magazine,* XXV (April), 852–67.

1883. "The Great South Gate," *Century Magazine,* XXVI (June), 218–32.

1883. An Address Delivered by Geo. W. Cable, at the Commencement Exercises of the Academical Department, of the University of Louisiana, June 15th, 1883. New Orleans, Board of Administrators of the University of Louisiana.

1883. "Flood and Plague in New Orleans," *Century Magazine,* XXVI (July), 419–31.

1883. " 'My Acquaintance with Cable,' " *Critic,* III (August 25, 1883), 348.

1883–84. Dr. Sevier, *Century Magazine,* XXVII (November–April), 54–68, 237–51, 422–30, 529–42, 753–65, 873–86; XXVIII (May–October), 70–81, 257–70, 418–26, 596–608, 698–711, 820–32.

1884. "The Convict Lease System in the Southern States," *Century Magazine,* XXVII (February), 582–99.

1884. " 'We of the South,' " *Century Magazine,* XXIX (November), 151–52.

1884. "New Orleans," in *Encyclopaedia Britannica,* 9th ed.

1885. "Margaret," *Christian Union,* XXXI (January 1), 7.

1885. "The Freedman's Case in Equity," *Century Magazine,* XXIX (January), 409–18.

1885. "New Orleans Before the Capture," *Century Magazine,* XXIX (April), 918–22.

1885. " 'Negro English' in Literature," *Critic,* VI (April 18), 185.

1885. "Professional Christianity," *Advance* (Chicago), II (July 30), 1–2.

1885. "The Silent South," *Century Magazine,* XXX (September), 674–91.

1885. "A Woman's Diary of the Siege of Vicksburg," *Century Magazine,* XXX (September), 767–75.

1886. "The Dance in Place Congo," *Century Magazine,* XXXI (February), 517–32.

1886. "International Copyright," *Century Magazine,* XXXI (February), 628–29.

1886. "Creole Slave Songs," *Century Magazine,* XXXI (April), 807–28.

1886. "The True South *vs.* The Silent South," *Century Magazine,* XXXII (May), 166–70.

1886. "Is It Sectional or National?" *Century Magazine,* XXXII (October), 962–63.

1887. "Carancro," *Century Magazine,* XXXIII (January, February), 355–65, 545–57.

1887. "Grande Pointe," *Century Magazine,* XXXIII (March), 659–84.

1887–88. "Au Large," *Century Magazine,* XXXV (November–March), 89–99, 213–26, 344–56, 548–55, 732–40.

1887. "The Busy Man's Bible," *Sunday School Times,* XXIX (December 10), 787.

1887–88. "A Layman's Hints," weekly item in *Sunday School Times,* XXIX (December 17–December 31, 1887), XXX (January 7–December 15, 1888).

1888. "The Negro Question in the United States," *Contemporary Review,* LIII (March), 443–68. (Published as "The Negro Question" in the Chicago *Inter-Ocean* and the New York *Tribune,* March 4, 1888.)

1888. "On the Writing of Novels," *Critic,* XII (March 24), 136.

1888. "What Shall the Negro Do?" *Forum,* V (August), 627–39.

1888. "Home Culture Clubs," *Century Magazine,* XXXVI (August), 497–507.

1888. "A Worthy Daughter of Her Race," *American Hebrew,* XXXVI (October 5), 130–31.

1888. "Strange True Stories of Louisiana: How I Got Them," *Century Magazine,* XXXVII (November), 110–14.

1888. "The Young Aunt with White Hair," *Century Magazine*, XXXVII (November), 114–16.

1888. "A Simpler Southern Question," *Forum*, VI (December), 392–403.

1888–89. "Françoise in Louisiana," *Century Magazine*, XXXVII (December–February), 254–60, 358–67, 512–20.

1889. Contribution to symposium, "Shall the Negro Be Educated or Suppressed?" *Independent*, XLI (February 21), 225–27.

1889. Tribute to James Russell Lowell, *Critic*, XIV (February 23), 94.

1889. "The History of Alix de Morainville," *Century Magazine*, XXXVII (March), 742–48.

1889. "Salome Müller," *Century Magazine*, XXXVIII (May), 56–69.

1889. "What Makes the Color Line?" *America* (Chicago), II (June 13), 325–26.

1889. "A Word About Dr. Holland," *Christian Union*, XL (July 25), 100.

1889. "The 'Haunted House' in Royal Street," *Century Magazine*, XXXVIII (August), 590–601.

1889. "The Nation and the Illiteracy of the South," *Independent*, XLI (August 29), 1106–7.

1889. "Attalie Brouillard," *Century Magazine*, XXXVIII (September), 749–57.

1889. " 'Strange True Stories of Louisiana,' " *Century Magazine*, XXXVIII (September), 798–99.

1889. "A National Debt," *Northwestern Congregationalist* (Minneapolis), I (September 6), 2–3. (Published in *The Negro Question* as "National Aid to Southern Schools.")

1889. "Congregational Unity in Georgia," *Congregationalist*, LXXIV (September 26), 317.

1889. "War Diary of a Union Woman in the South," *Century Magazine*, XXXVIII (October), 931–46.

1890. The Southern Struggle for Pure Government. Boston, The Massachusetts Club, 1890. (Published in abridged form as "Equal Rights in the South," New York *Tribune*, February 23; as "Pure Government: Free Government," *American,* XIX (March 1), 396–98; as "Solutions for Southern Problems," *Our Day,* V (April), 308–19.)

1890. "A Reply," *Century Magazine,* XXXIX (April), 958–59.

1891. "Address . . . at the Annual Meeting Held at Northampton, October 22, 1890," *American Missionary,* XLV (January), 8–13. (Published in pamphlet form as *What the Negro Must Learn,* New York, American Missionary Association, 1891[?].)

1891. "How to Teach the Bible," *Ladies' Home Journal,* VIII (February–April), 4, 6, 8 respectively.

1891. Introduction to Dora Richards Miller, "The Census As She Was Took," *Independent,* XLIII (December 17), 1865–66.

1892. "Does the Negro Pay for His Education?" *Forum,* XIII (July), 640–49.

1892. "Education for the Common People in the South," *Cosmopolitan,* XIV (November), 63–68.

1892. "A West Indian Slave Insurrection," *Scribner's Magazine,* XII (December), 709–20.

1893. "Mr. Cable as an Editor," *Critic,* XXII (February 4), 63–64.

1893. "The Taxidermist," *Scribner's Magazine,* XIII (May), 679–88.

1893. "New Orleans," *St. Nicholas,* XXI (November, December), 40–49, 150–54.

1893. "The Gentler Side of Two Great Southerners," *Century Magazine,* XLVII (December), 292–94.

1894. "After-Thoughts of a Story-Teller," *North American Review,* CLVIII (January), 16–23.

1894. John March, Southerner, *Scribner's Magazine,* XV (January–June), 53–68, 154–70, 380–93, 461–76, 554–64, 740–53; XVI (July–December), 49–62, 236–50, 371–88, 489–510, 634–56, 768–89.

1894. "The President's Address," Home Culture Clubs *Letter,* II, Supplement (May), 7–8.

1894. Introduction to Adelene Moffat, "The Story of a Club," *Cosmopolitan,* XVII (August), 435–36.

1894. Tribute to Oliver Wendell Holmes, *Writer,* VII (November), 162.

1895. "A Glance at the Month's Work," Home Culture Clubs *Letter,* III (March), 1.

1895. "May We Go Ahead?" Home Culture Clubs *Letter,* III (May), 4–5.

1895. Letter to David P. Todd, Home Culture Clubs *Letter,* IV (August 1), 13.

1895. Letter to Friede Row, Home Culture Clubs *Letter,* IV (September 1), 23.

1895. "Authors Who Ride," *Critic,* XXVII (October 12), 226.

1896. "Samuel L. Clemens," Home Culture Clubs *Letter,* IV (February 1), 70.

1896. "Richard Watson Gilder," Home Culture Clubs *Letter,* IV (March 1), 88.

1896. "Eugene Field," Home Culture Clubs *Letter,* IV (April 1), 109–10.

1896. "President Seelye," Home Culture Clubs *Letter,* IV (May 1), 133.

1896. "The Speculations of a Story-Teller," *Atlantic Monthly,* LXXVIII (July), 88–96.

1896. "Gregory's Island," *Scribner's Magazine,* XX (August), 149–59. (Published in *Strong Hearts* as "The Solitary.")

1896. "Extracts from a Story-Teller's Dictionary," *Chap-Book,* V (September 15), 411–23.

1896. "The Brown Ghost," *Symposium,* I (October), 16–19.

1896. "Thoughts and Views," *Symposium,* I (October–December), 36–38, 75–76, 125–27.

1896. "To See Our Life as Romance Sees It," *Symposium,* I (November), 59–66.

1896. "At the Edge of the Woods," *Bradley: His Book,* II (November), 3–7.

1896. "A Visit from Barrie," *Symposium,* I (December), 99–102.

1897. "The Portrait of a Life," *Book Buyer,* XIV (February), 65–66.

1897. "A Curious Misdemeanor in Letters," *Book Buyer,* XIV (March), 184–85.

1897. "Editor's Symposium," *Current Literature,* XXI (April–June), 290–93, 386–89, 514–17; XXII (July–September), 1–4, 97–104, 193–200.

1897. "Books of the Holiday Season," *Book Buyer,* XV (December), 479–507.

1897. "Art and Morals in Books," *Independent,* XLIX (December 16), 3–4.

1898. "Introduction," to Mary E. Burt and Mary B. Cable, eds., *The Eugene Field Book.* New York, Scribner's.

1899. "The Entomologist," *Scribner's Magazine,* XXV (January–March), 50–60, 220–27, 315–26.

1899. "Children of Jesus—A Christmas Carol," *Ladies' Home Journal,* XVII (December), 23.

1901. Letter on *Critic* anniversary, *Critic,* XXXVIII (January), 76.

1901. "Père Raphaël," *Century Magazine,* LXII (August), 545–61.

1901. "The Clock in the Sky," *Scribner's Magazine,* XXX (September), 327–32.

1901. "Some of My Pets," *Youth's Companion,* LXXV (September 5), 427.

1901. "The Angel of the Lord," in *A House Party* (a collection of anonymous stories). Boston, Small, Maynard.

1902. Bylow Hill, *Atlantic Monthly,* LXXXIX (March–May), 293–303, 452–65, 588–601.

1903. "Preface," to *The Cavalier* (Julia Marlowe Edition). New York, Scribner's.

1904. "Neighborly Gardens," *Good Housekeeping,* XXXVIII (April–May), 332–42, 419–21, 467–70.

1904. "The American Garden," *Scribner's Magazine,* XXXV (May), 621–29.

1905. Tribute to Mark Twain, in "Mark Twain's 70th Birthday," *Harper's Weekly,* XLIX (December 23), 1888–89.

1906. "Where to Plant What," *Century Magazine,* LXXII (May), 90–98.

1906. "The Home-Culture Clubs," *World's Work,* XII (October), 8110–14.

1909. "New Orleans Revisited," *Book News Monthly,* XXVII (April), 561–65.

1909. "Thomas Nelson Page: A Study in Reminiscence and Appreciation," *Book News Monthly,* XXVIII (November), 139–41.

1909. "The Northampton Prize Flower Garden Competition," in *Proceedings of the Convention at Which the American Federation of Arts Was Formed.* Washington.

1910. "The Midwinter Gardens of New Orleans," *Scribner's Magazine,* XLVII (January), 58–70.

1910. Tribute to Richard Watson Gilder, *Century Magazine,* LXXIX (February), 634–35.

1911. Tribute to Mark Twain, in a symposium, November 30, 1910, in *Proceedings of the American Academy and National Institute, New York,* III, 21–24.

1911. "The Cottage Gardens of Northampton," *Youth's Companion,* LXXXV (April 13), 190–91.

1911. Anecdote in "The Story-Tellers' Hall of Fun," *Cosmopolitan,* LI (July), 282–83.

1911. "William Cullen Bryant," in *Encyclopaedia Britannica,* 11th ed.

1912. Tribute to William Dean Howells, *Harper's Weekly,* LVI (March 9), 23.

1912. "Preface," to Lucy Leffingwell Cable Biklé, compiler, *The Voice of the Garden.* New York, John Lane.

1915. Letter to *Monthly News Letter* (American Association of Teachers of Journalism), I (April 15), no. 3.

1915. "My Philosophy," *Good Housekeeping,* LX (June), 628–33. (Published as "A Novelist's Philosophy," in *Proceedings of the American Academy and National Institute, New York,* VIII, 41–44.)

1915. Tribute to James Whitcomb Riley, *Writer,* XXVII (October), 149.

1917. "A Song for France," *Life,* LXIX (May 24), 896.

1918. "The Tocsin," *Outlook,* CXIX (June 12), 254.
1921. "Malvina," in *Liber Scriptorum: The Second Book of The Authors Club*. New York, The Authors Club.

II. REFERENCES

With a few exceptions, this list is restricted to published works to which specific footnote reference is made in this book. Newspaper articles and unpublished manuscripts are not included.

Abernethy, R. L., ed. Life and Lectures of Rev. John Moffat. Glen Rock, Pa., 1878.

Barrie, James M. "A Note on Mr. Cable's 'The Grandissimes,'" *Bookman,* VII (July, 1898), 401–3.

Bartlett, Rose. "How One Man Made His Town Bloom," *Ladies' Home Journal,* XXVII (March, 1910), 36, 80, 82.

Baskervill, William M. "George W. Cable," *Chautauquan,* XXV (May, 1897), 179–84.

——— "George W. Cable," *Vanderbilt Observer,* VI (March, 1885), 8–9.

Basso, Hamilton. "Letters in the South," *New Republic,* LXXXIII (June 19, 1935), 161–63.

Biklé, Lucy Leffingwell Cable. George W. Cable: His Life and Letters. New York, Scribner's, 1928.

——— "Introduction to New Edition," *Old Creole Days*. New York, Scribner's, 1937.

Bishop, David H. "A Commencement in the Eighties: George W. Cable's First Public Address," *Southwest Review,* XVIII (January, 1933), 108–14.

Bisland, Elizabeth. The Life and Letters of Lafcadio Hearn. 2 vols. Boston, Houghton Mifflin, 1906. Vol. I.

Bourne, Randolph. "From an Older Time," *Dial,* LXV (November 2, 1918), 363–65.

Boyesen, Hjalmar Hjorth. "The Chautauqua Movement," *Cosmopolitan,* XIX (June, 1895), 147–58.

——— Review of Cable's *John March, Southerner, Cosmopolitan,* XVIII (March, 1895), 633–34.

Bratton, Theodore DuBose. An Apostle of Reality: The Life and

Thought of the Reverend William Porcher DuBose. New York, Longmans, Green, 1936.
Brewster, Mary. "George W. Cable," *Congregationalist*, CX (December 10, 1925), 816–17.
Brown, Sterling A. "The American Race Problem as Reflected in American Literature," *Journal of Negro Education*, VIII (July, 1939), 275–90.
——— "The Negro Author and His Publisher," *Negro Quarterly*, I (Spring, 1942), 7–20.
——— "Negro Character as Seen by White Authors," *Journal of Negro Education*, II (April, 1933), 179–203.
——— The Negro in American Fiction. Washington, Associates in Negro Folk Education, 1937.
Brownlee, Fred L. "Moving In and Out," *Phylon*, IX (Second Quarter, 1948), 146–50.
Butcher, Philip. "George W. Cable and Booker T. Washington," *Journal of Negro Education*, XVII (Fall, 1948), 462–68.
——— "George W. Cable and Negro Education," *Journal of Negro History*, XXXIV (April, 1949), 119–34.
——— "George W. Cable: History and Politics," *Phylon*, IX (Second Quarter, 1948), 137–45.
——— "Some Dilemmas Resolved," *Phylon*, XII (Fourth Quarter, 1951), 390–92.
——— "Mutual Appreciation: Dunbar and Cable," *Free Lance: A Magazine of Poetry and Prose*, IV (First Half, 1957), 2–3. Reprinted in *CLA Journal*, I (March, 1958), 101–2.
"Cable at Vanderbilt," *Fisk Herald*, July, 1887.
Cable, Lucy Leffingwell. "The Story of the Author's Life," in *The Cable Story Book. Selections for School Reading*. Edited by Mary E. Burt and Lucy Leffingwell Cable. New York, Scribner's, 1899.
Cardwell, Guy A. "The First Public Address of George W. Cable," in *Studies in Memory of Frank Martindale Webster*. Washington University Studies, New Series, Language and Literature, No. 20. St. Louis, Washington University, 1951.
——— "George W. Cable Becomes a Professional Reader," *American Literature*, XXIII (January, 1952), 467–70.

Cardwell, Guy A. "Mark Twain's 'Row' with George Cable," *Modern Language Quarterly,* XIII (December, 1952), 363–71.

——— Twins of Genius. East Lansing, Michigan State College Press, 1953.

Cash, W. J. The Mind of the South. New York, Knopf, 1941.

Chase, Richard. "Cable and His *Grandissimes,*" *Kenyon Review,* XVIII (Summer, 1956), 373–83.

Chesnutt, Charles W. The Marrow of Tradition. Boston, Houghton Mifflin, 1901.

Chesnutt, Helen M. Charles Waddell Chesnutt: Pioneer of the Color Line. Chapel Hill, University of North Carolina Press, 1952.

Chittenden, Alice. "Home Culture for Busy Women," *Modern Priscilla,* X (January, 1897), 2–3.

Clemens, Samuel L. Life on the Mississippi. New York, Harper, 1917.

——— Mark Twain, Business Man. Edited by Samuel Charles Webster. Boston, Little, Brown, 1946.

——— Mark Twain's Autobiography. Edited by Albert Bigelow Paine. 2 vols. New York, Harper, 1929.

"Comment on Cable's Reply to the Attack Made on Him for Dining with Negro Family," *Fisk Herald,* February, 1890.

Connover, Charlotte Reeve. Some Dayton Saints and Prophets. Dayton, U. B. Publishing Co., 1907.

Cunningham, Virginia. Paul Laurence Dunbar and His Song. New York, Dodd, Mead, 1947.

Dabney, Virginius. Liberalism in the South. Chapel Hill, University of North Carolina Press, 1932.

DeMenil, Alexander Nicholas. The Literature of the Louisiana Territory. St. Louis, St. Louis News Co., 1904.

Dennis, Mary Cable. The Tail of the Comet. New York, Dutton, 1937.

Doherty, Herbert J., Jr. "Voices of Protest from the New South," *Mississippi Valley Historical Review,* XLII (June, 1955), 45–66.

Dunbar, Paul Laurence. Lyrics of the Hearthside. New York, Dodd, Mead, 1899.

"Editorial," *Vanderbilt Observer,* XII (February, 1890), 7–10.
"Edward H. R. Lyman," Home Culture Clubs *Letter,* IV (December 1, 1895), 42.
Eidson, John Olin. "George W. Cable's Philosophy of Progress," *Southwest Review,* XXI (January, 1936), 211–16.
Ekström, Kjell. "The Cable-Howells Correspondence," *Studia Neophilologica,* XXII (Spring, 1950), 48–61.
——— "Cable's *Grandissimes* and the Creoles," *Studia Neophilologica,* XXI (Autumn, 1949), 190–94.
——— "Extracts from a diary kept by Ozias W. Pond during the Clemens-Cable tour of readings in 1885," *Archiv für das Studium der neueren Sprachen,* CLXXXVIII (May, 1951), 109–13.
——— George Washington Cable: A Study of His Early Life and Work. Essays and Studies on American Language and Literature, X, The American Institute in the University of Upsala. Cambridge, Harvard University Press, 1950.
Flory, Claude Reherd. Economic Criticism in American Fiction: 1792 to 1900. Philadelphia, University of Pennsylvania, 1936.
Fortier, Alcée. A Few Words About the Creoles of Louisiana. Baton Rouge, Truth Book and Job Office, 1892.
——— Louisiana Studies. New Orleans, F. F. Hansell, 1894.
Franklin, John Hope. From Slavery to Freedom. New York, Knopf, 1947.
——— "George Washington Williams, Historian," *Journal of Negro History,* XXXI (January, 1946), 60–90.
"G. W. Cable," *Vanderbilt Observer,* IX (June, 1887), 13–14.
Gayarré, Charles. The Creoles of Romance and the Creoles of History. New Orleans, C. E. Hopkins, 1885.
——— "Mr. Cable's 'Freedman's Case in Equity,'" in Thomas M'Caleb, ed., *The Louisiana Book: Selections from the Literature of the State.* New Orleans, R. F. Straughan, 1894.
"George W. Cable," *Fisk Herald,* August, 1885.
"George W. Cable," *Fisk Herald,* December, 1889.
"George W. Cable and His Critics," *Fisk Herald,* March, 1885.
"George W. Cable as the Champion of the Negro," *Fisk Herald,* February, 1885.
"Grady Against Cable," *Fisk Herald,* May, 1885.

Grady, Henry W. "In Plain Black and White," *Century Magazine*, XXIX (April, 1885), 909–17.

Gray, Allison. "From the Steerage to a College Chair in 11 Years," *American*, XCVII (March, 1924), 46–47, 149.

Harris, Julia Collier. The Life and Letters of Joel Chandler Harris. Boston, Houghton Mifflin, 1918.

Haynes, Williams. "His Home and Gardens," *House & Garden*, XXXII (December, 1917), 28–29.

Hearn, Lafcadio. "The Scenes of Cable's Romances," *Century Magazine*, XXVII (November, 1883), 40–47.

Hemenway, Herbert D. "The Home-Culture Clubs, Northampton, Mass.," *Gentlewoman*, October 15, 1908.

Hendrick, Burton J. The Life and Letters of Walter H. Page. 2 vols. Garden City, N.Y. Doubleday, Page, 1923. Vol. I.

Howells, Mildred, ed. Life in Letters of William Dean Howells. 2 vols. Garden City, N.Y. Doubleday, Doran, 1928. Vol. I.

Howells, William Dean. Heroines of Fiction. 2 vols. New York, Harper, 1901. Vol. II.

——— Literature and Life. New York, Harper, 1902.

——— My Mark Twain. New York, Harper, 1910.

Hubbell, Jay B. The South in American Literature: 1607–1900. Durham, Duke University Press, 1954.

"James C. Napier," *Howard University Bulletin*, XX (July 1, 1940), 13.

Johnson, Clifton. "Home Culture," *Outlook*, LI (June 8, 1895), 952–54.

Johnson, Robert Underwood. "George Washington Cable," in *Commemorative Tributes to Cable, . . . Sargent, . . . Pennell.* New York, American Academy of Arts and Letters, Publication No. 57, 1927.

——— Remembered Yesterdays. Boston, Little, Brown, 1923.

Johnston, John W. "The True South *vs.* the Silent South," *Century Magazine*, XXXII (May, 1886), 164–66.

Kowaledsky, Waldemir. " 'My Acquaintance with Cable,' " translated and condensed by Charlotte Adams from the *Viestnik Evropii*, May, 1883, *Critic*, III (July 28, 1883), 316–17.

Le Jeune, Emilie. "Creole Folk Songs," *Louisiana Historical Quarterly*, II (October, 1919), 454–62.

Lorch, Fred W. "Cable and His Reading Tour With Mark Twain in 1884–1885," *American Literature,* XXIII (January, 1952), 471–86.

M'Caleb, Thomas, ed. The Louisiana Book: Selections from the Literature of the State. New Orleans, R. F. Straughan, 1894.

McIlwaine, Shields. The Southern Poor-White from Lubberland to Tobacco Road. Norman, University of Oklahoma Press, 1939.

McKay, Malcolm. "Dr. Sevier: A Protest," *Century Magazine,* XXVIII (October, 1884), 957.

McVicar, Landon, pseud., *see* Moffat, Adelene.

Manes, Isabel Cable. "George W. Cable, Fighter for Progress in the South," in *A Southerner Looks at Negro Discrimination: Selected Writings of George W. Cable.* New York, International Publishers, 1946.

Martineau, Harriet. Retrospects of Western Travel. 2 vols. London, Saunders and Otley, 1838. Vol. I.

The Meadow City's Quarter-Millennial Book. A Memorial of the Celebration of the Two Hundred and Fiftieth Anniversary of the Settlement of the Town of Northampton: Massachusetts. Northampton, the City of Northampton, 1904.

Meier, August. "Booker T. Washington and the Town of Mound Bayou," *Phylon,* XV (Fourth Quarter, 1954), 396–401.

Miller, Dora R. "Mr. Cable as an Editor Again," *Critic,* XXII (March 18, 1893), 167–68.

"Mr. George W. Cable at Vanderbilt University," *Christian Advocate,* XLVII (June 25, 1887), 1.

Mitchell, F. K. Review of Biklé's *George W. Cable: His Life and Letters, American Literature,* I (May, 1929), 217–19.

Moffat, Adelene. "Exhibition of Italian Arts and Crafts in Boston," *Survey,* XXII (April 3, 1909), 51–53.

——— "How Shall I Start a Club?" Home Culture Clubs *Letter,* IV (September 1, 1895), 24.

——— "Howard Pyle's Quality as an Illustrator," *Current Literature,* XXII (July, 1897), 42. Under pseud., Landon McVicar.

——— "Mountaineers of Middle Tennessee," *Journal of American Folklore,* V (October, 1891), 314–20.

——— "Northampton Clubhouse Work," Home Culture Clubs *Letter,* IV (January 1, 1896), 65–66.

Moffat, Adelene. "The Story of a Club," *Cosmopolitan,* XVII (August, 1894), 435–39.

——— "What Is a Home-Culture Club?" Home Culture Clubs *Letter,* IV (September 1, 1895), 23–24.

——— Views of a Southern Woman. An Address Before the Third Annual Conference of the National Association for the Advancement of Colored People. New York, National Association for the Advancement of Colored People, Publication No. 5, 1913.

——— Review of James Lane Allen's *The Choir Invisible, Current Literature,* XXII (August, 1897), 109. Under pseud., Landon McVicar.

Moffat, John. Our Nation's Peril and the Way of Escape. York, The Prohibition Committee of Chester County, Pa., 1879.

Moore, Rayburn S. " 'Don Joaquin,' a Forgotten Story by George W. Cable," *American Literature,* XXVI (November, 1954), 418–21.

Neilson, William Allan. In Memoriam: George W. Cable. 1925.

Nevins, Allan. "A Charming Personality," *Saturday Review of Literature,* V (February 2, 1929), 637, 640.

Nicoll, W. Robertson. "London Letter," *Bookman,* VII (July, 1898), 406–8.

The Northampton Book: Chapters from 300 Years in the Life of a New England Town, 1654–1954. Compiled and edited by the Tercentenary History Committee. Northampton, The Tercentenary Committee, 1954.

"The Northampton Home Culture Clubhouse," Home Culture Clubs *Letter,* IV (November 1, 1895), 37.

Nye, Russel B. "Mark Twain in Oberlin," *Ohio State Archæological and Historical Quarterly,* XLVII (January, 1938), 69–73.

Obituary notice, *Nation,* CXX (February 11, 1925), 133.

Ovington, Mary White. The Walls Came Tumbling Down. New York, Harcourt, 1947.

Pond, James B. Eccentricities of Genius. New York, G. W. Dillingham, 1900.

Powell, Lyman P. "The Home-Culture Clubs," *Booklovers Magazine,* V (March, 1905), 380–89.

Purnell, Elizabeth Wilkins. John Gamp: or Coves and Cliffs of the Cumberlands. Nashville, Gospel Advocate Publishing Co., 1901.

Russell, Mattie. "George Washington Cable Letters in Duke University Library," Duke University *Library Notes,* No. 25 (January, 1951), 1–13.

Sancton, Thomas. "A Note on Cable and His Times," *Survey Graphic,* XXXVI (January, 1947), 28.

Sawyer, Joseph Henry. A History of Williston Seminary. Easthampton, Mass., Published by the Trustees, 1917.

Scott, Arthur L. "The *Century Magazine* Edits *Huckleberry Finn,* 1884–1885," *American Literature,* XXVII (November, 1955), 356–62.

Simkins, Francis B. "New Viewpoints of Southern Reconstruction," *Journal of Southern History,* V (February, 1939), 49–61.

Stewart, Frank P. "Neighborhood Garden Clubs: What They Are Doing for a Massachusetts Town," *Suburban Life,* September, 1906, pp. 123–24.

Street, Appleton. "This Haunted House Has Only Happy Ghosts," *American,* CIV (September, 1927), 16, 118, 121, 124, 126.

Sykes, Lillian E. "James Carroll Napier," *Negro History Bulletin,* V (February, 1942), 114.

Taylor, Alrutheus Ambush. The Negro in Tennessee, 1865–1880. Washington, Associated Publishers, 1941.

Tinker, Edward Larocque. "Cable and the Creoles," *American Literature,* V (January, 1934), 313–26.

Turner, Arlin. George W. Cable. Durham, Duke University Press, 1956.

——— "George W. Cable, Novelist and Reformer," *South Atlantic Quarterly,* XLVIII (October, 1949), 539–45.

——— "George W. Cable's Beginnings as a Reformer," *Journal of Southern History,* XVII (May, 1951), 135–61.

——— "George W. Cable's Recollections of General Forrest," *Journal of Southern History,* XXI (May, 1955), 224–28.

——— "George W. Cable's Revolt Against Literary Sectionalism," *Tulane Studies in English,* V (1955), 5–27.

——— "George Washington Cable's Literary Apprenticeship," *Louisiana Historical Quarterly,* XXIV (January, 1941), 168–86.

——— "Mark Twain, Cable, and 'A Professional Newspaper

Liar,'" *New England Quarterly,* XXVIII (March, 1955), 18–33.

Turner, Arlin. "Notes on Mark Twain in New Orleans," *McNeese Review,* VI (1954), 10–22.

——— "A Novelist Discovers a Novelist: The Correspondence of H. H. Boyesen and George W. Cable," *Western Humanities Review,* V (Autumn, 1951), 343–72.

——— "Whittier Calls on George W. Cable," *New England Quarterly,* XXII (March, 1949), 92–96.

"Wallace Battle, the Episcopal Church and Mississippi," *Crisis,* XXXIV (October, 1927), 261–62, 282–83.

Waring, George E., Jr. "George W. Cable," *Century Magazine,* XXIII (February, 1882), 602–5.

Wetherill, J. K. "George W. Cable in New Orleans and Northampton," *Critic,* IX (October 9, 1886), 169–70.

White, Charles Fred. Plea of the Negro Soldier and a Hundred Other Poems. Easthampton, Mass., Published by the Author, 1908.

Willink, Cecile. "The Louisiana Historical Society Fifty Years Ago," *Louisiana Historical Quarterly,* VII (October, 1924), 667–71.

Wilson, Edmund. "Citizen of the Union," *New Republic,* LVII (February 13, 1929), 352–53.

——— "The Ordeal of George Washington Cable," *New Yorker,* November 9, 1957, pp. 172, 174–84, 189–96, 199–206, 209–16.

Woodward, C. Vann. Origins of the New South, 1877–1913. Vol. IX of *A History of the South,* ed. by Wendell Holmes Stephenson and E. Merton Coulter. Baton Rouge, Louisiana State University Press, 1951.

Index